Good Friends Great Tastes

A Celebration of Life, Food and Friendship

by Debbie Meyer

Published by

Good Friends Great Tastes™

Author: Debbie Meyer
P.O. Box 952
Grapevine, Texas 76099

debbiemeyer@sprynet.com
Email Debbie if you would like to be informed when she is in traveling to your vicinity for a
book signing or food related event. You are also invited to inform Debbie of stores in your area
that may be interested in hosting cooking classes or carrying *Good Friends Great Tastes*.

www.wimmerco.com/goodfriendsgreattastes
Fax 817-488-2368

1st Printing   April 2000   5,000 copies
2nd Printing   December 2000   5,000 copies
3rd Printing   May 2001   7,000 copies

Cover Design: Sarah Huerter
                Kansas City, Missouri
                Sarahhuert@earthlink.net
Photography: Joe Graber
                Arlington, Texas

Good Friends Great Tastes™
is a trademark of Good Friends Great Tastes, Grapevine, Texas

Copyright © 2000
by Debbie Meyer. All rights reserved.
ISBN 0-9676269-0-0

The author of this book has taken every precaution to ensure that all recipes have been
tested and are accurate. Contributors' recipes may have been changed slightly upon testing.

Printed in the USA by

WIMMER
The Wimmer Companies
Memphis
1-800-548-2537

Dear Friends,

My love and appreciation for food started very young. I grew up in Kansas City with three brothers, a European mother, and a father from the Kansas farmland. My mother didn't cook like all the other moms in the neighborhood. Instead, she cooked a lot of international recipes no one could pronounce. She is an excellent cook, so many of my recipes are credited to her.

In 1965, when we moved into the neighborhood where my parents still reside, they began holding elaborate dinner parties with several neighbors. They all used their best silver and decorated their tables beautifully, and I got to dress up just long enough to say hello, have dessert and scurry off to bed. It was Jody, our next door neighbor who was part of this dinner group, that gave me my first cookbook in 1971-*Kim's Cookbook for Young People*. This cookbook, along with the aspiration to be like the neighborhood entertainers, started me down the path of cooking and entertaining. Jody and her husband Jerry still live next door to my parents, and we continue to exchange recipes and entertaining ideas. Her youngest of five children, Sarah, did the artwork for *Good Friends Great Tastes*.

Throughout my years in school, from junior high to college, I hosted small gatherings that emulated what my parents had done. Since 1978 I have received cookbooks at holiday time and have also saved recipes from my friends and their parents. I still have these original cookbooks and hand-written recipe cards that I use today.

My palate continued to develop, when I studied a year abroad in college on a scholarship from Kansas State University and traveled to ten countries over the course of a year. From country to country the foods were vastly different and exciting. I lived in a co-ed dorm with people of all nationalities and we shared different foods and wines. My interest in food increased as a result. As an adult, I have continued to travel and learn more about new cuisines.

I also had the fantastic opportunity of being the food buyer for a gourmet store. It was there that I learned from customers' buying habits how our busy lives are affecting the way we cook and entertain. As most people are, I am extremely busy but do not want to sacrifice the details that make dining a memorable experience. I have learned to prepare in stages and through experience can quickly plan an impressive menu that balances taste, color, and texture. I am an every-day gourmet who wants to dine, rather than "just eat." Spending time visiting with my guests is more important to me than being in the kitchen. I am on a budget and cannot afford to buy elaborate napkins or floral arrangements for each gathering. Instead I search through my cabinets to create imaginative centerpieces. It is my attention to detail when friends gather that makes them feel pampered.

Good Friends Great Tastes provides balanced menus with wine selections and easy table decorating ideas. The menus and ideas are impressive but practical and not overly complicated for those who only occasionally entertain. I put my heart and soul into each menu and have tested every recipe In the book. I look forward to sharing my passion of over twenty-eight years with you.

Bon Appétit!

Debbie

Debbie
debbiemeyer@sprynet.com
www.wimmerco.com/goodfriendsgreattastes

Thank You

- to everyone who submitted old and new recipes for the cookbook and encouraged me to pursue my dream.

- to David Gore for his love and support, several test dinners each week and exchange of ideas. Thank you for the wonderful wine pairings for the book and extensive wine knowledge.

- to Joe and Jeanne Graber for the use of their home and a great amount of their time. Joe was the dedicated photographer for all the section dividers and my picture. Jeanne helped with the details, cleaned up and put up with our long photo sessions. She also made sure I got all my dishes and props back home.

- to Sarah Huerter for the wonderful logo and artwork. I was thrilled to have a lifelong friend to work with on such a heartfelt project. We shared ideas and emotions while working on the book. Her late nights and enthusiasm were greatly appreciated.

- to Macaire Hill for planting the seed that I should write a cookbook.

- to Markham Reilly, a business and entertainment consultant in Dallas, Texas. Markham encouraged me to make a living from my interests in food, people and travel through a class she teaches called Trust What You Love.

- to Marla Payne, Lynne Borkowski, Jane Langlais, Alexia Schuster and Becky Loboda for helping me proof the sections of the book.

- to Steve Harriman, of Pogo's Beverages in Dallas, Texas for the lessons in the up and coming wine regions and the availability of certain brands.

- to Brook and Michael Marsolek of Laurmar Designer Homes, Plano, Texas for allowing Joe and I to shoot the photograph for the back of the book in the kitchen of one of their spec homes.

- to my mom-Brigitte and Jody Huerter, the great cooks in my life that introduced me to gourmet foods and elaborate entertaining at a young age.

- to my dad-Louie, Ron, Steve, Tom, Renée and Audrey for being the test audience over the years and for their patience when I rambled on and on about food and recipes.

Table of Contents

Planning the Event

What type of event do you want to have? Do you want to have a sit down dinner? Will children be involved? Would a buffet be easier? What is the weather forecast? Should you have the event outside? How many people would you like to have as guests for this gathering? A rule of thumb is to give yourself two days to get everything done and three if possible. Of course there will be times that call for a spontaneous event-when you simply feel the need to be surrounded by friends or family. You may have little time to plan, but most people are thrilled to be treated to a home-cooked meal and don't mind eating off the everyday dishes.

Menu Tips

A well-planned meal should follow the basic food groups. A meat served with a vegetable and starch balances texture and nutrition, but color should also be a consideration. If your salad has a lot of yellow peppers in it, then yellow squash is not the best vegetable to serve. If you are making scalloped potatoes with cheese, then don't have a cheesy vegetable in the menu selection. Even the appetizer should avoid repetition of flavors. If the main dish has bacon crumbled on top then don't serve an appetizer with bacon. Consider the duplication of ingredients when planning your menu, balancing color and texture for presentation. Don't make all of your favorites at once, instead plan a menu where the prepared dishes complement the occasion, i.e. a cheese tray and other elegant appetizers for a wine tasting. Sometimes a little duplication is difficult to avoid and is acceptable. If your salad has nuts and so does the dessert, it is acceptable because they are served at different times and involve very different flavors. The table decorations and theme should coordinate with the menu and mood you are creating.

Outline your desired menu and consider the number of ovens you can access and the amount of time you have. Plan so that there are several things that can be made ahead of time. Consider using the shopping list (page 335) provided in the book and hang on to it until you are totally prepared for your event. The shopping list has a space for other errands to be added such as picking up a tablecloth from the cleaners, getting additional chairs or stopping to get liquor and mixers for the event. Think of the details all the way down to the ice needed, beverage napkins, flowers and candles. When you save trips to the store you save time. Think of the things that you can get done ahead of time or while the kids are in bed. Make your grocery list, set the table, pull out the dishes you will need, check your supplies in the bar, polish silver if necessary. The more organized you are the more fun you will have.

In order to save time in the kitchen, read through the entire recipe before you make your shopping list. The shopping list in the book is organized by aisle to avoid running all over the store. You may set this up on your own computer on a table and customize headings to suit your needs. Include non-food items on your list too, such as skewers, toothpicks or parchment paper. With an organized shopping list, you won't miss any items. If something in the recipe would taste better bought on the day of the event, then keep your list and circle that item or put a checkmark by it so you know you must go back to the store. There is also a space on the organized shopping list in the book that is designated for the ingredients you think you already have in stock. Check your cabinets before making a trip to the store. This helps you avoid duplication, saves money and unnecessary trips to the store that waste time.

Before food preparation begins, measure and chop ingredients, so that you can relax and have a good time while entertaining. Find opportunities to get things done early. Wash lettuce or toast nuts ahead of time. Consider this your party too, and minimize stress with early preparation. Clean up as you go and you won't have such a chore at the end of your preparation. This is a lesson that has taken me years to learn.

With an excellent menu, bread is not a necessity. If bread is served, find a great local bakery and select something interesting that goes with what you are serving. A great example would be jalapeño cheese bread with the Green Chili Breakfast Casserole or walnut scallion bread with a beef dinner entrée. If you choose to serve a sweet and a savory bread (such as raisin bread and walnut scallion bread) at the same meal, do not mix them in the same basket or they will take on the flavor of the stronger one. Cut the bread in thick slices instead of sandwich slices. Serve the bread with a good quality butter, slightly softened. It is not necessary to serve the bread warm, although it is a nice touch.

A good hostess will ask her guests if they have any food allergies before planning the menu. Shellfish can be hazardous to some, so be sure to inquire. When serving a seafood appetizer, it is nice to serve a non-seafood appetizer as well. Avoid duplication of ingredients when serving two appetizers. One may have meat and the other may have cheese or seafood. The number of appetizers you serve may depend on the time guests arrive and when you are sitting down for dinner. If you are planning to wait on late arriving guests, or introductions need to be made, additional time for appetizers may be needed. If the group hasn't seen one another in awhile, more than one appetizer may be needed to allow guests time to mingle.

Your invitation may prompt friends to ask "What can I bring?" If you decide to share the responsibility, select a menu and assign them a dish or let them be creative and use their own recipes. Let them know what you are serving and allow them to decide what is the best complement to the meal. If you are assigning something, be sure to send the recipe to them in enough time and include clear instructions. Assigning them their specialty will benefit you both. If you are unsure of their cooking abilities, allow them to choose what dish to bring, i.e. appetizer, salad, dessert. Ask the person bringing the appetizer to arrive earlier than the other guests.

Plan the event to reflect your personality and style. Your generosity of spirit when opening your home to friends is more important than having everything perfect. Written invitations are not necessary for every occasion, but are a nice touch when guests must plan ahead, or an accurate head count is needed. Request a reply whether the invitation is written or verbal. This helps to plan the seating arrangements and the amount of food needed.

Timing and Serving

Determine the approximate time you would like your meal to begin and outline (on paper) the time you need to prepare each item. Be sure and allow time for late arrivals, which may push back dinner. You will need time to dress the salad and complete any other menu items, open wine, etc. With your prepared outline you will stay on track and avoid frustration.

Wine and Beer

Ask a local merchant you can trust for advice when you are serving a group of people. Let the merchant know if your friends are knowledgeable of wine and indicate if cost is a consideration for you. There are wonderful white and red wines available that are not expensive but are considerably better than box wine. If wine comes in a magnum, it can be transferred to inexpensive carafes for easy serving. There are 5 glasses of wine per regular sized bottle; a magnum is equivalent to 2 bottles or 10 glasses. A wonderful recommendation for a magnum is La Vieille Ferme that comes in a red and white wine.

When serving beer, offer a variety of beers. Provide a selection that may be fun for experimenting and may stimulate conversation. I prefer glass bottles over cans. You might want to try Italian beer if the dinner is Italian or Mexican beer if you have a Southwest inspired menu. In most cases, both beer and wine should be offered since many guests may not drink wine.

After the Meal

For after dinner coffee, it is best to purchase whole beans and grind them yourself. Ground coffee should be used shortly after grinding because it loses flavor after about four hours. Do not store beans or ground coffee in the freezer. The freezing of beans changes the flavor due to condensation. Instead, store beans and ground coffee in an airtight container away from light. The ground beans may be stored in the refrigerator. Those that drink regular coffee seem to prefer unflavored blends and those that drink decaffeinated seem to drink flavored blends. Refrigerated flavored creamers or half-and-half are good in coffee and are a nice alternative to flavored coffees. To please both the serious coffee drinkers and those that like theirs doctored up, serve a flavored creamer.

Once you have planned a few events in your home and are pleased with the results, start keeping a notebook. List a few menus that you know you like in the notebook with the page number of the recipe and the book or magazine from which it came. Include the month and year of the publication for easy reference. List who came to dinner, what you served, and if you enjoyed the combination or what you would change. The exact menu can be duplicated for another group of friends and the event will come together more easily the next time you entertain.

Keep a camera on hand as you never know when there will be a great photo opportunity. These pictures can later be used for birthdays and celebrations.

Creating the Mood and Setting the Table

Creative Containers

You can find unique ideas for your table by thumbing through magazines and looking through your cabinets. There are some wonderful ways to make creative arrangements. Use a silver champagne bucket, silver mint julep cups, teapots, mason jars or rose bowls. The possibilities found in your own cabinets are endless. A candy dish turned over can make a base for another bowl to sit on top, which creates height and interest. You can fill containers with flowers, ornaments, fruits or vegetables depending on the occasion.

Arrange roses in a rose bowl by cutting stems short and using a fair amount of roses tightly tied together to create an elegant rounded arrangement. White roses and white tapers together on a table are very elegant. A mirror under a rose bowl with or without votives can create a dramatic ambience.

Candlelight

Candles can be used day or evening and add warmth and atmosphere. A votive by each place setting creates additional light and is a special touch. Scented votives should be avoided when serving food as the flavor of the food can be impaired.

Always use new candles on the table when entertaining. Be sure and trim the wicks so they don't sputter when lit. It is worth buying quality candles because they burn less quickly and you don't run the risk of losing the color coating when peeling off the tight plastic on the outside.

Use different heights of candleholders and put the same color and size candle in each one. My favorites are white, ivory and gold. Odd numbers are best for floral arrangements and candle arrangements. You can also create a beautiful table arrangement by arranging an odd number of flower filled vases of varying heights and shapes.

Displaying food on a footed cake plate can help you to add height to a table. Place vases or candleholders on top of the plate and surround the base with additional candles or vases for a unique centerpiece.

A rose bowl or tumbler can be used with a candle (in a glass holder) placed in the middle and greenery or flowers inserted between the outside glass and the votive in the glass holder. Add color to your table by coordinating napkins to the centerpiece.

Arrange trays of the same size or same type candles in varied heights to make a beautiful display on a coffee table or mantel.

Florist blocks can be cut in semi-circles to fit around the base of a tall candleholder or footed bowl. You can then push holly, greenery or flowers into the form. Secure the foam with florist tape and push tapers gently into foam. Put taller tapers to the inside and shorter to the outside. Fill in with holly, ivy, flowers or berries to hide the foam.

Natural Looks

Vegetables such as artichokes and small pumpkins can be hollowed out to hold a votive candle. Slide a tall taper inside a bundle of asparagus and tie with a ribbon. Look in your produce section at the grocery store for ideas to add seasonal color to your table.

Place a single rose on top of a napkin at each place setting for a personal touch.

Inexpensive flowers can be purchased at the grocery store. Arrange them yourself or provide your own vase or container and have them arranged while you shop.

Whole lemons, limes or cranberries add color to the bottom of a clear vase arranged with flowers. If you are ambitious, use a potato peeler or zester to create designs in the skins of the lemons and limes.

Nature can be an inspiration for adding color to any table. Gourds and pumpkins in various shapes and sizes make a beautiful table setting. Arrange in odd numbers and add ambience by placing small unscented votives in clear glass holders between the gourds to provide extra light. Gourds will spoil quickly so check your arrangement frequently, or use French leaves to line beneath the gourds.

For a more dramatic presentation, lightly spray fruits or vegetables with a gold or silver metallic paint.

A large bowl of fresh artichokes or a mixture of artichokes, lemons and avocados creates a refreshing centerpiece. I saw this on a trip to Napa Valley, California and it was on top of a natural wood table. Simple and elegant idea!

French leaves (decorative paper leaves found in gourmet or kitchen stores) make an excellent base for a platter with cheese. Place a single leaf on top of a plate and set a clear soup bowl on top for a simple autumn touch.

Napkins, Napkin Rings and Place Cards

Fun napkin rings are an easy addition to any table setting. Fresh small flowers or greenery may be easily wrapped around a napkin ring by using thin florist wire and a pliable stem like something from a birch tree. Twist birch into circles and twist with florist wire. Group foliage into small bunches and bind stems with wire. The same technique can be used to slip over tapers.

Make a place card out of small flowerpots for a spring party by gluing a place card to one side and tie with raffia or ribbon. Attach a pack of seeds to napkin rings made from raffia or wire for a garden meeting or a spring brunch.

Chili peppers tied together with raffia makes a festive southwest napkin holder.

Make place cards out of small pumpkins by writing names on them with a metallic pen.

At holiday time, ornaments are an inexpensive way to add color. Add a decorative ornament to each person's wineglass as a party favor. They also make easy place card

holders by writing the person's name on a solid color ornament with a special metallic marker. Jody Huerter of Kansas City, Kansas fills the ornaments with salt and uses a paperclip where the hook would go to hold a place card. In order for the ornament to sit upright you may need a small circle of wire covered with metallic stars (as seen at holiday time in craft stores) to hold the ornament in place on top of the table.

A small stocking with names written in glitter and filled with candy is a great place card idea for kids or adults.

Cloth napkins are best. Simple white restaurant napkins can be purchased at specialty kitchen stores.

A napkin folded into the shape of a square and tied like a present, with a beautiful ribbon is a nice touch for a holiday or birthday table. Cut a piece of cardboard in a square to insert in the napkin to help maintain consistent size and shape while folding. Carefully slide the cardboard out once the ribbon is tied. For a dessert party, add a delicate dessert fork to the napkin and ribbon ensemble (see Dessert Section photograph).

Buy an assortment of festive beverage napkins (paper and cloth) and keep them on hand for casual and elegant dining.

Festive Ideas

Assorted colors of small jellybeans or runts (a brightly colored hard-coated candy) add color to the bottom of a glass vase. Add Gerber daisies (without water) for an easy centerpiece at a child's party.

A buffet set with a nice white tablecloth and a large bow (placed slightly off center) with extra streamers makes the table look like a large gift. This is a festive idea for birthday or holiday gatherings.

A large wicker basket (painted or not) can be lined with a garbage bag and filled with ice for a cute holder for wines. Carafes or open wine can be immersed in the ice and guests can serve themselves.

For a picnic celebration, line a terra cotta pot with foil and the outside edges with romaine lettuce leaves. Fill center with salad and tie raffia around the outside of the pot. It is a fun and unique presentation and if you forget to take it home, the cost is minimal. Square wire baskets (normally used for organization) make great containers for vegetables that have been julienned for dipping. Be creative in your use of serving containers!

Music played softly on the stereo or radio helps fill the voids in conversation when not all guests have arrived and some of the guests do not know each other. Choose background music that doesn't interfere with talking until the guests get comfortable. Turning the television on when entertaining is inappropriate unless the theme of the party centers around the event, i.e. Super Bowl, Kentucky Derby, Oscars.

Make the presentation on the dinner plates uniform in appearance. If the vegetable is on the right of the meat then do this same way on every plate. When guests look around

the table this is visually pleasing. Wipe off any dribbles of sauces with a napkin before serving. The entire meal will be more appetizing when you follow these steps.

Themed Parties

For an Octoberfest theme (celebrated in Munich, Germany) a menu of Rouladen or Wiener Schnitzel can be prepared. A more casual evening would consist of sauerkraut, bratwurst, crusty dinner rolls, Hot German Potato Salad and beer. In Bavaria, royal blue and white checked tablecloths are common table coverings. In German restaurants a colored square tablecloth is placed diagonally over a white tablecloth or a white square over a colored tablecloth. A variety of German beers can be found in most liquor stores. Taped accordion music of German songs helps create a festive atmosphere. (Refer to menu 15 in the Menus and Wine Pairings section.)

For Italian parties use red and white checked tablecloths. When hosting a themed gathering choose authentic menu items from the country or region including the beverages served. To add to the atmosphere, play background music that is consistent with the theme. Sending invitations to your guests may inspire their contributions to the "Evening in Italy" and encourage suggestions to carry out the theme. (Refer to menu 24 in the Menu and Wine Pairings section.)

The Spanish practice of serving tapas dates back to King Alfonso the 10th. Due to an illness he was required to take small bites of food with wine between meals. Once recovered, he mandated that wine be served with small bites of food in the region of Castille where he governed. The tradition continues throughout Spain although some question the origin of the tradition. Tapas are often served in taverns "tabernas" and some restaurants accompanied by wine or sherry. Olives, nuts, cured hams, regional sausages and manchego cheese are some of the common items that are available and may be found in gourmet specialty stores. A tapas party can be a fun gathering where dinner consists only of a variety of appetizers. Button mushrooms sautéed with olive oil and garlic, tuna salad on toast points, potato croquettes, calamari and fried or marinated sardines are some of the other delicious items found on a tapas menu.

For a bistro atmosphere, string small white lights in the trees on a patio and use white tablecloths. A gazebo lined with lights also creates a beautiful setting.

For economical decorations at a wine tasting dinner, fill a champagne bucket to overflowing with red and green grapes. Tie each white cloth napkin with a floral pick of grapes. Try a wine with each course, pairing each wine to complement the food. Avoid preparing spicy foods for a wine tasting because they deaden the palate and certain wines will be less appealing than if paired with milder foods.

A festive Cajun party can be staged to resemble a dark intimate Cajun restaurant. Put black lace over white tablecloths and hang crystals on candelabras. Serve hurricanes and play authentic Cajun music. Hurricane mix is a powdered drink mix that can be found in many liquor stores. (For menu ideas refer to menu 7 or 25 in the Menu and Wine Pairings section.)

Vicki Morgan, a friend since childhood, entertained her Bunco group in Little Rock, Arkansas with a unique theme dinner. She planned a menu with a safari theme and renamed all the courses. The main course was "Wild and Cheesy Chicken Casserole" and "Safari Slaw" was the salad. She turned sturdy boxes upside down and arranged them in different heights on each guest table and for the buffet. She draped the boxes with different animal print fabrics with burlap underneath and a lighter colored burlap was the tablecloth over the entire table. She placed wooden animal figures and painted flowerpots on top of the table. The flowerpots were painted with animal print designs and animal print tissue was used inside (greenery could also be used) of the centerpieces. Each table had a mix of animal prints and was slightly different. Naming the items on the menu for a buffet is a good idea when you mark each one with a place card. It is nice to know what is being served in a buffet whether or not it is a themed dinner.

For a humorous baby shower idea, use the smallest disposable infant diapers and put them around mason jars as vases or use them as coozies for canned beverages. Rattles and baby trinkets can also be tied to each napkin with ribbon and given to the mother-to-be at the end of the shower. To create a diaper holder for nuts or mints, cut 4 inch triangles from white paper, fold the bottom point up and bring the other two sides to the middle and fasten with a tiny safety pin.

For outdoor parties, galvanized buckets, wheelbarrows or wagons make great coolers for beverages. Create a beach party cooler out of a round galvanized bucket by tying a grass skirt around the outside.

Glassware and Silver

Serving magnums of wine is more economical, especially for large groups. Transferring the wines from the magnum to carafes is more appealing and also easier to handle.

Brandy snifters, martini glasses and open face champagne glasses can double as dessert dishes. For a decorative touch, tie a wire edge ribbon to the stem. Martini glasses or similar shaped margarita glasses are wonderful for individual portions of shrimp cocktail. Hang large peeled shrimp on the edge of the glass and put the sauce in the center.

China, silver and crystal do not have to be used only at the holidays. If you feel that just getting together is a special event, then by all means use them. Toasting is acceptable but clinking glasses is not recommended when using fine crystal or antique stemware. Both are delicate and chip easily.

Many antique China sets have wide mouth coffee cups and these are perfect for appetizer portions of soups.

Use silver spreaders to serve dips for dressy or casual entertaining. These also make a great hostess gift.

Chargers are normally used as decoration under a dinner plate, but are big enough to make great serving pieces. Line them with kale or lettuce for cheese or appetizer platters. Place a pedestal cake plate under a charger to create height.

For breakfast use a footed cake plate to serve bagels, muffins or danishes. Taking time to add interest to everyday meals makes guests feel very special. It is a nice touch and no more difficult than serving breakfast pastries on a dinner plate. Topping a footed cake plate with a smaller footed cake plate makes a creative tiered serving piece for appetizers and assorted desserts. Garnish with fresh flowers.

I recommend putting salad dressings, mayonnaise, mustard, ketchup or any other condiments in glass bowls, divided dishes or glass banana split dishes. These inexpensive dishes are more sanitary than dipping knives in jars and much more visually appealing.

Glass banana split dishes are the perfect size for dips, crackers and olives for two.

Setting the Table

The difference in formal and informal table settings is the number of utensils used. The setting should always be traditional.

The pattern of the plate should face the guest.

Wineglasses should be placed with the largest in front above the knife, working down to the smallest on the outside. Additional glasses are positioned in order of use and the course they are accompanying. If using a water glass, this should be the first glass above the knife. If serving champagne, the glass should be placed behind and between the water and white

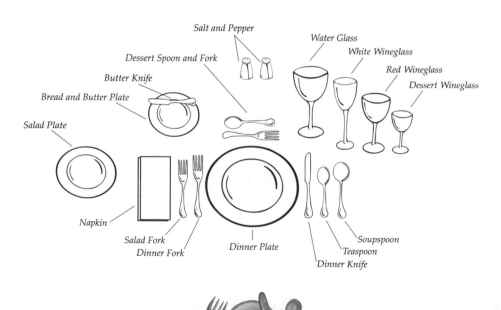

wineglass. Wines are generally not poured until everyone is seated, the host has checked the flavor, and the appropriate course is presented.

Knives are on the right and forks on the left. Knife blades should always be turned toward the plate.

A rule of thumb for properly setting the table is that the utensils are placed in the order they will be used, working from the outside in. The salad fork is placed to the left of the dinner fork, which is next to the plate.

The butter knife should sit straight across the top of the butter plate.

A teaspoon is placed to the right of the knife with the soupspoon to the right of the teaspoon.

Dessert forks and spoons may be placed horizontally above the plate with the fork facing right and the spoon facing left. An alternative is to serve the dessert with the dessert fork or spoon on the dessert plate and a spoon on the saucer with the coffee, handle parallel to the handle of the cup. Do not place the coffee cup and saucer on the table until dessert is served.

The host should announce dinner, tell guests where to sit or have place cards to avoid confusion. Once all the guests are seated, the host serves the guests from the left. If the host chooses to pass the serving pieces, passing begins with the person to the right of the host. All platters and bowls are passed to the right and the host is the last one served. To signify the start of the meal, the host puts their napkin in their lap and all guests should follow the host's lead. When the host begins to eat, guests should begin their meal.

Let the host or waitperson know you are finished with your meal by laying down your utensils properly. Place them side by side, handles of your utensils diagonal in the lower right hand quarter of the plate. Your knife should be on the outside with the blade turned in toward the fork on the left. Dishes should be removed from the right by your host or waitperson.

Menus and Wine Pairings
♦ denotes may be prepared ahead

Chicken Menus

Menu 1
Crab Stuffed Mushrooms, p. 66 ♦

Bibb Lettuce with Feta, Sautéed Apples and Pears with Red Wine Vinaigrette, p. 135

Red Wine Vinaigrette, p. 135 ♦

Cornish Game Hens with Honey Glaze and Caramelized Onions, p. 182

Honey Glaze, p. 182 ♦

Sautéed Spinach, p. 182

Rice Medley, p. 182

Chocolate Sacks Filled with White Chocolate Mousse, p. 256 ♦

Wine recommendation for appetizer: Champagne

Wine recommendations for dinner: White Burgundy or Chardonnay

Menu 2
Spicy Shrimp Dip, p. 72 ♦

Bibb Lettuce with Maple Raspberry Vinaigrette, p. 134

Maple Raspberry Vinaigrette, p. 134 ♦

Baked Sour Cream Marinated Chicken, p. 173 ♦

Wild Rice with Fresh Corn and Shallots, p. 221

Pineapple Carrot Cake with Cream Cheese Frosting, p. 266 ♦

Wine recommendations for appetizer: Gewürztraminer, Viognier

Wine recommendations for dinner: Pinot Noir or Chardonnay

Menu 3

Cheddar Stuffed Mushrooms, p. 45 ♦

Puffed Salami and Cheese Rolls, p. 57

Romaine and Red Leaf Lettuce with Caramelized Pecans and Gorgonzola, p. 131

Caramelized Pecans and Vinaigrette, p. 131 ♦

Basil Pesto Stuffed Chicken Breasts with Sun-Dried Tomato Cream, p. 172 ♦

Lemon Rice Pilaf, p. 221

Fruit Torte with Mascarpone Cream, p. 276 ♦

Wine recommendations for appetizers: Pinot Grigio or Orvieto

Wine recommendation for dinner: Chianti

Menu 4

Appetizer Brie Cheesecakes, p. 42 ♦

Crab Cakes with Rémoulade, p. 68 ♦

Strawberry Romaine Salad, p. 137

Cajun Chicken à la King, p. 181 ♦

Flourless Chocolate Torte with Vanilla Cream and Fresh Berries, p. 262 ♦

Wine recommendations for appetizer and first course: Chenin Blanc or Riesling

Wine recommendations for dinner: Pinot Noir or Fumé Blanc

Menu 5

Danish Meatballs in Sour Cream Dill Sauce, p. 55 ♦

Red Leaf Lettuce with Walnuts and Shallot Vinaigrette, p. 129

Shallot Vinaigrette, p. 129 ♦

Chicken Cordon Bleu, p. 176 ♦

GRAND MARNIER® Strawberry Napoleons, p. 272 ♦

Wine recommendation for appetizer: Pinot Noir

Wine recommendations for dinner: Chardonnay or Côtes du Rhône

Seafood Menus

Menu 6

Blue Cheese and Date Spread, p. 49 ♦

Romaine Salad with Pine Nut Vinaigrette, p. 126

Pine Nut Vinaigrette, p. 126 ♦

Salmon with Gorgonzola Cream Sauce, p. 202

Tomato Pie, p. 238

Fresh Fruit Tarts with GRAND MARNIER® Cream, p. 274

GRAND MARNIER® Cream, p. 274 ♦

Wine recommendations for appetizer: Sonoma Chardonnay or Conundrum

Wine recommendation for dinner: Fumé Blanc

Menu 7

Bacon Tomato Tartlets, p. 61 ♦

Green Olive Dip, p. 38 ♦

Mesclun Salad with Stilton, Grapes and Honey Vinaigrette, p. 139

Honey Vinaigrette, p. 139 ♦

Cajun Spiced Shrimp with Mushrooms, p. 212

White Chocolate Bread Pudding, p. 260 ♦

Wine recommendation for appetizers: Champagne

Wine recommendation for dinner: Chardonnay

Lamb Menus

Menu 8

Artichoke Dip, p. 37 ♦

Baked Brie with Pesto and Mushrooms, p. 43

Fresh Tomato, Kalamata and Feta Salad with Shallot Herb Vinaigrette, p. 120

Shallot Herb Vinaigrette, p. 120 ♦

Rosemary Grilled Lamb with Port Wine Sauce, p. 196 ♦

Port Wine Sauce, p. 196 ♦

Potatoes Gruyère, p. 223

Baklava with Vanilla Ice Cream, p. 286 ♦

Wine recommendations for appetizers: Fumé Blanc, Chardonnay

Wine recommendation for dinner: Rioja

Menu 9

Olive Stuffed Meatballs with Yogurt Sauce, p. 56 ♦
Romaine Salad with Fresh Basil Vinaigrette and Homemade Croutons, p. 127
Fresh Basil Vinaigrette and Homemade Croutons, p. 127 ♦
Grilled Lamb Chops with Peppercorn Currant Glaze, p. 193 ♦
Feta Potatoes, p. 231 ♦
Baklava, p. 286 ♦
Wine recommendations for appetizer: Petit Syrah or Côtes du Rhône
Wine recommendation for dinner: Cabernet

Beef Menus

Menu 10

Pineapple Shrimp Skewers with Honey Marinade, p. 74 ♦
Orange and Romaine Salad with Lime Vinaigrette and Sugared Pecans, p. 136
Lime Vinaigrette and Sugared Pecans, p. 136 ♦
Tropical Fiesta Steak with Island Marinade and Caribbean Salsa, p. 157 ♦
Caribbean Salsa, p. 157 ♦
Black Beans with Cilantro Pesto Rice, p. 222
Cilantro Pesto, p. 222 ♦
Chocolate Mango Parfait, p. 275
Beverage for appetizer and dinner: Beach Buzzes, p. 105
Beverage with dessert: Rum Mint Coolers, p. 106

Menu 11

Smoked Gouda and Prosciutto Puffs, p. 58 ♦
Smoked Salmon Spread, p. 71 ♦
Baked Goat Cheese Salad with Herb Vinaigrette, p. 128
Herb Vinaigrette, p. 128 ♦
Beef Tenderloin with Bordelaise Sauce, p. 152 ♦
Mashed Potatoes with Caramelized Onions, p. 229 ♦
Green Bean Bundles, p. 239 ♦
Pecan Crust Ice Cream Pie with Caramel Sauce, p. 283 ♦
Wine recommendations for appetizers:
Sauvignon Blanc, White Bordeaux, Italian Vernaccia
Wine recommendations for dinner: Bordeaux or Cabernet-Merlot Blend

Menu 12

Escargot with Shallot Cream in New Potatoes, p. 77 ♦

Sage Sausage Stuffed Mushrooms, p. 62 ♦

Hearts of Palm, Artichoke, Olive Salad with Red Wine Vinaigrette, p. 123 ♦

Beef Tenderloin with Mustard Brown Sugar Glaze, p. 155

Garlic Chive Mashed Potatoes, p. 228 ♦

Marinated Green Been Bundles, p. 240 ♦

Best Rolls Ever, p. 100 ♦

Strawberry White Chocolate Mousse Cake, p. 270 ♦

Wine recommendation for appetizers: Slightly chilled Pinot Noir

Wine recommendation for dinner: Australian Cabernet

Menu 13

Crab Artichoke Dip, p. 65 ♦

Thai Chicken Strudel, p. 65

Baked Goat Cheese Salad with Herb Vinaigrette, p. 128

Herb Vinaigrette, p. 128 ♦

Beef Tenderloin with Red Zinfandel Sauce, p. 151

Zinfandel Sauce, p. 151 ♦

Potato, Mushroom and Spinach Tart, p. 224

Bacon-Brown Sugar Carrots, p. 243

Tumbleweed Pie, p. 284 ♦

Wine recommendation for appetizers: Fumé Blanc

Wine recommendation for dinner: Red Zinfandel

"Nothing makes you more tolerant
of a neighbor's noisy party than being there."

Menu 14

Warm Spinach Artichoke Dip, p. 36 ♦

Shrimp Tartlets, p. 71 ♦

Frisée with Pistachios, Pears and Sherry Vinaigrette, p. 133

Sherry Vinaigrette, p. 133 ♦

Herb Crusted Prime Rib with Port Wine Sauce, p. 160 ♦

Port Wine Sauce, p. 160 ♦

Julienne Vegetable Medley, p. 232

Cambozola Mashed Potatoes, p. 226

Almond Lace Cookie Ice Cream Torte with Chocolate Sauce, p. 285 ♦

Wine recommendation for appetizers: Champagne

Wine recommendation for dinner: Australian Shiraz

Menu 15

Sausage En Croûte with Homemade Mustard, p. 60

Homemade Mustard, p. 60 ♦

Spiced Peaches, p. 138 ♦

German Rouladen with Rich Brown Gravy, p. 158 ♦

Red Cabbage, p. 248 ♦

Potato Dumplings

Amaretto Cheesecake, p. 249 ♦

Wine recommendation for appetizer: Riesling

Wine recommendation for dinner: Gewürztraminer

Menu 16

Chilled Artichoke Vegetable Dip, p. 38 ♦

Smoked Salmon Spread, p. 71 ♦

Mesclun Salad with Grapes, Stilton and Honey Vinaigrette, p. 139

Honey Vinaigrette, p. 139 ♦

Stovetop Beef Tenderloin with Rosemary Red Pepper Sauce, p. 154

Gruyère Butternut Squash Gratin, p. 247 ♦

Chokahlúa Cheesecake, p. 250 ♦

Wine recommendations for appetizers: White Bordeaux or Savignon Blanc

Wine recommendation for dinner: California Cabernet Sauvignon

Menu 17
Hearts of Palm and Artichoke Crostini, p. 35 ♦
Crab Tartlets, p. 67 ♦
Warm English Salad with Bacon, Stilton and Mushrooms, p. 130
Pepper Crusted Beef Tenderloin with Pinot Noir Sauce, p. 153
Pinot Noir Sauce, p. 153 ♦
Potatoes Gruyère, p. 223
Green Beans with Balsamic Brown Butter, p. 239
Bananas Foster with Vanilla Ice Cream, p. 281
Wine recommendation for appetizers: White Burgundy
Wine recommendation for dinner: California Pinot Noir

Casual Menus

Menu 18
Cheese Pecan Spread, p. 46 ♦
Easy Southwest Dip, p. 46 ♦
Southwest Caesar Salad with Homemade Croutons, p. 125
Dressing and Homemade Croutons, p. 125 ♦
Grilled Pork Tenderloin with Chili Maple Glaze, p. 165 ♦
Black Beans with Cilantro Pesto Rice, p. 222
Cilantro Pesto, p. 222 ♦
Pecan Lace Tacos with Lime Mousse Filling, p. 288 ♦
Wine recommendations for appetizers: Pinot Blanc, Viognier, Dry Riesling
Wine recommendations for dinner: Tempranillo, Grenache, Côtes du Rhône

Menu 19
Sun-Dried Tomato Spread, p. 40 ♦
Zucchini Bites, p. 39 ♦
Stuffed Portobello Mushrooms, p. 236
Garlic Rosemary Chicken, p. 180 ♦
Potatoes Gruyère with Shallots, p. 223 (variation)
Homemade Vanilla Ice Cream and Praline Grahams, p. 282, 299 ♦
Wine recommendation for appetizers: Champagne
Wine recommendation for dinner: Australian Chardonnay

Menu 20
Southwest Layer Dip, p. 51 ♦
Spicy Chicken Wings with Blue Cheese Dip, p. 63
Blue Cheese Dip, p. 63 ♦
Award winning Chili with Red Wine and Steak Tips, p. 118 ♦
Jalapeño Cornbread, p. 102 ♦
Buttermilk Brownies, p. 292 ♦
Beverage recommendation for appetizer and dinner: Assorted beers

Menu 21
Boiled Shrimp with Homemade Cocktail Sauce, p. 75 ♦
Marinated Pork Tenderloin with Molasses Barbecue Sauce, p. 166 ♦
Molasses Barbecue Sauce, p. 166 ♦
Corn Maque Choux, p. 244
Baked Mashed Potatoes Supreme, p. 227 ♦
Strawberry Lemon Poppy Seed Cake with White Chocolate Frosting, p. 268 ♦
Wine recommendation for appetizer: Sauvignon Blanc
Wine recommendation for dinner: Chateauneuf-du-Pape

Menu 22
Spinach Dip with Crudités, p. 37 ♦
Horseradish Shrimp Dip, p. 76 ♦
Garlic Marinated Pork Tenderloin, p. 164 ♦
Simple Garlic Potatoes, p. 232
"Jiffy's®" Cornbread Casserole, p. 245
Butterscotch Apple Crisp with Vanilla Ice Cream, p. 279 ♦
Wine recommendation for appetizers: Côtes du Rhône
Wine recommendation for dinner: Chateauneuf-du-Pape

Menu 23
Andouille and Shrimp Crostini, p. 70 ♦
Tortilla Roll Ups with Texas Salsa, p. 53/p. 52 ♦
Brisket with Honey Barbecue Sauce, p. 162 ♦
Broccoli Salad with Nuts and Raisins, p. 142 ♦
Picnic Potato Salad, p. 143 ♦
Chocolate Flower Pot Dessert, p. 258 ♦
Beverage recommendations for appetizers: Beer and Margaritas on the Rocks, p. 107
Wine recommendation for dinner: Grenache Shiraz

Pasta Menus

Menu 24

Puff Pastry Prosciutto Pinwheels, p. 59 ◆

Tomato Basil Bruschetta ◆ (serve along with Caesar Salad and Carbonara), p. 41

Caesar Salad with Homemade Croutons, p. 124

Homemade Croutons, p. 124 ◆

Carbonara, p. 216

Tiramisu, p. 290 ◆

Wine recommendation for appetizer: Vernaccia

Wine recommendation for dinner: Chianti

Menu 25

Hot Crab Dip, p. 69 ◆

Salad with Mandarin Oranges, Capers and Red Onion with a Spicy Vinaigrette, p. 148

Spicy Vinaigrette, p. 148 ◆

Pasta with Chicken, Cream and Creole Spice, p. 218

Creole Spice, p. 218 ◆

Rum Bundt Cake with Whipped Cream, p. 259 ◆

Wine recommendations for appetizer: Viognier, Riesling

Wine recommendation for dinner: Gewürztraminer

Brunch Menus

Menu 26

Hot Pepper Peach Dip, p. 45 ◆

Spinach Salad with Balsamic Maple Vinaigrette with Sugared Pecans, p. 132

Balsamic Maple Vinaigrette and Sugared Pecans, p. 132 ◆

Chicken and Shrimp in Puff Pastry, p. 88 ◆

Amaretto Cake, p. 267 ◆

Beverage recommendations for brunch: Champagne and coffee

Menu 27

Fruit Ambrosia, p. 83 ♦

Sausage and Spinach Quiche, p. 89

Rosemary Potatoes, p. 233

Baked Apple Donuts, p. 95

Beverage recommendations for brunch:
Spicy Bloody Mary Pitchers (p. 105) and coffee

Menu 28

Quick Eggs Benedict, p. 83

Fruit with Lime Cream, p. 81

Lime Cream, p. 81 ♦

SHAKE'N BAKE® Perfect Potatoes

Sour Cream Coffee Cake, p. 98 ♦

Beverage recommendations for brunch: Mimosas (p. 32) and coffee

Menu 29

Hashbrown Egg Pie, p. 93 ♦

Chorizo, Tortilla, Fresh Tomato Quiche, p. 90

Sausage Crescents, p. 96 ♦

SHAKE'N BAKE® Perfect Potatoes

Raspberry Streusel Muffins, p. 94

Beverage recommendations for brunch:
Spicy Bloody Mary Pitchers (p. 105), Mimosas (p. 32) and coffee

Menu 30

Fresh Fruit Mélange, p. 81 ♦

Spinach and Egg Pinwheel with Shrimp Sauce, p. 84 ♦

Tomato Tartlets, p. 61 ♦

Rosemary Potatoes, p. 233

Gingerbread with Pear Brandy Sauce, p. 264 ♦

Beverage recommendations for brunch: Champagne and coffee

Secrets from the Kitchen

Throughout the years I have been cooking I have learned helpful tips and have some recommendations for ingredients. I would like to share these discoveries with you so you may also enjoy them. Some of these tips are repeated in recipes in this book where applicable, along with other useful information.

Taste Tips

A good quality butter such as LAND O LAKES® is necessary. Some of the house brands seem to have too much water and not enough flavor. I don't use margarine unless specified by a recipe contributor.

I use HELLMANN'S® Real Mayonnaise only.

Pomi Tomatoes are shelf stable fresh tomatoes. They taste great in soups and sauces. They are found with the canned tomatoes but come in a shelf stable cardboard box.

Tomato paste and anchovy paste come in resealable tubes that are great because recipes usually call for such small amounts. The tomato paste is generally found on the aisle with the canned tomatoes and the anchovy paste is with the canned tuna and other fish products. They will need to be refrigerated once opened.

Chopped or minced garlic in a jar is wonderful for marinades or meatballs. For sauces and other recipes, I chop fresh garlic.

Parmigiano-Reggiano would be my recommendation for any recipe that uses Parmesan but sometimes it is difficult to find. I have specially noted several recipes where I would not substitute. Grate your own even if is not Parmigiano-Reggiano. U.S. renditions are aged 14 months and the Parmigiano-Reggiano is aged 2 years. The flavor of pre-grated Parmesans does not compare to freshly grated.

I cook with sea salt and keep both coarse and fine salt on hand. Sea salt has been used through the ages and is a result of the evaporation of seawater; the salt is a residue. It doesn't have the tang of regular table salt. Kosher salt is coarse grained and doesn't have any additives. Don't over salt. Put shakers on the table so guests may add additional salt to their taste. Try your sauces as you are cooking to determine if extra salt is needed.

Have you ever felt like something is missing from a recipe? When this happens, I use a sprinkle of *Tony Chachere's®*. *Tony Chachere's® Creole Seasoning* is a combination of salt, red pepper and other spices. *Tony Chachere's®* is in the spice section of most grocery stores or visit their web site at www.cajunspice.com or call 1-800-551-9066 to find a store that carries Tony's in your area.

A few drops of Tabasco® pepper sauce in chicken soup enhances the flavor.

Good stocks are always needed and they can be used when a recipe calls for broth. Keep a good chicken and lobster base on hand. Each must have water added according to the directions. If you can't find a good one in your grocery store ask a local restaurant or specialty store if they can order them for you in a size manageable for the home. Broth can be used from a can, but is not as rich in flavor.

Demi-glace is used in recipes when making a brown sauce. Most come as a concentrate and will need water added. In a store bought demi-glace, the complicated process has been done for you. A beef or veal reduction was made from boiling the bones for a 24 hour period to form a thick glaze. Vegetables and spices and a small addition of Madeira or sherry are added during the process to give the reduction a unique flavor.

Kitchen Bouquet® Browning and Seasoning Sauce adds color to your sauce. You only need a few drops for Rich Brown Gravy or a Balsamic Sauce.

Deli bacon tastes best, is thicker, and is less fatty. You can purchase the exact amount needed from the butcher at the grocery store meat counter.

Chocolate chip cookies taste better when they are made with shortening rather than butter. A few drops of butter flavoring can be added or butter flavored shortening is also good. Cookies hold up better over several days and stay moist without tasting stale.

All-purpose flour is used in all recipes in *Good Friends Great Tastes* unless otherwise noted.

Lightly salted butter is used when butter is called for unless otherwise noted.

Unsweetened coconut milk can be purchased in Asian grocery stores and might be found in the Asian section of your grocery store. The sweetened type on the beverage aisle cannot be substituted.

Whipping cream is such a wonderful treat especially in the summer over fresh strawberries. For two cups whipping cream, whip one cup (½ pint) heavy cream in a bowl that will hold at least 2 cups. (Heavy cream doubles in volume, when whipped.) Chill the heavy cream in the bowl you are whipping it in along with the beaters for 10 minutes in the freezer for best results. Whip with a hand mixer and as it starts to form soft peaks add one tablespoon of powdered sugar and one teaspoon vanilla. Taste and add more sugar if needed. Whip until it forms peaks. Do not over whip or it will turn to butter. To intensify the flavor of the berries toss them in a small amount of superfine sugar.

Light olive oils have been put through a filtration process but are no lighter in calories or fat. They will have a lighter, less classic olive oil flavor. Virgin olive oil and extra virgin olive oil have been cold pressed which is a chemical free process that involves only pressure and a lower level of acidity. The lower the acidity the higher the grade. Extra virgin olive oil is the finest and fruitiest of the olive oils and is less acidic. The deeper the color the more intense the flavor. Those olive oils that just state "olive oil" on the label are a combination of refined olive oil and virgin or extra virgin olive oil.

Oil is the last thing added to a salad dressing that you are trying to emulsify or thicken. Oil is added slowly in a thin stream at the same time as mixing rapidly either in a blender, processor or with a whisk. This is usually done with ingredients such as vinegar and oil that do not normally combine smoothly. This process disperses and suspends minute droplets of one liquid throughout the other to create a thick and satiny texture.

Balsamic vinegar is made from the Italian white Trebbiano grape and is aged in barrels to give it the dark color and pungent sweetness. Balsamic vinegar is great in salad dressings or drizzled over mozzarella and tomatoes and sprinkled with fresh chopped basil and olive oil.

Salad dressings are easy to make especially if made from vinegar and oil. Experiment. Oil and vinegar based dressings are much healthier than prepared versions. Salad is meant to be dressed lightly with a salad dressing. Do not drench. If you have any doubt that you put enough on, offer additional dressing in a small glass bowl with a spoon. Toss salad just before serving unless otherwise stated or greens will be limp. Some vinaigrettes will solidify due to the temperature in the refrigerator and the type oil used. If this happens, run warm water over the jar to melt the build-up and re-whisk.

Ice glazed frozen, boneless skinless chicken breasts bought in bulk are great for chicken dishes. One breast is equivalent to 1 cup when cubed or sliced. When grilling, grill extra chicken breasts and freeze them. You can defrost them later and add them to a casserole. The fresh grilled flavor tastes better than boiled or microwaved chicken.

White pepper is usually used instead of black in cream sauces. The flavor is slightly milder than black pepper, and it is more appealing than having dark flecks in your sauce.

Spices do have a shelf life. For best flavor replace ground spices after 3 years, whole spices 4 years, leafy herbs and seasoning blends after 2 years, seeds 4 years and extracts 4 years.

When cooking with eggplant, cut it open lengthwise and salt it. The salt draws out the bitter flavors as it sweats. Wipe off bitter juice and proceed.

Preparation

One of my biggest secrets for everyday meals is to keep my favorite cookbook and a blank pad and pencil in the car. I find I am more likely to cook something good if I can run into the store directly after work or running errands without having to go home. I will sit in the car in the parking lot, make a shopping list, shop and be ready to cook when I get home. You can keep copies of my "organized shopping list" in the car or create one on your computer.

When a recipe using a cake mix requires you to flour the pan, use a bit of the cake mix instead.

Sifting passes ingredients through fine mesh to remove large pieces. It incorporates air and will change measurements. Measure ingredients after they are sifted and that is the correct amount that should be added to the recipe, unless otherwise stated.

Devein shrimp by removing the gray-black vein from the back of the shrimp. You can do this with a sharp tip of a knife or the prong of a fork. This is optional on small and medium shrimp but recommended on large shrimp.

A tip from Linda Gore, Colleyville, Texas. It is sometimes hard to know how much of the asparagus you should trim off. If you take the asparagus and bend it, it will break where the tender stalk meets the tough stalk.

Chicken and Shrimp in Puffed Pastry or Cajun Chicken à la King is elegant enough for company because it is served in puffed pastry shells. The frozen puffed pastry dough also

comes in sheets and can be cut into shapes such as stars and flowers. Use the shapes as a topping for fresh fruit. Cut into a shape and sprinkle with regular sugar before baking, or sifted powdered sugar after baking, for a tasty addition to a fruit dessert.

Instead of relying on package labels, always use a measuring cup. It is best to measure liquids in glass measuring cups and solids in metal or plastic measuring cups. Solids can then be leveled off with a knife to ensure proper measurements.

If you accidentally over salt a dish while it is still cooking, drop in a peeled potato to absorb the excess salt. It is a quick fix. Remove potato before serving.

Although recipes state oven temperatures and cooking time, they are not always exactly accurate for your oven. Be sure to set your timer a few minutes earlier than the completed cooking time so that you can check the dish and avoid burning accidents. In turn, you may have to leave the dish in a little longer if oven is not as hot as the oven in which the recipe was tested. I recommend having your oven calibrated to the correct temperature if it isn't new. A magnetic mounted oven thermometer will also work and can be left in the oven to check the temperature to see how closely your controls are to the actual temperature.

A small amount of oil added to butter keeps the butter from burning.

Use a plastic sandwich bag pulled over your hand to reach into the shortening can to scoop up shortening for greasing pans.

When thickening sauces, there are several agents typically used. Arrowroot or arrowroot flour is probably the least called for but can be found in health food stores, Asian markets and some supermarkets. It is a rootstalk, dried and ground to a fine powder and has twice the thickening power of cornstarch. It should be mixed with a cold liquid and added to a hot mixture. Cornstarch is blended the same way with an equal part cold water blended with the dry powder. It should be blended to the consistency of heavy cream. When using flour and water as a thickener it should have the consistency of a thick paste.

When serving alcohol, always have bottled waters available or offer guests a glass of water with dinner. Sparkling waters (flavored/unflavored) are great to have on hand and are festive for those not drinking.

Kitchen Tools, Storage and Keeping Things Clean

A pepper mill is necessary for recipes that call for freshly ground or cracked pepper.

Kitchen shears are a great asset. They make cutting basil in strips or mincing parsley easier. You can use them to trim pie crusts too.

A portable egg timer allows you to time things that are in the oven when you need to go to another room in the house where the oven timer cannot be heard. The extra timer and the oven timer can both be used when you are timing more than one recipe.

Zyliss makes a cheese grater for fresh Parmesan. I can't be without it! Visit their web site at www.zylissusa.com or call customer service toll free at 1-888-794-7623 for a store near you that sells Zyliss.

Quiche dishes, pie plates and springform pans often have a size of 9 or 10 inches stated in a recipe. I have never experienced a problem using a 9 inch plate for a 10 inch or vice versa.

Meta West, Abilene, Kansas, informed me the ideal temperature for your refrigerator thermostat is 37 degrees Fahrenheit. This temperature will preserve foods better and keep foods from freezing.

Refrigerate fresh basil with a damp paper towel inside a plastic bag for up to 4 days. It will turn brown if you store it in the store container.

Ice that sits too long in the freezer takes on the flavor of what is being stored. When entertaining, be sure to have fresh ice, or buy a bag to use for the party.

When making potato dishes ahead, be sure and cook them and reheat before serving. Potatoes will turn brown over time if exposed to air when they are raw.

Brown sugar sometimes gets hard when stored in the box. It is best to store it in an airtight container. If it does become hard, peel half an apple and put it in the box for several hours or overnight. The sugar will soften and can be transferred to an airtight container.

Food storage is made easy and visible if you use self-sealing plastic bags. Several sizes are good to have on hand. Use one food item for each bag. Self-sealing plastic bags can be used to marinate meats too. Seal well before putting in the refrigerator. Get a step ahead in your recipes by storing pre-measured ingredients in plastic bags (grated cheese, chopped nuts, minced onions) so recipes can quickly be assembled the day of the event. Glass canning jars with lids are useful for storing your homemade vinaigrettes. Use canning labels to identify.

Wrap celery in foil before placing it in the refrigerator. It will stay fresh longer.

When storing potatoes, place an apple in the potato bag to keep them from budding.

Spray plastic storage dishes with cooking oil before pouring tomato-based sauces in them. It will keep them from staining.

Meta West, a Family and Consumer Science teacher, from Abilene, Kansas, passed on this tip for cleaning up after cooking. It is best to use cold water to soak dishes that held eggs, flour, starch, cream and milk. Hot water is best for those dishes that have contained oils, butter, sugar and syrup. Meta suggests using a paper towel to wipe away excess butter and oil prior to soaking. After dishes are soaked, all dishes should be washed with soap in hot water for sanitary purposes.

My friend Irem Himam from Balikesir, Turkey, taught me to remove burnt foods from saucepans and skillets. Add a drop of dish soap and enough water to cover the pan. Bring to boil on the stove and the pan will be easier to clean.

To get red wine stains off counter tops, sprinkle with baking soda and leave for a few minutes. Wipe away the stain with a wet dishcloth and stain should disappear. For red wine on carpets, sprinkle with iodized table salt and let sit. The salt will absorb the red wine. Scoop the excess off the carpet after several minutes and vacuum. If you get wine or coffee on table linens or clothing, don't pre-treat with bar soap, instead launder in detergent in warm or hot water. If stain remains, soak article in an all-fabric bleach before laundering again. Point out all stains to the dry cleaners if you are letting them care for your tablecloths and napkins.

Time Savers

Appetizers

Crostini is a great appetizer! Cut a baguette into ¼ inch slices. Slice one large tomato into 10 individual ¼ inch slices and chop. Brush one side of bread with olive oil and sprinkle with dried oregano. Mix chopped tomatoes with ½ cup fresh basil and 2 minced garlic cloves. Arrange a layer of tomatoes on top of baguette slice. Top with a thin slice of fresh mozzarella. Broil on cookie sheet until cheese melts. Serve immediately. Makes 24. You can use Gruyère cheese for a variation.

Need a super quick appetizer? Buy a can of refrigerated pizza dough. Buy some thinly sliced Cajun ham from the deli, and thinly sliced mozzarella. Roll up to the size of a fat cigar. Bake according to bread directions and slice into 1 inch slices. Serve with a side of warmed spaghetti sauce.

Would you like a great tasting salsa? Add to a large bottled picante sauce, 1 bunch fresh chopped green onions, six chopped tomatoes, one clove minced garlic and three chopped avocados. Mix up a few minutes before your event. It adds a homemade flavor.

Everyone loves chili con queso. Melt a large block of processed American cheese and a (10 ounce) can of Ro*Tel® Diced Tomatoes and Green Chiles over a double boiler or in a crockpot. Serve warm with tortilla chips. If you want a variation or to add some pizzazz fry hot sausage, drain and crumble and add this to the cheese-Ro*Tel® queso. For another great combination, defrost and squeeze all the water out of a (10 ounce) box of spinach and add to the cheese-Ro*Tel® tomato mixture or add a can of chili without beans. Combinations of onion and jalapeño will add more spice and can be included in any of these combinations. For a special treat, put a cool scoop of guacamole in the bottom of a bowl. Pour warm chili con queso over the top. Serve with tortilla chips.

For an elegant and easy sandwich for a buffet, serve beef tenderloin with horseradish or for a colorful combination, try thinly sliced cooked pork loin on mini rye breads with a small dollop of Red Cabbage. For tenderloin or pork, allow about a quarter pound of meat per person for a buffet of several meats and appetizers and ½ pound per person if it is dinner.

Cynthia Seymour, a friend from the Knots Landing Dinner Group, (a group of us that watched the television series together for years) uses regular biscuits from the refrigerator section as a bun for appetizer ham sandwiches. Bake according to package directions and brush with melted butter and sprinkle with dried dill weed. Serve with sweet, hot mustard and thinly sliced ham. Delicious!

Joe Graber, my friend and the photographer for this book, created this easy and elegant appetizer. He uses fresh Basil Pesto as the bed for sea scallops that have been sautéed in butter approximately 2 minutes on each side or until translucent. Allow three large sea scallops per guest.

Salads and Vegetables

Make a great summer salad by layering fresh sliced tomatoes with fresh mozzarella slices so they slightly overlap, and sprinkle with fresh chopped basil, balsamic vinegar and lightly drizzle with olive oil. For an elegant and colorful presentation alternate tomato and mozzarella in a circle, drizzle with oil and vinegar and add a basil leaf in the middle.

For a quick egg salad, hard boil 4 eggs and grate into a bowl. Mix ¼ cup HELLMANN'S® Real Mayonnaise, 2 tablespoons sweet pickle relish, a pinch of sugar, salt and pepper to taste. Serve warm on fresh wheat bread. A pinch of sugar added to the water keeps the shells from cracking when the eggs are boiled.

David Gore makes a great squash side dish. Cut up unpeeled yellow squash and zucchini (approximately 6 whole vegetables.) Chop one medium onion and dice 2 slices bacon. Cook bacon and onion together until the onion is translucent. Add one (10 ounce) can Ro*Tel® Diced Tomatoes and Green Chiles and the squash. Simmer covered, until squash is tender. Taste and if salt is needed, sprinkle with *Tony Chachere's® Creole Seasoning* to taste. If not using Ro*Tel®, add ½ cup water so that the vegetables steam.

Brunch

Fun brunch idea...no time to bake homemade muffins, but want a special touch? Mix together ½ cup good jam with 1 stick soft butter. Form into cylinder on wax paper and refrigerate. Slice off and this is a wonderful tasty, colored butter.

SHAKE'N BAKE® makes a great seasoning for fresh potatoes called Perfect Potatoes. Cut unpeeled potatoes in cubes and toss with seasoning. Bake on a cookie sheet with oil. These are great for brunch.

Sara Lee makes a frozen croissant that is a special treat. They get crispy on the outside and are soft in the middle. Serve with real butter and preserves.

My dad, Louie, makes a wonderful pancake treat. He uses pancake batter and makes the thin pancake recipe. He then rolls canned or fresh peach slices up inside and places seam side down on the plate. He rubs butter across the top and sprinkles them with sugar. They are great!

For a breakfast treat, butter Jewish rye bread on one side and spread with cream cheese on the other side. Put buttered side down in a pan as though you are making a grilled cheese sandwich. Top with thin sliced pastrami and warm in skillet, toasting the buttered side. Simultaneously fry eggs and top pastrami with a fried egg. This combination is delicious.

For a festive holiday brunch idea, arrange canned unbaked cinnamon rolls on a cookie sheet (approximately 17 rolls) in the shape of a Christmas tree and bake according to directions. Drizzle with frosting to look like lights strung on a tree. Use red and green gumdrops in between rolls as ornaments.

Champagne drinks are popular for brunch. Pour a glass of champagne and top off with a small amount of orange juice for a mimosa or cranberry juice for a poinsettia.

Dinner

Hamburgers don't have to be boring! My friend Jeanne Graber's mother, Claudette Patane, from Midlothian, Texas mixes in a (2.2 ounce) package dry beefy onion soup mix with 2 pounds ground beef or try mixing with a drained (10 ounce) can Ro*Tel® Diced Tomatoes and Green Chiles. Both are great!

Defrost boneless skinless chicken breasts and marinate overnight in Italian dressing and then roll in a stuffing mix. Drizzle 2 tablespoons butter mixed with one chopped garlic clove over the top and bake at 350 degrees approximately 25 to 30 minutes. These can also be sliced and added to a salad.

Dessert

Need a quick but elegant dessert? Mix 2 cups vanilla ice cream with 2 tablespoons KAHLÚA® and 4 tablespoons either Amaretto or Frangelico. Pour into a brandy snifter or open face champagne glass that has been tied with a foil edged ribbon at the base. Use the large side of your cheese grater to grate white chocolate on top. This will make 2 servings.

Simple Garnishes

Purple or green kale is a leafy vegetable that makes a wonderful liner for a plate of appetizers, sandwiches or vegetables. Most upscale grocery stores sell kale. To revive limp leaves, let them soak in cool water 30 minutes. Dry with paper towels before placing on the serving platter.

During the holidays, add greenery from the Christmas tree to your appetizer and cake platters. Add colorful pinecone ornaments to dress up the greenery.

A small hollowed out pumpkin or red cabbage is a fun way to serve a dip. A small pumpkin can be used as a soup bowl in the fall months.

Miniature vegetables are unusual and appealing. You can find these at upscale grocery stores. They require less preparation since they are used whole. Squash, zucchini and carrots are usually available in this size.

Grapes cut into small bunches are quite decorative on a cheese tray. Fill in bare areas on the cheese tray, piling up the small clusters and hiding stems. The guests can put a small cluster on their appetizer plate, rather than struggling to pull single grapes off. For frosted grapes, dip the grapes in egg whites and then sprinkle them with superfine sugar. Let them harden and they will have the appearance of a first winter frost. To tell if grapes are fresh, shake them. If they cling to their stems, they're fresh; if they fall off, they're past their prime. Champagne grapes are tiny grapes that are beautiful on a cheese platter and can be found at a upscale grocery stores that carry specialty produce.

If apples or pears are used, brush them lightly with lemon juice to keep them from discoloring. Dip tips of thinly sliced green apple in paprika and add to a cheese platter for color and interest. Add shredded purple cabbage beneath the fanned slices to create a colorful bed for the apples.

Star fruit or carambola is a wonderful garnish when cut crosswise into ¼ inch thick slices. It is yellow and resembles a star. Add as an edible decoration to cheese trays, desserts or salads.

Edible flowers have several decorative uses. You can mix an egg white with a few drops of water and brush the mixture onto all surfaces of the flower. Sprinkle with superfine sugar and let dry for a special look. They may be used in this way or directly from the package to decorate the top of white frosted mini cupcakes. Edible flowers may also be used to dress up a salad, to garnish a plate of cookies or glued to a place card as decoration. Use a Bundt cake pan to make an ice ring for a punch bowl, add edible flowers to the water before freezing.

Flowers of any kind add color and style to appetizer and dessert platters. Pastel roses are especially good for showers, weddings and teas.

A Bundt cake looks festive when the center of the cake is filled with fresh flowers. Crumble foil and put in the center so you have a base for the stems and fewer flowers will be needed.

Make leaves of chocolate to dress up simple desserts. Mix 8 ounces bittersweet chocolate with 1 ½ teaspoons shortening. Melt in double boiler. Paint the underside of a camellia, ivy or gardenia leaf and lay chocolate side up on a pan and put in refrigerator or freezer. Once hardened, peel leaf away and use the chocolate leaf as a garnish.

Chop fresh parsley and sprinkle it around the outside edge of a plate for added color.

When using fresh herbs in a main dish, reserve sprigs to later garnish the plates. It is best to use herbs found in the recipe for garnish; parsley is the exception. If it is necessary for presentation to add color to the plate, choose flavors that are complementary, i.e. finely chopped green and red pepper with the Shrimp with Cilantro Pesto Cream Sauce. When serving a sauce, try pouring the sauce outside of the meat rather than on top. Fanning meat over a mound of potatoes with sauce drizzled around the outside makes a nice presentation. Pay attention to plate presentation in restaurants and collect new ideas.

Purchase empty condiment bottles (squeeze variety) to create edible plate designs. Fill bottle with a thick enough sauce from your menu and draw designs on the outside edge of the plates you are using to serve the food. The sauce must be a consistency that won't run. Raspberry Sauce or Vanilla Sauce are often used as a decorative accent on a dessert plate. To paint heart shapes on a dessert plate, place a dollop of Vanilla Sauce in the center of the plate (creating a circle) and dot drops of Raspberry Sauce 1 inch apart at the edge of the circle. Stick a toothpick in the center of each dot, pull each up or down to form a heart. The slice of dessert is then placed on top of the sauce. Practice on a separate plate before decorating the guest's plates.

Appetizers

Kitchen tools needed

May be prepared ahead

Puff Pastry Prosciutto Pinwheels, page 59 ~ Appetizer Brie Cheesecakes, page 42
Horseradish Shrimp Dip, page 76 ~ Warm Spinach Artichoke Dip, page 36
Assorted Cheeses

Hearts of Palm and Artichoke Crostini

Makes: 36

1   baguette cut into ¼ inch
    slices
2   (6 ounce) jars marinated
    artichokes, drained and
    chopped
3   stalks hearts of palm
¾   cup **HELLMANN'S®** Real
    Mayonnaise
¼   cup sour cream
1¼ cups freshly grated
    Parmesan cheese
2   cloves garlic, chopped
⅛   teaspoon Tabasco® pepper
    sauce
¼   teaspoon *Tony Chachere's®*
    Creole Seasoning

Place all ingredients other than baguette in blender or processor. If bread seems too moist, toast slightly without mixture under broiler and turn over. Put mixture on top and broil until edges start to become golden. Try one in broiler since it is a quick appetizer. It would be best for you to know how long your broiler takes to toast. Temperatures of ovens vary! Continue to broil the remainder of the batch. Sprinkle lightly with *Tony Chachere's®* before serving. These are a great alternative to artichoke dip.

If baguette slices are large cut them in half. Women tend to eat appetizers that are smaller in size. Make filling up to a day ahead of time and keep in the refrigerator, covered. The day of the gathering purchase the bread from the store bakery or specialty baker. This is also great with walnut scallion bread, if available in your area.

blender or food processor
cheese grater

Warm Spinach Artichoke Dip

Serves: 6

2   (10 ounce) packages chopped frozen spinach
1   (14 ounce) can artichokes, drained and chopped
1   tablespoon fresh jalapeño, seeded
1   teaspoon minced garlic
¼   cup minced onion
2   cups Monterey Jack cheese, grated
1   (8 ounce) package cream cheese
1   cup freshly grated Parmesan cheese
1   teaspoon Tabasco® pepper sauce
½   teaspoon *Tony Chachere's® Creole Seasoning*
1   cup half-and-half
½   cup **HELLMANN'S®** Real Mayonnaise
1   small tomato chopped or cherry tomato fanned for garnish

Defrost spinach and squeeze out all water. Mix with all other ingredients. Bake at 350 degrees until bubbly, approximately 30 minutes. Sprinkle top lightly with additional *Tony Chachere's®* and garnish with tomato for added color. Serve with tortilla chips and side of salsa for a casual gathering. Serve without salsa and offer guests crackers instead of chips if the meal is more elegant. Make ahead and refrigerate. Heat before the guests arrive.

Goat cheese (½ cup) can be substituted for the Parmesan. Fried, crumbled bacon (4 slices) may also be added to either mixture. Bacon adds excellent flavor.

cheese grater

Carrie Hoffman:
Overland Park, Kansas

Carrie took me under her wing during high school. Our friendship continued when we both attended Kansas State. On this recipe the combination of ingredients grew from her original recipe after experimenting. Freshly grated Parmesan and Monterey Jack combined with cream cheese is a tasty combination.

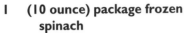

Spinach Dip with Crudités

Serves: 8

1   (10 ounce) package frozen
    spinach
1   (16 ounce) container sour
    cream
1   cup **HELLMANN'S®** Real
    Mayonnaise
3   green onions, chopped
1   (8 ounce) can drained,
    chopped water chestnuts
    (optional)
1   package **KNORR®**
    **Vegetable Soup, Dip and
    Recipe Mix**

Thaw spinach and squeeze as much water as possible out of spinach. Blend all ingredients together, cover and refrigerate. Make this a minimum of 2 hours ahead. Stir before serving. Serve with crackers or vegetables. Everyone should have this in their collection of recipes if they don't already!

Crudités are raw seasonal vegetables.

Artichoke Dip

Serves: 6

2   (14 ounce) cans artichoke
    hearts, drained
1   cup **HELLMANN'S®** Real
    Mayonnaise
1   cup freshly grated
    Parmesan cheese
3   cloves garlic, minced
    Dash Tabasco® pepper
    sauce

Chop the artichokes and mix with remaining ingredients. Bake at 350 degrees until thoroughly heated and bubbly 30 to 45 minutes. I prefer to mix this together and let it sit overnight. Bake before serving.

Lynne Borkowski, a friend from working together at Caviar to Cabernet, cooks, drains and crumbles 16 ounces of bacon and sprinkles this on top before baking. It makes a hearty appetizer and the bacon adds great flavor. For a southwest flair, I have also made this recipe and added a (7 ounce) can of chopped green chiles. Cooked, chopped shrimp (1 cup) adds a seafood twist!

cheese grater

Chilled Artichoke Vegetable Dip

Serves: 6

1 **(14 ounce) can artichoke hearts**
1 **package Hidden Valley® Original Ranch® dry dressing mix**
2 **cups sour cream**
⅛ **teaspoon Worcestershire sauce**
⅛ **teaspoon lemon juice**

Drain and chop artichokes. Combine with remaining ingredients. Refrigerate at least one hour or overnight. Serve with fresh vegetables.

Miniature vegetables are unusual and appealing. You can find these at upscale grocery stores. They require less preparation since they are used whole. Squash, zucchini and carrots are available in this size.

Green Olive Dip

Serves: 8

2 **(8 ounce) packages cream cheese**
¼ **cup HELLMANN'S® Real Mayonnaise**
⅓ **cup grated freshly grated Parmesan cheese**
¼ **cup chopped green onion**
6 **slices deli bacon, cooked and crumbled**
1 **(5 ounce) jar pimento stuffed olives, drained and chopped**
¼ **teaspoon Tabasco® pepper sauce**

Soften cream cheese in microwave 15 seconds. Combine with the other ingredients. Refrigerate until ready to serve. May be made up to 2 days ahead. If desired, cook an additional strip of bacon or reserve one strip to crumble over the top.

Deli bacon tastes best, is thicker, and is less fatty. You can purchase the exact amount needed from the butcher at the grocery store meat counter. Serve dip with water crackers. Water crackers or biscuits are a bland, crisp cracker that allows the flavor of the dip to be appreciated!

cheese grater

Lynne Borkowski: Grapevine, Texas

This recipe is easy and delicious. It is great with cocktails. Lynne and her husband Richard are friends that don't mind unannounced guests. We have had quite a few impromptu gatherings to taste new recipes.

Zucchini Bites

Serves: 4

2   **medium zucchini, washed and unpeeled**
⅓   **cup HELLMANN'S® Real Mayonnaise**
½   **cup freshly grated Parmigiano-Reggiano cheese**
I   **teaspoon fresh basil**
     Paprika

Score sides of zucchini with a channel knife starting at the top of the zucchini and scraping down in 3 straight lines, each a third of the way around. Slice zucchini in ¼ inch slices. Mix together the mayonnaise, Parmigiano-Reggiano and basil. Spread each slice with a thin layer of mixture. Arrange on foil covered cookie sheet. Preheat broiler. Broil approximately 30 seconds or until cheese slightly browns. Sprinkle with paprika. Mayonnaise, cheese and basil may be mixed ahead of time and refrigerated until ready to use.

¼ cup chopped kalamata olives can be added to this mixture. Chopped red pepper can be used as a garnish for a more colorful combination once they are removed from the broiler. To add spice, omit basil and use chopped jalapeño and ½ cup chopped onion. Melba toast rounds can be substituted for zucchini.

A channel knife is a kitchen tool that has a small sharp "v" that peels the skin away, creating a design in the surface of the vegetables.

channel knife
cheese grater

Sun-Dried Tomato Spread

Serves: 8

2 tablespoons pine nuts, toasted

2 large cloves chopped, fresh garlic

½ cup chopped drained sun-dried tomatoes (oil packed)

2 tablespoons fresh, chopped basil

1 (8 ounce) package cream cheese at room temperature

¼ teaspoon *Tony Chachere's®* *Creole Seasoning*

⅛ teaspoon cayenne

Toast pine nuts 3 minutes in 350 degree oven or until lightly golden. Remove from baking sheet immediately. Mix pine nuts with next 3 ingredients in blender or food processor. Soften cream cheese in microwave 15 to 20 seconds and mix with tomato mixture and spices. Taste, and if more salt or spice is needed add more Tony's seasoning. If more spice rather than salt is preferred add more cayenne. Transfer into the bowl you would like to serve in and garnish with parsley, basil or good quality black olives. Serve slightly chilled with water crackers. Make 8 to 12 hours ahead.

blender or food processor

Shelley Castor: Phoenix, Arizona

Shelley and I used to room together on business trips. We bonded immediately and food was definitely a topic of many of our conversations. This recipe is a neighborhood favorite.

Tomato Basil Bruschetta

Serves: 6

4 ripe tomatoes, cored
2 sprigs basil, leaves only, finely chopped
1 tablespoon fresh parsley, chopped
½ red onion, peeled and finely chopped
3 shallots, peeled and finely chopped
½ teaspoon sea salt
½ teaspoon freshly ground pepper
1½ cups olive oil
½ cup water
1 teaspoon fresh oregano, finely chopped
1 tablespoon red wine vinegar
1 loaf Italian bread or a French baguette
3 garlic cloves, peeled and split

Chop the tomatoes with skin and seeds into ¼ inch cubes and place in a large bowl. Add the basil, parsley, onion and shallots. Season with salt and pepper to taste. Pour in olive oil, water, oregano and vinegar. Marinate for 3 hours at room temperature. Refrigerate prior to serving. May be made a day ahead, but refrigerate after it marinates 3 hours. Cut bread into 1 inch slices. Toast slightly in oven and rub top and sides with split garlic cloves. When ready to serve, top with generous amount of tomato mixture. Serve immediately.

Kitchen shears are a definite asset. They make cutting basil in strips or chopping parsley much easier.

Appetizer Brie Cheesecakes

Makes: 24

4	**crispy cracker breads, zwieback or Melba toasts**
2	**tablespoons melted butter**
6	**ounces cream cheese**
4½	**ounces Brie cheese, with rind**
1	**egg**
1	**tablespoon dry sherry**
⅛	**teaspoon salt**
⅛	**teaspoon garlic powder**
⅛	**teaspoon pepper**
24	**small fresh basil leaves**
6	**cherry tomatoes, quartered**
	Small basil leaves for garnish
	Cooking spray

Spray 24 mini muffin tins with cooking spray. Put crackers in blender to crush. Put crushed crackers in a bowl and add the melted butter to the crumbs. Press into the bottom of muffin tins. Beat together cream cheese, Brie, egg, sherry, garlic powder, salt and pepper with a hand mixer until combined. This may be made 1 day ahead, covered and refrigerated. The mixture will be lumpy. Place one teaspoon in each muffin tin. Place a basil leaf on top. Top with more cheese mixture and bake at 350 degrees for 10 to 12 minutes. Cool slightly. Remove from tins and top each with a cherry tomato wedge and additional basil leaf. Serve slightly warm. Cracker bread can be found with the specialty crackers.

blender
hand mixer
mini muffin tins

This idea of mini cheesecakes can be used for a sweet dessert cheesecake as well. Substitute a recipe from the dessert section. The decoration on top could be an edible flower or fruit. The cracker base can be made from graham crackers or gingersnaps mixed with butter for a dessert cheesecake. Bake mini dessert cheesecakes 10 to 12 minutes or until edges are slightly golden. I would not recommend the batter for Chokahlúa Cheesecake be used for this procedure.

Baked Brie with Pesto and Mushrooms

Serves: 6

1	tablespoon butter
¾	cup sliced mushrooms
1	clove garlic, minced
1	(8 ounce) wheel of Brie
2	teaspoons pesto, from a jar
8	sheets phyllo dough, thawed
	Fresh basil sprig for garnish
	Butter flavored cooking spray

Melt butter in saucepan and sauté mushrooms and garlic. Set aside. Slice Brie horizontally through the middle and spread pesto on the inside bottom layer. Spread mushrooms evenly over the pesto. Put other half of Brie back on top. Remove phyllo from the refrigerator and unwrap. As you work, keep it covered with a damp dish towel. On a baking sheet, lay out one sheet of phyllo and spray with cooking spray. Place Brie in center of sheet and wrap phyllo around Brie. Each time you wrap the Brie in the individual sheets, spray with cooking spray and turn the Brie completely over. Repeat this procedure three more times. Spray a sheet of phyllo with oil and stack another one on top of it, spray with oil. Layer a total of 4 sheets together. Place the wrapped Brie in the center of these and bring the corners to the center of the Brie, gathering it up in the center with your fingers. Use kitchen string and secure it so it looks ruffled at the top like a package. Bake at 350 degrees 15 minutes, until lightly golden. Remove the string and replace it with a ribbon and a fresh sprig of basil.

kitchen string
ribbon

If phyllo dough is frozen, thaw completely in the refrigerator before using. Thawing at room temperature makes dough difficult to handle. Refreeze any unused phyllo after thawing.

Baked Brie with Peach-Port Preserves

Serves: 6

Peach with Port Preserves

1 **(16 ounce) bag of frozen peaches**
½ **cup brown sugar**
½ **cup white sugar**
1 **teaspoon orange zest**
½ **orange, squeezed**
½ **cup port wine**

Brie

1 **(8 ounce) wheel of Brie**
¼ **cup chopped pecans, toasted**
8 **sheets phyllo dough**
Butter flavored cooking spray
4 **tablespoons Peach-Port Preserves (recipe above)**

In a medium saucepan, add the peaches, brown and white sugar, orange zest, juice from the orange and port wine. Cook until thickened, approximately 15 minutes. Place in refrigerator until ready to use. Slice Brie horizontally through the middle so you have a top and a bottom. Measure out preserves and finely chop the peaches (use minimal juice). Spread this on top of the sliced Brie and top with the pecans. Remove phyllo from the refrigerator and unwrap. As you work, keep it covered with a damp dish towel. On a baking sheet, lay out one sheet of phyllo and spray with cooking spray. Place Brie in center of sheet and wrap phyllo around Brie. Each time you wrap the Brie in the individual sheets, spray with cooking spray and turn the Brie completely over. Repeat this procedure three more times. Spray a sheet of phyllo with oil and stack another one on top of it, spray with oil. Layer a total of 4 sheets together. Place the wrapped Brie in the center of these and bring the corners to the center of the Brie, gathering it up in the center with your fingers. Use kitchen string and secure it so it looks ruffled at the top like a package. Bake at 350 degrees 15 minutes, until lightly golden. Remove the string and tie with a ribbon for garnish. Remaining preserves can be used as a topping for muffins as well. Keep leftover preserves refrigerated.

Slivered almonds may be substituted for pecans as well as Bing cherries, pears or apples in place of peaches.

kitchen string
ribbon
zester or cheese grater

Cheddar Stuffed Mushrooms

Serves: 6

I	**pound mushrooms**
6	**tablespoons unsalted butter**
½	**cup walnuts**
I	**yellow onion, chopped**
I	**cup grated cheddar cheese**
½	**cup bread crumbs**
½	**cup fresh parsley, chopped**
¼	**teaspoon salt**

Preheat oven to 350 degrees. Remove stems from washed mushrooms and chop. Melt butter. With a pastry brush, brush butter over mushrooms. Arrange caps on a baking sheet. Toast walnuts on a baking sheet for 3 minutes in oven. Chop fine. Sauté onion and stems in remaining butter. Remove from heat and stir in remaining ingredients. Divide mixture among mushroom caps, mounding slightly. These can be made 4 hours ahead. Refrigerate. Bake 20 to 25 minutes.

pastry brush
cheese grater

Hot Pepper Peach Dip

Serves: 12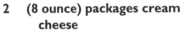

2	**(8 ounce) packages cream cheese**
I	**(7.6 ounce) jar Rothchild Hot Pepper Peach Preserves**
I	**tablespoon seeded, chopped jalapeño**
I	**teaspoon paprika**
I	**teaspoon chopped parsley**
I	**teaspoon dry minced onion**
8	**ounces shredded mozzarella cheese**

Set aside approximately I cup shredded cheese to sprinkle over dip. Mix remaining ingredients together with a hand mixer. Put dip in one to two bowls depending on the size. Sprinkle shredded cheese on top and refrigerate. This dip is spicy yet slightly sweet. It is delicious! A large (II ounce) jar will make two batches.

The best cracker for this dip is called Neva Betta. It doesn't have salt, but has great flavor and is good for dips. Check your local grocery store, specialty cheese or gourmet retailer. If you are unable to find, call Joel at 954-458-8080. The Hot Pepper Peach Jam can be found at gourmet retailers or call Rothchild Berry Farms for a store near you at 1-800-356-8933. For a variation, try the Hot Pepper Raspberry Jam in place of peach.

cheese grater
hand mixer

Cheese Pecan Spread

Serves: 8

½ cup coarsely chopped pecans
2 cups grated cheddar cheese
¾ cup **HELLMANN'S®** Real Mayonnaise
2 tablespoons chopped green onion
4 strips cooked bacon, drained and crumbled

Chop nuts coarsely with a sharp knife. Combine all ingredients and chill 12 hours. Serve with bagel chips or water crackers. The green onions and bacon are delicious mixed with the cheddar.

 cheese grater

Beth Lemaster, Carrollton, Texas

Beth was thrilled when she took this spread to several gatherings and got calls from friends, asking her for the recipe. Beth joined our Girl's Dinner Club as a guest of a member years ago when her husband was working in Los Angeles. We are happy they didn't have to move and we continue to get together.

Easy Southwest Dip

Serves: 6

1 (16 ounce) carton sour cream
½ cup **HELLMANN'S®** Real Mayonnaise
1 package **KNORR®** Vegetable Soup Dip and Recipe Mix
1 cup chunky salsa
2 teaspoons chili powder
¼ cup chopped fresh cilantro (stems removed)

In a bowl, combine sour cream, mayonnaise, dry soup mix, salsa, chili powder and cilantro. Cover and refrigerate a minimum of 2 hours. Serve with tortilla chips.

Goat Cheese and Olive Finger Sandwiches

Serves: 6

½ **cup good quality ripe black olives**
2 **ounces mild goat cheese**
I **green onion, minced**
½ **clove garlic, chopped**
⅛ **teaspoon Tabasco® pepper sauce**
I **loaf good quality sliced white bread (sour dough is firm and works well)**
¼ **cup minced parsley**

Remove pits from the olives if necessary and chop the olives. Put the olives, goat cheese, green onion, garlic and Tabasco® sauce in a blender or food processor or use a hand mixer to blend. Use cookie cutter to cut out shapes in the bread. Do not use crusts. Cut out the bread shapes and spread goat cheese, olive mixture on one side of bread shape. Top with another bread cutout. The filling should spill out the sides enough that chopped parsley will outline the shape when you dip them. Dip the edge of the sandwiches in the minced parsley. The olive mixture can be made ahead. Bring to room temperature before using. The bread can be cut out and stored overnight in an airtight container.

This is a great holiday tea or party item. It can be used for any occasion or served as a spread. If these ingredients don't appeal to you, use a chicken salad with finely chopped ingredients or some other filling. Garnish the plate with fresh greenery and cranberries during the holidays.

holiday or other 2 inch cookie cutter
blender, food processor or hand mixer

To easily remove pits from olives, place them on a work surface and roll over them with a rolling pin, then pick out the pits.

Pistachio-Crusted Goat Cheese with Roasted Garlic and Apricot Chutney

Serves: 6

Goat Cheese
1   (10 ounce) log plain Montrachet goat cheese
1   cup shelled pistachios, chopped
¼   cup bread crumbs

Roasted Garlic
2   bulbs garlic
⅛   cup olive oil

Apricot Chutney
1   tablespoon butter
1   clove garlic, minced
½   cup sugar
½   cup brown sugar
½   teaspoon salt
3   tablespoons white balsamic vinegar
½   cup dried apricots, chopped
1   Granny Smith apple, peeled and chopped
½   teaspoon, peeled fresh ginger, chopped
½   orange, squeezed
1   thinly slice baguette or water crackers

Chop pistachios in blender or food processor and mix with bread crumbs. Roll the goat cheese in this mixture. Gently press pistachios into surface and refrigerate. Make chutney up to 3 days ahead and refrigerate. Melt butter in saucepan and add garlic. Sauté until fragrant and butter golden. Do not burn butter. Add the sugars, salt and vinegar. Cook over low until the sugar is dissolved. Add the apricots, apple, ginger and juice from the orange. Cook the mixture until it coats the back of the spoon, about 15 minutes. Do not overcook. Set aside and refrigerate once cooled. An hour before serving the appetizer, preheat the oven to 350 degrees. Cut ¼ inch off the heads of garlic to expose the cloves. Place garlic in a baking dish, drizzle with oil and toss to coat. Place cut side up and cover tightly with foil. Roast the garlic until the skins are golden and garlic is tender, approximately 55 minutes. Cool slightly before serving. Place the log of goat cheese on a baking dish and place in the oven to warm for 5 to 7 minutes, while garlic is cooling. Serve on a platter with a garlic bulb on each side. Serve the chutney in a dish on the side with a spreader for serving. Spread a thin slice of baguette with roasted garlic, a generous amount of goat cheese and a top with chutney. The sweet chutney with the goat cheese and garlic is delicious. You may experiment with serving technique. You may choose to spread these for the guests prior to serving and place on platter or drizzle the chutney over the top of the goat cheese log before serving with the garlic bulbs on the side.

Montrachet cheese is a white chèvre (goat cheese) from Burgundy, France. It is soft, moist and has a creamy texture and tangy flavor.

blender or food processor
vegetable peeler

Blue Cheese and Date Cheese Spread

Serves: 12

3   (8 ounce) packages cream
    cheese
4   ounces blue cheese
2   cups sharp cheddar cheese,
    grated
1   (8 ounce) package dates,
    chopped
1   cup pecans, toasted

Preheat oven to 300 degrees and toast pecans 3 to 4 minutes. Mix cream cheese, blue cheese, cheddar cheese and chopped dates together. You may make this as a spread or make into one large or two small cheese balls. Coarsely chop pecans. If making into cheese balls, roll in pecans, otherwise sprinkle nuts on top of spread. This can be made 2 days ahead. Do not roll or sprinkle nuts on top until the day you are serving.

A small hollowed out pumpkin or red cabbage is a colorful way to serve a dip.

cheese grater

Jeanne Graber: Arlington, Texas

Jeanne is a dear friend. We used to spend every Tuesday evening visiting over wine and appetizers when she worked near my house. She made this fabulous mixture as a cheese ball when my parents came in town to visit and she and Joe invited us for dinner. I love the blue cheese and date combination.

Black Bean Dip

Serves: 6

2   **(15.5 ounce) cans of black beans, drained and rinsed**
8   **Roma tomatoes, seeded**
2   **tablespoons red wine vinegar**
3   **tablespoons olive oil**
1   **cup chopped, green onions**
1   **tablespoon fresh cilantro, chopped**
¼   **teaspoon ground cumin, or more to taste**
2   **cloves garlic, minced**
1   **fresh jalapeño, seeded and finely chopped**
  Salt and freshly ground black pepper, to taste

Mix ingredients together and chill. Serve with tortilla chips. Additional fresh seeded, minced jalapeño may be added if more spice is preferred.

Donna Edwards, Dallas, Texas

Donna made this several years ago for a "Dinner Club" gathering and I put the recipe in my collection. I love this as an alternative to cheesy southwest dips.

Tomatoes are the fruit of a vine native to South America. It was not until 1893 that the tomato was given a classification of vegetable. This was done for trade purposes. Roma tomatoes or "Italian plum tomatoes" are egg shaped and flavorful.

Southwest Layer Dip

Serves: 8

3 ripe avocados
2 tablespoons lemon juice
1 clove fresh garlic, chopped
1 (8 ounce) carton sour
    cream
1 (1.25 ounce) package taco
    seasoning
2 (9 ounce) cans bean dip
8 ounces grated cheddar
    cheese
1 bunch green onions
1 medium tomato, chopped
1 (4.25 ounce) can ripe black
    olives, chopped

Mash the avocados with the lemon juice and garlic. Set aside. Mix the taco seasoning with the sour cream and set aside. In a decorative large glass bowl or a 9 x 13 inch pan, spread the bean dip on the bottom of dish. Layer the guacamole over the bean dip, then the sour cream mixture. Sprinkle the cheese over these mixtures and sprinkle the tomatoes, black olives and green onions over this for color. You may make 24 hours ahead. Serve this with tortilla chips.

The mashed avocados, lemon and garlic are the start of a great Guacamole. Laurie Martell Pino of Denver, Colorado is a friend from college. She increases the number of avocados to 4 or 5 and adds 1 to 3 tablespoons total garlic, depending on your taste, ½ of a chopped red onion, ⅓ cup salsa and black pepper, to taste. Sour cream may be added to the Guacamole if you like a creamier consistency. Fresh seeded, minced jalapeño can be added if you want to add spice.

 cheese grater

Texas Salsa

Makes 5 cups

2   **fresh tomatoes**
2   **(14.5 ounce) cans of Mexican stewed tomatoes with peppers and spices**
2   **yellow or white onions, chopped**
5   **jalapeños with seeds**
4   **serrano peppers with seeds**
5   **large cloves garlic**
1½ **tablespoons cumin seed**
2   **teaspoons salt**

Put the tomatoes in the blender to chop. Add the cans of tomatoes with juice and onions. Keep a large bowl near so when blender gets full you may dump some of the salsa out and add additional ingredients. Add jalapeños, serranos and garlic. Add the cumin seed and the salt. Stir all ingredients together. Make sure that all flavors blend and everything is chopped. Keep refrigerated in a sealed container and serve with tortilla chips, Mexican casseroles or eggs.

The hot flavor of this salsa comes from the jalapeños and serrano peppers that can vary in strength each time you buy them. If you prefer a milder sauce, then start with 3 jalapeños and 2 serrano peppers and work your way up. You can always add more. Color of the sauce will vary due to the ripeness of the tomatoes.

 blender

Tommy and Vivie Dodd, Plano, Texas

Tommy and Vivie Dodd make this and give it as gifts, besides using it on everything from chips to baked potatoes. They came over one Sunday afternoon for barbecue and we all made it together. This is easy and fun to make. You may want to wait until guests arrive and include them in preparing this sauce. It can be eaten immediately.

White and yellow onions are considered to be mild flavored onions. They can be used interchangeably.

Tortilla Roll Ups

Serves: 8

1 **package flour tortillas**
2 **(8 ounce) packages of cream cheese**
4 **green onions, chopped**
½ **cup cheddar cheese**
1 **clove minced garlic**
¼ **cup salsa**
   Extra salsa for dipping

Mix together cream cheese, onions, cheddar, garlic and salsa. Thinly spread on one side of a flour tortilla. Roll up to the size of a cigar. Be sure ends have enough filling. Wrap and refrigerate overnight or until firm. Slice in ½ inch slices and serve with extra salsa.

Chopped black olives, fresh, seeded and minced jalapeño, drained green chiles or canned, drained, black beans are also great additions to the basic mixture.

 hand mixer

When planning your appetizers balance the ingredients so there is a variety. Don't have them all be cream cheese based. Look at what ingredients are overlapping and choose things that complement one another and are not too similar in color, taste or texture.

Tamale Dip

Serves: 8

2 **(15 ounce) cans tamales, with juice**
1 **(16 ounce) can chili without beans**
1 **(8 ounce) jar picante sauce**
2 **(5 ounce) jars old English cheese**
1 **chopped onion**

Chop tamales and mix together with all other ingredients. This may be made ahead and refrigerated. Bake in a quiche pan for 15 to 20 minutes or until heated and bubbly. Serve warm with tortilla chips. As an alternative you may heat over double boiler and serve out of a fondue pot or crockpot, but I think a quiche pan or pie plate is more appealing. A processed American cheese can be substituted for old English cheese.

You may be able to get homemade tamales with some gourmet variations in your area. I have used spinach tamales made with cream cheese for this recipe and it was exceptional.

Cocktail Meatballs

Serves: 8

Meatballs
- 1½ **pounds ground chuck**
- 6½ **ounces evaporated milk**
- 1 **cup instant rice**
- 1 **egg**
- ½ **cup chopped onion**
- ½ **teaspoon salt**
- 1 **teaspoon minced garlic**
- ¼ **teaspoon chili powder**

Sauce
- 2 **cups catsup**
- ½ **cup brown sugar**
- 2 **tablespoons liquid smoke**
- 1 **teaspoon minced garlic**
- ½ **cup chopped onion**

Mix ground chuck with next 7 ingredients and shape into balls. For a cocktail party they should be walnut size. Combine sauce ingredients in medium saucepan and heat slowly to dissolve the brown sugar. Put meatballs in a baking dish and pour the sauce over them. Bake 1 hour at 350 degrees. Remove meatballs with a slotted spoon into a serving dish that continues to warm, such as a chafing dish or crockpot. Stir sauce so juices of meatballs blend with the sauce. Spoon over meatballs. Serve with toothpicks. These may be made ahead and frozen. Defrost and reheat. Serve warm.

These meatballs are dual purpose. Substitute the meatballs for the ground beef in the recipe (p. 217) for spaghetti with meatballs.

chafing dish or crockpot
slotted spoon
toothpicks

Melissa Weikel: Topeka, Kansas

Melissa and I have been friends since college. After graduation we both lived in Dallas and were able to get together fairly often. Now we live in separate cities. We only get together once a year, but we always manage to enjoy a new restaurant and good conversation. Everyone loves these bite size meatballs with their slightly sweet flavor.

Chopped or minced garlic in a jar is great for marinades or meatballs. For sauces and other recipes, I chop fresh garlic.

Danish Meatballs with Dill Sauce

Makes: 80 meatballs

Meatballs
1	**pound ground beef**
½	**pound ground veal**
½	**pound ground pork**
2	**teaspoons salt**
¼	**teaspoon pepper**
2	**eggs**
⅓	**cup chopped onion**
½	**cup heavy cream**
1	**cup bread crumbs**
	Additional salt and pepper, to taste

Sauce
1	**cup butter**
¼	**cup flour**
2	**cups chicken broth**
16	**ounces sour cream**
¼	**cup chopped fresh dill or 1½ tablespoons dried dill weed**
	Salt and pepper, to taste

Mix ground meats, salt, pepper, eggs, onion and cream. Make meatballs and roll in bread crumbs. Bake meatballs at 375 degrees for 35 minutes. Taste meatballs and add a sprinkle of salt and pepper if needed. Melt butter in a large pan. Whisk in flour and gradually stir in broth. Cook over low heat stirring constantly until sauce bubbles and thickens. Stir in sour cream and dill. I prefer fresh dill. Add salt and pepper, to taste. Pour sauce over meatballs. Meatballs can be made ahead and frozen (without sauce) or refrigerated with sauce. For frozen meatballs, thaw, heat in oven and make sauce. Serve warm in a chafing dish or crockpot. For refrigerated meatballs with sauce, heat in double boiler. Serve with toothpicks.

---

whisk
chafing dish or crockpot
double boiler
toothpicks

Joan Willhite: Yellow Springs, Ohio

Joan was my work counterpart in Ohio. When we all met for corporate gatherings it was like family getting together. Joan doubles this recipe because these meatballs get eaten so quickly.

Olive Stuffed Meatballs with Yogurt Sauce

Makes: 50 meatballs

Meatballs
I	**pound ground beef**
2	**eggs**
I	**cup dry bread crumbs**
2	**cups lemon-lime carbonated drink**
I	**(10 ounce) jar pimento stuffed green olives**
I	**teaspoon garlic salt**
I	**teaspoon onion salt**

Yogurt Sauce
2	**cucumbers**
I	**cup plain yogurt**
2	**teaspoons vinegar**
I	**tablespoon olive oil**
½	**teaspoon salt**
2	**garlic cloves, pressed**

Rinse olives under cold water to remove brine and salt. Dry on paper towels. Combine all meatball ingredients except olives, and mix well. Mold meat mixture around each olive to make a meatball. Broil in a jelly-roll pan on top rack in oven about 2 inches from the heat for 8 minutes, turning once. To make Yogurt Sauce, peel the cucumber and halve lengthwise removing all of the seeds. Grate cucumber and drain off excess liquid. Combine with remaining sauce ingredients and mix until smooth. Serve warm meatballs with toothpicks and chilled sauce on the side. The meatballs can be made ahead and reheated. Sauce should be refrigerated until ready to serve.

For Chicken Souvlaki, marinate chicken breasts in ½ cup olive oil, ¼ cup lemon juice, ½ cup red wine, 3 cloves chopped garlic and ½ chopped onion. Sprinkle with oregano and grill. To serve, cube chicken and place on warm pita bread. Top with Yogurt Sauce, chopped red onion and lettuce and fold over for a delicious sandwich.

jelly-roll pan
cheese grater
garlic press
toothpicks

Sami El-Beheri:
Colorado Springs, Colorado

Sami made these meatballs for us when he was in town visiting his daughter, Twila. Sami travels around the world and keeps me informed on money exchange and car rental tips. He has many wonderful recipes and enjoys cooking.

Puffed Salami and Cheese Rolls

Serves: 6

1   sheet frozen puffed pastry
4   ounces thinly sliced hard
      salami with exterior
      casing removed
2   slices Swiss cheese
8   good quality pitted black
      olives, halved
1   egg beaten with 1 teaspoon
      water

Thaw pastry 20 minutes and cut into 16 squares. Top each square with a piece of salami, a piece of cheese and an olive half. Pull two opposite corners over salami mixture. Brush corners of pastry with egg to seal and secure with a wooden toothpick. Brush with more egg and place on baking sheet. Bake at 400 degrees for 10 minutes until golden. Serve warm.

This is another appetizer where you can use your imagination. Try pepperoni and mozzarella or ham and cheddar. The opportunities are endless and the puffed pastry creates an elegant appetizer.

"That is the happiest conversation where there is no competition, no vanity, but a calm, quiet interchange of sentiments."

Samuel Johnson

Smoked Gouda and Prosciutto Puffs

Puffs

1	**stick butter**
1	**cup water**
1	**cup flour**
½	**teaspoon salt**
4	**eggs**

Filling

4	**ounces smoked Gouda cheese, grated or cut in small pieces**
6	**tablespoons heavy cream**
3	**tablespoons softened butter**
3	**tablespoons minced prosciutto**
1	**tablespoon Dijon mustard**
½	**teaspoon drained, bottled horseradish**
	Fresh chopped parsley

Bring water and butter to boil in saucepan over medium heat. Add flour and salt; reduce to low and stir until mixture leaves the sides of pan. Remove from heat and stir in eggs one at a time, beating well after each addition. Drop ½ teaspoonfuls onto lightly greased baking sheet. Bake at 400 degrees 20 to 30 minutes until light golden brown. These may be frozen and filled later if you have more than needed. Puree the cheese in the blender or food processor with the whipping cream and butter. If you don't have a food processor you can use a blender or hand mixer. When smooth, add prosciutto, mustard and horseradish and process again. The filling may be made up to two days ahead. Stir fresh parsley into mixture for color. Cut puffs open, but not in half. Pipe filling into puffs. Serve within 30 minutes or they will get soggy.

These puffs can be used for other fillings or for mini sandwiches. This same dough can be used as an eclair dessert puff filled with pudding and glazed with chocolate. They are impressive yet very simple, used either way!

cheese grater
blender or food processor
pastry bag

Puff Pastry Prosciutto Pinwheels

Serves: 6

1 **sheet frozen puff pastry, thawed**
2 **tablespoons honey mustard**
¼ **pound thinly sliced prosciutto, chopped**
1 **cup freshly grated Parmesan cheese**

Thaw pastry according to package directions (approximately 30 minutes). Preheat oven to 400 degrees. Lay pastry out flat. Press dough with fingers to smooth out where it has been folded. Spread mustard on top of pastry. Arrange the prosciutto evenly to cover all the pastry; sprinkle evenly with cheese. Lightly press the cheese into the prosciutto with a rolling pin. Starting at the long end, roll up the pastry like a jelly roll just to the middle of the dough (3 times), roll the other side the same way. Where the two rolls meet in the center, pinch together lightly and if needed, use a small amount of water to seal. These cut slightly easier if refrigerated before cutting, but it is not necessary. You may freeze at this point if you are making ahead. Defrost before trying to cut. Using a serrated knife, cut the rolls into ½ inch slices. Place the slices flat on a lightly greased cookie sheet. Flatten slightly with spatula. Bake at 400 degrees 10 minutes until lightly golden. Turn the pinwheels over and bake 5 minutes more. Serve warm or at room temperature.

Once cooled, these may be cut in half to serve more people.

A tall bottle works for a rolling pin if you don't have one.

rolling pin
serrated knife

Sausage En Croûte with Homemade Mustard

Serves: 6

1   **sheet frozen puffed pastry**
2   **pieces kielbasa or Polish sausage, each 6 inches long**
1   **egg beaten with 1 tablespoon water**
    Homemade Mustard (recipe follows)

Homemade Mustard
2   **(2 ounce) containers dry mustard**
1   **cup white vinegar**
2   **beaten eggs**
1   **cup white sugar**
    Pinch salt

Thaw pastry 20 minutes; unfold and roll out on a lightly floured surface to a 12 x 11 inch rectangle. Cut pastry crosswise in half. Wrap each piece of sausage in pastry, trimming pastry as necessary and sealing edges with egg mixture. Use pastry trimmings and small cookie cutters to decorate Sausage En Croûte. Brush with more egg and place on ungreased cookie sheet. Bake at 375 degrees for 35 to 40 minutes or until browned and puffed. Remove from oven and let cool slightly. To serve, cut each in 1 inch slices and serve with Homemade Mustard. Combine dry mustard and white vinegar and let sit overnight. The next day add sugar, salt and eggs and heat to the desired consistency. Refrigerate. Serve with the Sausage En Croûte.

mini cookie cutters
pastry brush

"*Live Life to the Fullest. You have to color outside the lines if you want to make your life a masterpiece. Laugh some everyday. Keep growing, keep dreaming, follow your heart. The important thing is not to stop questioning.*"

Albert Einstein

Bacon Tomato Tartlets

Makes: 24

1 **(12 ounce) can flaky biscuits**
6 **slices deli bacon, cooked, drained and crumbled**
1 **medium tomato, seeds removed, chopped**
3 **ounces mozzarella cheese, grated**
½ **cup HELLMANN'S® Real Mayonnaise**
1 **teaspoon dried basil leaves**
¾ **teaspoon garlic salt**
1 **teaspoon dried thyme**
½ **teaspoon dried oregano**

Split the biscuits into 3 pieces. (The flaky biscuits pull apart easily into their natural layers.) Spray muffin tins lightly with cooking oil. Press split biscuits into mini muffin tins. You will not use entire can of biscuits. Mix remaining ingredients together and fill each of the pastries with mixture. Bake at 350 degrees for 10 to 12 minutes. These can be frozen and reheated for unexpected guests.

If you want to serve these for breakfast, but you already have bacon as an ingredient in another dish, make them without bacon and sprinkle the top with fresh chopped parsley. For blue cheese lovers this version makes a great appetizer with a heavy beer or red wine. Eliminate the tomato and spices, replace the mozzarella with 4 ounces blue cheese and replace spices with 3 chopped green onions. Chopped walnuts (¼ cup) make a nice addition to the blue cheese mixture.

mini muffin tins
cheese grater

Frank and Darrel Kutcher:
Frisco, Texas

While Frank and I worked together, we often discussed his family's culinary creativity. He and his wife have twins but still manage to cook great meals and entertain friends frequently.

Sage Sausage Stuffed Mushrooms

Makes: 40 mushrooms

40 mushrooms, stems removed
¼ cup butter, melted
10 ounces sage bulk sausage
1 tablespoon chopped green onions
¼ teaspoon pepper
1 clove garlic
1 tablespoon fresh parsley
1 (8 ounce) package cream cheese

Place mushrooms in shallow baking dish. Brush with melted butter. You may use less butter if preferred. Brown sausage and onions in skillet. Drain. Mix in the spices, parsley and cream cheese. Heat to blend all ingredients and melt cheese. Stuff mushrooms with filling. These may be made up to one day ahead and refrigerated until ready to bake. Bake 20 minutes at 325 degrees when ready to serve.

Use your imagination and experiment with hot sausage or andouille sausage as a substitute for the sage sausage. Recipes are only a guideline for cooking. By changing the type cheese or meat in a recipe you can become the inventor! Look at your recipes in a new light. What can you change to expand your own collection? This filling is also delicious mixed into scrambled eggs.

Spicy Chicken Wings with Blue Cheese Dip

Serves: 8

Wings/Drumettes

4	pounds chicken wings or drumettes
3	tablespoons Tabasco® pepper sauce
3	tablespoons butter

Blue Cheese Dip

1	tablespoon lemon juice
½	cup **HELLMANN'S®** Real Mayonnaise
½	cup sour cream
1	clove garlic
⅓	cup crumbled blue cheese

Fry chicken wings or drumettes in hot oil for 10 minutes. Drain. Melt butter and add Tabasco® sauce. Brush on fried wings or drumettes with a pastry brush. Mix sauce ingredients together and use as a dipping sauce for chicken. Make sauce ahead and refrigerate.

This Blue Cheese Dip is also a tasty dip for vegetables.

pastry brush

Tom Scherer: Kansas City, Kansas

My brother Tom gave me this recipe years ago. These spicy wings taste like the hot wings served in bars. The recipe can be slightly jazzed up with thin strips of celery and served on a bed of gourmet lettuce such as mesclun. We had these in a Dallas restaurant served this way. Tom and I have dined on a lot of bar food throughout the years! This recipe remains a favorite.

Thai Lettuce Folds

Serves: 6

Chicken

4   **boneless chicken breasts, thawed**
2   **tablespoons peanut or vegetable oil**
2   **cloves garlic, minced**
⅓   **cup chicken broth**
2   **green onions with tops, chopped**
1   **tablespoon fresh cilantro, chopped (stems removed)**
1   **tablespoon fresh lime juice**
½   **teaspoon cayenne**
¼   **teaspoon ground ginger**
    Salt, to taste

Cucumber Dipping Sauce

½   **cup water**
¼   **cup sugar**
¼   **cup rice wine vinegar**
1   **tablespoon honey**
¼   **teaspoon crushed red pepper**
⅛   **teaspoon salt**
½   **cup peeled, grated cucumber**
1   **tablespoon cilantro, chopped (stems removed)**
3   **heads Bibb lettuce**
½   **pound bean sprouts (for garnish)**

Make sauce and chill while cooking chicken. For sauce, mix together the first 6 ingredients and bring to boil. Reduce heat and cook an additional 3 minutes. Remove from heat and refrigerate until cool. While the sauce is cooling, grate a cucumber and set aside ½ cup. Add cucumber and cilantro to the sauce when cool. Cut chicken into small cubes. Heat oil in a skillet over medium heat one minute. Add garlic and chicken; cook, stirring constantly 3 to 5 minutes or until chicken is lightly browned. Add broth and cook over medium heat until most of the liquid evaporates. Stir in green onions, cilantro, lime and spices. Toss to coat. Salt to taste. To serve, wash and dry the largest leaves of Bibb lettuce. You will need a total of 12 leaves. Put the chicken mixture in a bowl. Let guests fill leaves with mixture, top with bean sprouts and drizzle sauce over. Fold over so it is like eating a fajita. These are best eaten off small cocktail plates.

cheese grater

Thai Chicken Strudel

Serves: 6

10 sheets phyllo dough
2 large boneless, skinless chicken breasts, boiled with a carrot and celery stalk or chicken broth
¾ cup bottled oriental peanut sauce
2 carrots julienned or grated
2 green onions, chopped
1 cup grated Monterey Jack cheese
2 tablespoons chopped cilantro (stems removed)
1 stick butter, melted

Keep phyllo dough covered with damp dish towel while working. Boil chicken breasts in water that is seasoned with carrot and celery, or boil in chicken broth. Shred chicken and mix with the peanut sauce, carrots, onions, cheese and cilantro. Filling may be made ahead and refrigerated. Butter baking sheet and lay out 1 slice phyllo, brush with butter. Repeat until all 10 sheets are used. Sprinkle the chicken mixture along the long side of the dough. Roll up and bake seam side down on a jelly-roll pan because the peanut sauce is oily. Bake at 375 degrees 20 to 30 minutes until golden. Slice in 1 inch slices and serve warm on small plates with forks.

pastry brush
jelly-roll pan
cheese grater

Crab Artichoke Dip

Serves: 6

1 (14 ounce) can artichoke hearts, drained and chopped
2 cups **HELLMANN'S®** Real Mayonnaise
4 ounces fresh lump crabmeat
⅓ cup freshly grated Parmesan cheese
½ cup white onion, sliced paper thin
2 tablespoons melted butter
½ cup bread crumbs
½ fresh lemon
   Tony Chachere's® Creole Seasoning

Squeeze out moisture from lump crabmeat or if using canned crabmeat, rinse and squeeze out the moisture. Mix together first 5 ingredients. Mix melted butter with the bread crumbs. Top the mixture with the bread crumbs and bake in a quiche pan or pie plate until bubbly at 350 degrees. Squeeze with lemon and sprinkle lightly with *Tony Chachere's®* Creole Seasoning. Serve with water crackers.

cheese grater

Crab Stuffed Mushrooms

Serves: 6

1½ **pounds medium size fresh mushrooms (30 to 35)**
5 **tablespoons butter, divided use**
½ **cup chopped onion**
1 **garlic clove, minced**
½ **cup bread crumbs**
¼ **cup chopped fresh parsley**
2 **tablespoons dry sherry**
½ **teaspoon Worcestershire sauce**
½ **teaspoon salt**
¼ **teaspoon cayenne pepper**
¼ **cup HELLMANN'S® Real Mayonnaise**
3 **tablespoons grated Parmesan cheese**
8 **ounces fresh lump crabmeat**
Tony Chachere's® Creole Seasoning

Remove and chop mushroom stems and set aside. Melt 3 tablespoons butter in a large skillet. Add chopped mushroom stems, onion, and garlic. Sauté 3 to 5 minutes or until tender. Stir in the bread crumbs and next 7 ingredients until well blended; gently stir in crabmeat. Spoon crab mixture evenly into mushroom caps and place on a rack in a broiler pan. (This will eliminate mushrooms getting soggy in their own juices.) Drizzle with remaining 2 tablespoons butter. Sprinkle lightly with *Tony Chachere's® Creole Seasoning*. Bake at 350 degrees, 20 minutes. Make the crabmeat filling a day ahead. Fill caps and broil as guests arrive. Serve warm.

This filling can also be used with portobello mushrooms and served as a side dish with a grilled steak.

 cheese grater

"Be at peace with God. Whatever you conceive him to be, and whatever your labors and aspirations, in the noisy confusion of life keep peace with your soul."

Found in Old Saint Paul's Church, Baltimore, Dated 1692.

Crab Tartlets

Serves: 6

1	**(12 ounce) can flaky biscuits**
6	**ounces canned crab or fresh lump crabmeat**
2	**green onions, chopped**
¼	**cup Monterey Jack cheese, grated**
¼	**cup cheddar cheese, grated**
¼	**cup HELLMANN'S® Real Mayonnaise**
½	**teaspoon lemon juice**
⅛	**teaspoon curry powder**
⅓	**cup drained, chopped water chestnuts (½ of an 8 ounce can)**
	Paprika
	Fresh chopped parsley
	Cooking spray

Split the biscuits into 3 pieces. The flaky biscuits pull apart easily into their natural layers. Spray muffin tins lightly with cooking spray. Press split biscuits into mini muffin pans. If using fresh lump crabmeat, squeeze moisture out. If using canned crabmeat, rinse and squeeze moisture out. Mix crab with next 7 ingredients. Fill each of the pastries with mixture. Sprinkle with paprika and fresh parsley. Bake at 350 degrees for 10 to 12 minutes. These freeze well. Reheat in same temperature oven. If frozen in center, it may take 10 to 20 minutes. Try one before serving or cut one in half to be sure center is warm.

mini muffin tins
cheese grater

Crab Cakes with Rémoulade

5 tablespoons butter, divided use
1 celery stalk, minced
½ small red pepper, minced
½ small onion, grated
1 tablespoon flour
1 teaspoon dry mustard
½ teaspoon *Tony Chachere's®* Creole Seasoning
½ cup milk
8 ounces fresh lump crabmeat (canned crabmeat may be substituted)
¾ cup dry bread crumbs (start with ½ cup if mixture is not making firm patties add additional ¼ cup)
1 tablespoon fresh lemon juice
1 tablespoon fresh, chopped parsley

Rémoulade
3 tablespoons Creole mustard
1 cup HELLMANN'S® Real Mayonnaise
2 tablespoons drained chopped capers
1 tablespoon chopped fresh parsley
Juice of one fresh lemon
¾ teaspoon cayenne pepper
¼ teaspoon *Tony Chachere's®* Creole Seasoning

Biscuits for Mini Crab Cakes
1 cup biscuit mix
½ cup butter, melted
½ cup sour cream

Heat 2 tablespoons butter and cook the celery, pepper and onion until tender. Stir in flour, mustard and *Tony Chachere's®*. Cook 1 minute. Gradually stir in milk and cook until mixture thickens. Remove from heat and add crab, bread crumbs, parsley and lemon. Form into 2 to 3 inch round patties if you are serving as a sit down appetizer, or into bite size patties if you are serving them on the mini biscuits. Cook in 3 tablespoons butter until brown. For Rémoulade combine all ingredients and chill. Serve as a sauce for crab cakes or any other seafood. Both the crab cakes and the Rémoulade can be made ahead. The Rémoulade can be stored in the refrigerator for 4 days and crab cakes can be made a day ahead, refrigerated and reheated in the oven. If you would like mini crab cakes on a flaky biscuit, combine the biscuit ingredients and turn onto floured surface. Knead five or six times. Roll into ½ inch thickness and cut with a 1 inch round cookie cutter. Place on lightly greased cookie sheet and bake at 450 degrees, 8 to 10 minutes or until lightly browned. Cool. Split biscuits and put a small amount of Rémoulade on the inside of each biscuit and a mini crab cake on each. The mini biscuits can be made ahead and frozen.

Hot Crab Dip

Serves: 12

6	tablespoons butter
½	cup chopped green onion
2	tablespoons flour
1	(8 ounce) bottle clam juice
1	cup half-and-half
1	(8 ounce) package cream cheese
1½	cups grated **Swiss** cheese
1	tablespoon prepared horseradish
2	teaspoons **Worcestershire** sauce
1	teaspoon cayenne pepper
1	pound fresh lump crabmeat
¼	cup fresh chopped parsley

Melt butter and add green onions. Add flour and whisk 1 minute. Gradually whisk in clam juice. Boil until mixture thickens, stirring often, approximately 3 minutes. Whisk in half-and-half and bring to boil. Boil 1 minute, stirring constantly. Reduce to low. Add cheeses, horseradish, Worcestershire sauce and cayenne. Stir until cheese melts. Mix crab and ¼ cup parsley into dip. Put in chafing dish to serve. Serve warm with crackers. This can be made a day ahead, refrigerated and heated on the stove before transferring into chafing dish.

If canned crabmeat is substituted, rinse and squeeze all moisture out.

chafing dish
cheese grater

"What I am most attracted to in my friends are their spirits: they are people who love life, who are passionate, who take risks to live fully, who are sensitive to feelings and idiosyncrasies, who share this goodness with me."

Alexandra Stoddard

Andouille and Shrimp Crostini *Makes: 24*

1	baguette, sliced in ½ inch diagonal slices
¾	cup fresh andouille sausage
6	ounces uncooked shrimp
1	tablespoon olive oil
¼	cup diced shallots
¼	cup roasted red bell peppers from a jar, drained and chopped
2	tablespoons fresh parsley
1	tablespoon chopped fresh thyme
1	tablespoon Dijon mustard
¼	cup mozzarella cheese, grated (optional)
½	teaspoon *Tony Chachere's® Creole Seasoning*

Slice baguette and set aside. Peel casing off andouille and chop. Peel, devein and coarsely chop shrimp. Heat the oil over medium high heat and add sausage. Cook 2 minutes until golden, breaking up sausage with the spoon. Using slotted spoon, transfer sausage to a bowl. Drain on paper towel if necessary. Add shallots to the same skillet with oil from sausage and sauté 3 minutes. Add the shrimp and sauté until cooked through, 3 minutes. Mix in drained, chopped peppers, chopped parsley, fresh thyme, mustard, sausage and cheese. Add *Tony Chachere's® Creole Seasoning*. Toast baguette in broiler on cookie sheet, 2 to 3 minutes. Top with the warm shrimp and sausage mixture. If cheese is used, broil crostini again with sausage, cheese and shrimp mixture, until cheese melts. Either mixture can be made ahead and refrigerated. Toast one side of crostini, turn and add the shrimp mixture and place under broiler to warm.

slotted spoon
cheese grater

"Strangers are just friends waiting to happen."

Author Unknown

Shrimp Tartlets

¼ **pound shrimp**
1 **(3 ounce) package crab boil**
¾ **cup HELLMANN'S® Real Mayonnaise**
⅓ **cup shredded Swiss cheese**
⅓ **cup freshly grated Parmesan**
½ **teaspoon Worcestershire sauce**
¼ **teaspoon Tabasco® pepper sauce**
1 **(12 ounce) can flaky biscuits Paprika Cooking spray**

Cook shrimp as directed on crab boil package with the crab boil spice package. Peel, devein and chop. Split each biscuit into 3 pieces in their natural layers. The flaky biscuits pull apart easily. Spray muffin tins lightly with cooking spray. Press dough into lightly greased mini muffin pans. Mix shrimp, mayonnaise, cheeses, Worcestershire and Tabasco®. Fill each of the pastries with the mixture. Sprinkle with paprika. Bake at 350 degrees for 10 to 12 minutes. These freeze well. Reheat in same temperature oven. If frozen in center, it may take 10 to 20 minutes to heat. Try one before serving or cut one in half to be sure the center is warm.

mini muffin tins

Smoked Salmon Spread

1 **(4 ounce) package fresh smoked salmon**
1 **(8 ounce) package cream cheese**
4 **tablespoons chopped red onion**
1 **tablespoon capers**
2 **tablespoons fresh chives**
2 **teaspoons lemon pepper**
1 **teaspoon dried dill weed**
2 **tablespoons milk**

Finely chop salmon. Soften cream cheese 15 to 20 seconds in microwave. Mix together all ingredients. Refrigerate until ready to serve. This spread can be made 24 hours ahead. Serve with water crackers.

As an alternative you may blend all ingredients except smoked salmon. Spread pumpernickel cocktail bread slices with cream cheese mixture. Neatly arrange thin strips of smoked salmon in a rosette on top of bread and serve.

Spicy Shrimp Dip

Serves: 12

2 **pounds uncooked shrimp**
1 **(3 ounce) package crab boil**
8 **ounce package cream cheese at room temperature**
½ **cup HELLMANN'S® Real Mayonnaise**
1 **cup Thousand Island dressing**
¼ **cup minced green onion**
1 **small onion, grated**
4 **teaspoons Tabasco® pepper sauce**
1 **tablespoon seasoned salt**
1 **tablespoon prepared horseradish, drained**
Fresh parsley, chopped (for garnish)

Boil shrimp in water according to crab boil directions. (Crab boil is found in the spice section of the grocery store.) Peel, devein and chop shrimp. Use a hand mixer to blend cream cheese, mayonnaise and Thousand Island dressing. Stir in shrimp, green onion and grated onion, Tabasco® sauce, seasoned salt and horseradish. Serve with crackers or vegetables. Make at least 8 hours ahead of serving time so flavors blend.

 hand mixer

Mary King: Coppell, Texas

Mary and I sat across from each other when we were buyers together. When there was a birthday celebration, everyone would bring an appetizer or dessert. This was an office favorite and I have held onto her recipe for years!

Devein shrimp by removing the gray-black vein from the back of the shrimp. You can do this with a sharp tip of a knife or the prong of a fork. This is optional on small and medium shrimp, but recommended on large shrimp.

Calypso Pineapple Shrimp

Serves: 4

2	**pineapples**
½	**cup toasted almonds**
I	**tablespoon butter**
I	**tablespoon oil**
I	**large onion, minced**
¼	**teaspoon curry powder**
¼	**teaspoon saffron**
	Pinch cayenne pepper
24	**shrimp, peeled and deveined**
I	**tablespoon lemon juice**
I¼	**cups heavy cream**
I	**teaspoon coarse black pepper, or more to taste**
	Salt, to taste

Cut the pineapples in half lengthwise, up through the leaves. Using a small sharp knife, cut out the pineapple flesh and chop in ½ inch cubes. Set aside. Toast nuts in 300 degree oven 3 to 5 minutes. Place the hollowed out pineapples on a serving platter. Heat the butter and oil in a large skillet over medium heat. Add the onion and sauté for 5 minutes. Stir in the curry, saffron and cayenne. Cook for 2 minutes. Add the shrimp and lemon juice to the skillet and stir-fry 5 minutes. Pour the cream into the pan. Add the almonds and the pineapple to the pan. Add pepper and salt to taste and cook 5 minutes longer, stirring constantly. Remove the mixture from the skillet and serve in the hollowed out pineapple as an appetizer. Serve with small plates and forks along with a spoon to scoop, if adding to an appetizer buffet or passing as an appetizer.

Saffron is the yellow-orange stigmas from a purple crocus and each flower only produces 3 stigmas. It is a very labor-intensive process and it takes over 14,000 of these stigmas for one ounce of saffron. Because of this, saffron is the world's most expensive spice and sold in very small quantities.

Pineapple Shrimp Skewers with Honey Marinade

Serves: 4

24 large shrimp, tails intact

Marinade
¼ **cup chopped green onions**
1 **teaspoon chopped garlic**
1 **tablespoon chopped fresh ginger**
¼ **cup rum**
⅓ **cup honey**
1 **tablespoon whole black peppercorns**
1 **teaspoon crushed red pepper**
2 **tablespoons sesame oil**
1 **tablespoon Chinese plum sauce**
1 **fresh pineapple for garnish**

Rinse, peel and devein shrimp, keeping tail intact. Mix marinade ingredients, excluding the pineapple and add shrimp. Toss to coat. Let them sit overnight. Prepare grill. Core pineapple and cut pineapple into chunks to use on skewers. Alternate shrimp and pineapple on skewers using 3 shrimp and 4 chunks pineapple per skewer. Grill until shrimp turns pink, 2 to 5 minutes on each side.

Use the leftover hollowed out pineapple for Black Beans with Cilantro Pesto Rice.

 8-6 inch bamboo skewers, soaked in water

"Wrinkles only go where smiles have been."

Jimmy Buffett

Homemade Cocktail Sauce for Boiled Shrimp

Makes 1¼ cups

¾ cup good quality catsup
½ cup prepared horseradish, drained
½ fresh lemon, squeezed
1 teaspoon sugar
1 teaspoon Worcestershire sauce

Mix ingredients together and refrigerate until ready to serve. If horseradish causes water to accumulate at the top, carefully drain or mix into sauce. This sauce is best if made fresh, just before serving.

*Mary Pat Johnston:
Overland Park, Kansas*

Mary Pat made this for me when I visited her in D.C. Through her 7+ moves we have managed to stay in touch regularly. She left this recipe on my answering machine after I requested it and when I went to make it, I couldn't find the recipe. I made it from memory and was very pleased with the results. It is spicy and much better than bottled.

Use crab boil when boiling shrimp for extra flavor. It can be found with the spices.

Martini glasses or similar shaped margarita glasses are wonderful for individual portions of shrimp cocktail. Hang large peeled shrimp on the edge of the glass and put the sauce in the center.

Horseradish Shrimp Dip

Makes: 3 cups

1	**pound shrimp, uncooked (reserve 5 for garnish)**
1	**(3 ounce) package crab boil**
¾	**teaspoon *Tony Chachere's® Creole Seasoning*, divided use**
4	**green onions, sliced**
3	**tablespoons prepared horseradish, drained**
3	**tablespoons HELLMANN'S® Real Mayonnaise**
1	**(8 ounce) package cream cheese, softened**
¼	**cup chopped celery**
½	**yellow bell pepper, chopped**
1	**tablespoon lemon juice**
¼	**teaspoon dried dill**
¼	**teaspoon cayenne pepper**
1	**tablespoon chopped fresh parsley**
	Fresh parsley for garnish

Cook shrimp according to crab boil directions, drain. Peel, devein (reserve 3 to 5 whole shrimp for garnish) and chop. Mix together shrimp with ½ teaspoon of the Tony's seasoning and remaining ingredients. Chill for at least 3 hours. Taste and if more salt is needed, add *Tony Chachere's®* for salt and spice. If only spice is needed, add a bit more cayenne. Put in serving dish or hollowed out cabbage and garnish edge by alternating shrimp and parsley leaves. Sprinkle dip with remaining ¼ teaspoon *Tony Chachere's®* for color. Serve with vegetables and crackers.

hand mixer

Cayenne Toasts

Serves: 8

1	**baguette, sliced in ¼ inch slices**
½	**cup olive oil**
2	**teaspoons cayenne pepper**
1	**teaspoon salt**
1	**teaspoon sugar**
½	**teaspoon paprika**
1½	**teaspoons garlic powder**

Preheat the oven to 200 degrees. In a blender or a jar with a tight lid, combine oil and seasonings. Lay the bread slices on a jelly-roll pan and brush one side with the flavored oil. Bake one hour until they are crisp. Cool. Serve with an appetizer buffet and those that like spicy food can eat them with anything from Sun-dried Tomato Dip to Spinach Artichoke Dip or spread them with goat cheese. These are wonderful!

jelly-roll pan
pastry brush

Escargot with Shallot Cream in New Potatoes

Makes: 12 escargot

1	**(7 ounce) can large snails**
6	**small new potatoes**
1	**tablespoon olive oil**

Shallot Cream

½	**cup dry white wine**
½	**cup chicken broth**
3	**tablespoons minced shallots**
½	**teaspoon dried thyme**
1	**small bay leaf**
1	**teaspoon cornstarch, dissolved in 2 teaspoons cold water**
1	**cup heavy cream**
2	**garlic cloves, minced**
1	**tablespoon butter**
½	**teaspoon pepper**
¼	**teaspoon salt**
2	**tablespoons minced parsley, divided use**
	Tony Chachere's® Creole Seasoning

Rinse snails and let dry on a paper towel. Wash the potatoes and cut in half. Put potatoes raw side down on jelly-roll pan that has been coated with 1 tablespoon oil. Preheat oven to 400 degrees and bake on middle rack 30 to 35 minutes until potatoes are tender. Make sauce while potatoes are baking. Combine the wine, broth, shallots, thyme and bay leaf in a skillet and boil over high heat. Reduce to 3 tablespoons liquid. Add the cornstarch mixture, cream and garlic and boil until reduced to ⅔ cup. Stir in the snails, butter, pepper, salt and 1½ tablespoons parsley. Remove the bay leaf. Scoop out the meat of the potato so you can put the escargot in the center. If necessary cut off rounded side of potato so they may sit evenly on plate. Spoon a snail with the sauce into center of scooped out potato and sprinkle lightly with *Tony Chachere's®* and remaining minced parsley.

This sauce is divine! The escargot may be served as a seated first course on a piece of toasted baguette with the sauce spooned over the toast and snails.

jelly-roll pan

Jerie Wylie: Keller, Texas

Jerie is a friend from my first job out of college. She explained her recipe for escargot on a drive out to Napa Valley with the Knots Landing Dinner Group for her 40th birthday celebration. I came home and experimented with her recipe and this recipe is the result. The group gets together once every few months for dinner and at her home for an annual holiday celebration.

Marinated Smoked Salmon

Serves: 16

Salmon

2 pounds fresh salmon

Marinade

1 teaspoon cloves
½ teaspoon cinnamon
1 teaspoon allspice
¼ cup sugar
1 cup water

Pull out any bones that were not removed by the fish department. Mix marinade together and marinate salmon 24 hours. Smoke on grill for 1 hour or broil in oven for 10 to 20 minutes until it flakes easily. Do not turn, it falls apart easily. Check after 10 minutes and again at 15 minutes as broilers vary. (A rule of thumb is 10 minutes per pound.) Serve as a buffet appetizer with crème fraîche or sour cream mixed with dill, chopped red onion and capers. Serve crackers and bread on the side.

Carol Provost, Colleyville, Texas

Carol is a friend from our days at Caviar to Cabernet. We had a great time at work talking to customers and to each other about food. We enjoy the salmon prepared with this marinade because the flavor is so unique.

Crème fraîche is a matured, thickened cream with a slightly nutty flavor. You can make it at home by mixing 1 cup whipping cream with 2 tablespoons buttermilk in a glass container. Cover and let it stand at room temperature for 8 to 24 hours or until very thick. Stir well and refrigerate for up to 10 days. Prepared crème fraîche is also sold in some grocery stores in the specialty cheese section.

Beer Cookies

Serves: 12

1   **stick butter plus**
     3½ tablespoons butter
1½ **cups flour before sifting**
2   **cups grated medium or**
     sharp cheddar cheese
1   **teaspoon baking powder**
1   **teaspoon salt**
1   **teaspoon cayenne**

Soften butter in microwave for 10 seconds. Sift the 1½ cups flour. Using the entire sifted amount, add remaining ingredients. A pastry bag is used to form the cookies, but the end may need to be removed as the mixture is very thick. (Whatever works to get a 1 inch by ½ inch strip or a round mini cookie is also fine.) Bake at 350 degrees on an ungreased cookie sheet, 15 to 20 minutes. They should be light and golden but not browned on the bottom. Store them in an airtight container.

These are great for a brunch where Bloody Marys are served, as a snack with beer or when a variety of appetizers are served together.

pastry bag
sifter

Cajun Pecans

Serves: 6

4   **tablespoons unsalted butter**
1   **tablespoon chili powder**
1   **teaspoon coarse sea salt**
1   **teaspoon dried basil**
1   **teaspoon dried oregano**
1   **teaspoon dried thyme**
½   **teaspoon onion powder**
¼   **teaspoon garlic powder**
¼   **teaspoon cayenne pepper**
1   **pound pecan halves**

Melt butter over low heat. Add all spices. Stir together and add pecans. Keep heat on low and stir together to coat all pecans with butter mixture. Spread on jelly-roll pan in a single layer. Bake at 350 degrees for 5 minutes. Remove from oven and toss pecans so all have a chance to roast. Roast an additional 5 minutes. Cool and store in an airtight container. If you prefer a little saltier taste, sprinkle with more fine sea salt.

Chop and use in salads or as a snack.

jelly-roll pan

Pita Toasts

Serves: 6

3   pita breads
6   tablespoons unsalted
       butter, room
       temperature
1   tablespoon fresh parsley,
       minced
1   teaspoon fresh chives
1½ teaspoons lemon juice
1   large clove garlic, minced
       Salt and freshly ground
         pepper, to taste

Halve each pita bread crosswise and then into quarters. Separate into 24 pieces. Blend softened butter with other ingredients and let mixture stand at room temperature, one hour. Spread on the inside of the bread. Bake at 450 degrees for 5 minutes or until crisp. The butter mixture can be made ahead and brought to room temperature.

These are a great accompaniment to a salad or with hummus. The herb butter can be used with any bread for a special touch.

Pecan Crunch

Serves: 6

⅔   cup pecan halves
2   tablespoons butter
1   tablespoon sugar
½   teaspoon salt
       Freshly ground black
         pepper, to taste
¼   teaspoon cayenne

Combine the pecans with the butter, sugar, salt, black pepper and cayenne in a small, heavy saucepan. Cook over low heat, stirring occasionally until the sugar caramelizes. Place mixture in a small paper bag to cool. Shake to break up the pieces. These may be stored in an airtight container for one month.

These are a great snack as well as a perfect topping for a salad with blue cheese and a Shallot, Red Wine or Spicy Vinaigrette. They are slightly sweet with a pepper finish. Increase quantity significantly for snacking.

Brunch,
Breads &
Beverages

Kitchen tools needed

May be prepared ahead

Cranberry Juice and Champagne ~ Bacon Tomato Tartlets (variation page 61)
Fresh Fruit Mélange, page 81 ~ Rosemary Potatoes, page 233
Spinach and Egg Pinwheel with Shrimp Sauce, page 84 ~ Amaretto Cake, page 249

Fresh Fruit Mélange

Serves: 8

Salad

- 1 **pint sliced strawberries**
- 1 **pint blueberries**
- 3 **kiwis peeled and sliced**
- 1 **medium cantaloupe, cut into uniform chunks or balls**
- 1 **medium honeydew, cut into uniform chunks or balls**
  Mint leaves as garnish

Dressing

- ½ **cup orange juice**
- ¼ **cup fresh lemon juice**
- 3 **tablespoons sugar**

Gently toss strawberries, blueberries, kiwis, cantaloupe and honeydew together. Combine dressing ingredients and pour over fruit mixture. Serve chilled and garnish with mint leaves.

Any fruit combination is good in this salad. Oranges, pineapple, or blackberries can be added or substituted. Varying the color is the most important thing for presentation.

melon baller (optional)

Lime Cream

Makes: 1 cup

- 2 **teaspoons grated lime peel**
- 1 **(8 ounce) carton sour cream**
- 2 **tablespoons sugar**
- 1½ **tablespoons fresh lime juice**
  Assorted fruit (see hint)

Grate lime peel on the smallest side of grater. Mix lime peel with all ingredients. Refrigerate. Recipe can be made 24 hours ahead. This may be used as a dip for mixed fruits such as strawberries, bananas, cantaloupe, honeydew, kiwi or any other fruit. If using fresh apple or pear you will need to brush them with a small amount of lemon juice so they do not discolor.

To serve, cut slivers of cantaloupe that have been topped with mixed berries and a slice of kiwi. Drizzle a small amount of lime cream over top. Fruit can also be put on wooden skewers for a buffet.

cheese grater or zester

Overnight French Toast

Serves: 6

4 eggs, slightly beaten
¼ cup sugar
¼ teaspoon ground nutmeg
⅔ cup orange juice
⅓ cup milk
½ teaspoon vanilla
½ teaspoon ground cinnamon
1 (16 ounce) loaf French bread
⅔ cup butter, melted
½ cup chopped macadamia nuts (optional)
Powdered sugar for garnish
Syrup

Combine first seven ingredients. Grease 9 x 13 inch pan. Cut bread into 1 inch slices. Put bread into 9 x 13 inch pan and pour eggs over bread. Turn to coat bread with egg mixture, cover and refrigerate overnight. Melt butter into jelly-roll pan, put bread on this and bake at 400 degrees 10 minutes. Sprinkle with nuts and bake 10 minutes more. Garnish with sifted powdered sugar. Serve with warm syrup.

This is a great basic recipe, or you can take it a step further and serve with fresh berries, a raspberry sauce, or sauté apples to accompany the French toast. Various fruits or nuts can be used too, the opportunities are endless. A raspberry liqueur, amaretto, GRAND MARNIER® or Frangelico can be substituted for a quarter cup of orange juice, but reduce the amount of sugar used. Pair nuts with a similar flavored liqueur, e.g., Frangelico with hazelnuts or amaretto with almonds.

jelly-roll pan
sifter for powdered sugar

Marla Payne: Coppell, Texas

Since this wonderful French Toast is made ahead of time, it alleviates morning confusion when you have visitors. A few of us got together and cooked an extravagant New Year's Eve dinner and then we stayed up all night. Marla made this for New Year's Day. It is delicious!

Fruit Ambrosia

Serves: 4

3 medium oranges, peeled
2 bananas, sliced
½ cup orange juice
3 tablespoons honey
1 tablespoon lemon juice
¼ cup flaked coconut
   Maraschino cherries,
      optional

Combine sliced oranges and bananas and toss gently. Combine orange juice, honey and lemon juice in small bowl; stir well and pour over fruit. Toss gently. Sprinkle with coconut and top with halved cherries.

Quick Eggs Benedict

Servings: 6

2 (10 ounce) packages frozen
   puffed pastry shells
   (12 shells)
12 eggs
12 slices tomato
12 slices Canadian bacon,
   warmed slightly in
   microwave, skillet or oven
1 packaged hollandaise sauce,
   prepared according to
   directions
   Pimento strips
   Sliced black olives
   Fresh parsley

Bake pastry shells, according to directions on a cookie sheet, but undercook slightly so shells are light brown. Cool. Cut off tops and scoop out middle dough, being careful not to make holes in shell. Place shells on large cookie sheet. Carefully crack 1 raw egg into each shell. Bake at 325 degrees until egg is set, 20 to 25 minutes. Heat Canadian bacon in skillet while eggs are cooking. Remove from oven. To serve, place tomato slice on slice of heated Canadian bacon, top with cooked shell. Spoon hollandaise sauce over egg baskets and garnish with crossed strips of pimentos, black olive slices and sprigs of parsley.

A Crab Cake (page 68) would accompany this meal nicely. Serve alongside Quick Eggs Benedict (without Rémoulade) and omit the Canadian bacon.

Spinach and Egg Pinwheel with Shrimp Sauce

Serves: 8

Egg Pinwheel

7   **eggs, separated**
¼   **teaspoon cream of tartar**
¾   **teaspoon salt (divided use)**
⅓   **cup butter**
6   **tablespoons unsifted flour**
     Dash of cayenne
1¼   **cups milk**
½   **cup medium cheddar,**
     coarsely grated
½   **cup fresh Parmesan, grated**
     Butter or shortening to
     grease pan

Filling

2   **(10 ounce) packages frozen,**
     chopped spinach
2   **tablespoons butter**
¼   **cup onion, chopped**
¼   **teaspoon *Tony Chachere's®***
     Creole Seasoning
¼   **cup medium cheddar**
     cheese, grated
½   **cup sour cream**
2   **tablespoons freshly grated**
     Parmesan cheese

If you are planning to serve the pinwheel immediately after baking, make sauce ahead of time. The pinwheel only takes 15 minutes to bake. Place egg whites and eggs in separate bowls. Let egg whites warm for one hour. Grease bottom of a jelly-roll pan and line with wax paper. Grease wax paper. Heat oven to 350 degrees. With mixer at high speed beat egg whites with ¼ teaspoon salt and cream of tartar until stiff. Peaks should form when beaters are removed. Melt ⅓ cup butter in large saucepan. Remove from heat. With wire whisk, stir in flour, cayenne and ½ teaspoon salt until smooth. Gradually stir in milk. Bring to boil, stirring constantly. Reduce heat, simmer, stirring until thick and leaves the bottom of the pan. Beat in cheeses. With whisk, beat egg yolks, then beat into cheese mixture. With under and over motion, fold ⅓ egg whites into cheese mixture. Carefully fold in remaining whites to combine. Turn into prepared pan. Bake 15 minutes, or until surface is puffed and firm to fingers. While baking, make filling by cooking spinach according to the package directions. Drain. In medium skillet, sauté onion until golden in 2 tablespoons butter. Add spinach, *Tony Chachere's®*, cheddar and sour cream. Mix well. With spatula loosen edge of soufflé; invert on waxed paper sprinkled with freshly grated Parmesan. While warm, peel off wax paper. Spread evenly with filling. From longer side, roll up. Place seam side down on cookie sheet. Slice. This freezes well. Spray foil heavily with cooking spray and sprinkle with additional Parmesan to keep foil from sticking. Take from freezer and place in refrigerator for 24 hours. Reheat in foil on cookie sheet 30 minutes at 325 degrees to

Spinach and Egg Pinwheel *continued*

Shrimp Sauce

1   **tablespoon butter**
1   **tablespoon flour**
2½ **ounces half-and-half**
1   **(10½) ounce can cream of
      shrimp soup**
¾   **cup grated medium cheddar
      cheese**
2   **tablespoons Sauterne
      (sweet wine)**
6   **ounces peeled, cooked fresh
      shrimp, chopped (reserve
      8 whole shrimp for
      garnish)**
1   **(3 ounce) package crab boil**

350 degrees. If you refrigerate overnight it will not take as long to reheat. For Shrimp Sauce, boil shrimp in crab boil, peel and devein. Make a roux of butter and flour. Mix in half-and-half and whisk to thicken. Add soup, cheese, and wine. Whisk until thick and cook over low heat. Add cooked shrimp. Bring to boil. Spoon over sliced egg pinwheel. Garnish with a whole shrimp.

If you prefer cheese sauce, mix 2 cups cheddar with 1 cup milk and heat over double broiler. Add 1 tablespoon butter, salt and pepper to taste. Add dash cayenne and ¼ teaspoon dry mustard. Cook until melted. Remove from heat and beat until smooth. A packaged hollandaise sauce is a quick alternative to the shrimp or cheese sauce.

whisk
jelly-roll pan (11½ x 17)
cheese grater
hand mixer
wax paper

"We cannot tell the precise moment when friendship is formed.
As in filling a vessel drop by drop.
There is at last a drop which makes it run over;
so in a series of kindnesses there is
at least one which makes the heart run over."

James Boswell

Creole Pork with Garlic Grits

Serves: 4

2 teaspoons salt
1 teaspoon black pepper
¼ teaspoon cayenne pepper
2 tablespoons butter
1 tablespoon vegetable oil
2 pounds pork sirloin or pork scaloppine, cut in 2 inch squares
1 cup flour
5 cloves garlic, minced
1½ cups onion, finely chopped
¾ cup celery, finely chopped
½ cup green pepper, finely chopped
1 pound fresh tomatoes, finely chopped
1½ cups chicken stock
4 tablespoons prepared roux

Garlic Grits

2 cups quick grits
2 quarts water
3 teaspoons salt
6 ounces grated sharp cheddar cheese
3 cloves garlic, minced
1 stick butter
3 eggs, slightly beaten
2 cups milk
¼ cup freshly grated Parmesan cheese

For the Creole Pork, mix together the salt, and peppers and rub into the meat with your fingers and coat with the 1 cup flour. Melt the 2 tablespoons butter and the vegetable oil together in a large skillet. Turn heat up to medium. Thoroughly brown meat in the butter and oil mixture. Remove the meat from the skillet and drain on paper towels. In the pan drippings, sauté the garlic, onions, celery and green pepper until they are soft. Add the meat back to the skillet and add tomatoes and chicken stock. Simmer on low heat one hour until meat is tender. Ten minutes before serving, thicken the sauce with the prepared roux. For Garlic Grits, cook grits in the 2 quarts water, seasoned with the 3 teaspoons salt until tender yet still pourable. Remove from heat and add cheese, garlic and butter. Let grits cool and with a hand mixer beat in the eggs and milk. Pour into two 2 quart casserole dishes that have been greased. Bake at 325 degrees for 50 to 60 minutes. Remove from oven and sprinkle with Parmesan cheese. Bake for an additional 10 minutes. The Garlic Grits may be made ahead, refrigerated and baked before serving. Serve the Creole Pork over the Garlic Grits.

You may prepare your own roux from the Chicken Gumbo recipe or find prepared roux in a jar at some grocery stores and Cajun shops. Southern Seasonings out of Broussard, Louisiana makes one called Bootsie's Cajun Creole Roux for Gumbos & Stews. Call to see if it is available in a store in your area. Their number is 1-800-879-5129. A crockpot (or Dutch oven placed in a warm oven) works well for simmering if you cannot tend to a pot on the stove.

Creole Pork *continued*

This dish is a classic Creole dish of New Orleans called Grillades and Grits but is most commonly made from veal and veal stock. This version is also delicious and makes an outstanding brunch entrée. Scaloppine (often spelled scaloppini) is a term for Italian cookery describing a thin scallop of meat (usually veal) dredged in flour before sautéing.

cheese grater

Julie and Joe Lancaster:
Grapevine, Texas

This delicious dish was served at a party hosted on a Sunday afternoon. The flavor of the slow cooked pork with the garlic and tomatoes is fabulous! Joe and Julie have plenty of space to entertain so they served this buffet style for over 30 people, along with several other brunch dishes. This is always a huge hit!

Chicken and Shrimp in Puffed Pastry

Serves: 6

¼ **cup butter**
½ **pound fresh sliced mushrooms**
2 **tablespoons sliced green onions**
2 **(10¾ ounce) cans cream of chicken soup**
½ **cup sherry**
½ **cup half-and-half**
1 **cup grated cheddar cheese**
2 **cups cooked chicken, diced**
2 **cups fresh shrimp cooked, deveined and chopped**
1 **(3 ounce) package crab boil**
½ **teaspoon Tabasco® pepper sauce**
2 **tablespoons chopped fresh parsley**
1 **(10 ounce) package frozen puffed pastry shells**

Boil shrimp in crab boil and peel, devein and chop. Melt butter. Sauté mushrooms and onions 5 minutes. Add soup and gradually whisk in the sherry and the half-and-half. Heat over low, stirring occasionally. Add cheese and stir until melted. Add chicken and shrimp and heat to serving temperature, but do not boil. Add Tabasco® pepper sauce. Just before serving, stir in parsley. This can be made ahead and reheated. Prepare pastry shells just before serving. Generously spoon mixture into baked shells. Mixture should overflow onto plate.

Cheese grated yourself melts more easily than the grated packaged cheese.

 whisk
cheese grater

Brigitte Scherer:
Kansas City, Kansas

My mother makes this for holidays when she wants to serve an easy but special brunch. The puff pastry makes an impressive presentation. The Tabasco® pepper sauce enhances all of the flavors.

Sausage and Spinach Quiche

Serves: 8

8 ounces sausage fried, drained and crumbled
3 tablespoons chopped green onion
2 tablespoons butter
½ cup grated cheddar cheese
¾ cup grated **Swiss** cheese
1 teaspoon Italian seasoning (you can use ½ teaspoon oregano, ½ teaspoon basil)
1 cup fresh spinach, chopped (cooked measurement)
1 garlic clove, chopped
8 beaten eggs
½ cup half-and-half
1 (3 ounce) package cream cheese, softened

Preheat oven to 350 degrees. Crumble sausage and fry. Drain well. In the same pan slightly sauté chopped green onion in 2 tablespoons butter. Mix sausage, onion, cheddar, Swiss cheese and Italian seasonings. Spread on bottom of greased 10 inch quiche dish. Using the same pan as you cooked the sausage, steam the spinach. Spread cooked chopped spinach over the top of the sausage mixture and sprinkle with chopped garlic. Beat eggs and half-and-half together with whisk. Soften the cream cheese in the microwave 15 to 20 seconds. Add softened cream cheese to the egg mixture. Beat again and pour over spinach. Bake until set, approximately 45 minutes.

Five ounces of fresh spinach before it is steamed is equivalent to one cup cooked spinach. Choose any sausage you prefer– i.e., spicy, regular, sage or turkey.

cheese grater
whisk
glass pie plate or quiche pan

"Cooking is an uncertain art, hostage to the quality of ingredients you are able to obtain, the temperament of your oven, the weather, even your mood."

Ruth Reichl

Chorizo, Tortilla, Fresh Tomato Quiche

Serves: 8

8	**ounces chorizo**
¾	**teaspoon vegetable oil**
2	**corn tortillas cut in 1 inch strips**
¼	**cup flour**
¾	**teaspoon chili powder**
½	**teaspoon salt**
1	**medium tomato, chopped**
⅓	**cup salsa**
3	**green onions**
1	**jalapeño, seeded, minced**
5	**slightly beaten eggs**
¾	**cup milk**
5	**ounces frozen chopped spinach**
1	**cup grated Monterey Jack cheese**

Thaw spinach and squeeze out moisture. Remove casing from sausage and crumble. Fry chorizo and drain. Lightly brush the bottom of a 9 inch pie plate with oil. Place the strips of tortillas in the bottom of the dish, slightly overlapping. Combine the flour, chili powder and salt. Sprinkle ½ of flour mixture over tortillas. Combine the tomatoes, salsa, green onions and jalapeño. Layer the tomato mixture over the flour mixture. Sprinkle the tomato mixture with the remaining flour. Sprinkle chorizo on top of the flour mixture. In a medium size bowl combine the eggs, milk and spinach and ½ cup of cheese. Pour egg mixture evenly over the tomato mixture. Bake uncovered at 350 degrees for 30 minutes. Sprinkle with remaining cheese and bake 5 minutes longer.

cheese grater
quiche pan or pie plate

Chorizo is a coarsely ground pork sausage flavored with garlic, chili powder and other spices.

Breakfast Pie

Serves: 8

1	pound spicy sausage (any flavor sausage can be used)
1½	cups grated Swiss cheese
1	(9 inch) refrigerated pie crust
4	eggs, lightly beaten
¼	cup green bell pepper, chopped
¼	cup red bell pepper, chopped
2	tablespoons chopped onion
1	cup half-and-half

Cook sausage thoroughly, drain and crumble. Prepare crust according to package directions. Do not bake. Mix cheese and sausage. Sprinkle in shell. Lightly beat eggs in bowl. Combine remaining ingredients and add to egg mixture. Pour into shell. Bake at 375 degrees for 40 to 45 minutes. Cool on rack 10 minutes before serving.

cheese grater
glass pie plate

*Julie McAllister:
North Richland Hills, Texas*

Julie is one of the original Dinner Club members that still gets together from my first job out of college. It started as a Knots Landing watch party and blossomed from there. We still enjoy our eating adventures and take pride in the recipes. I requested this from Julie after she made it for a baby shower and I had a second helping. It is delicious!

Green Chili Egg Strata

Serves: 12

6   slices French bread
3   tablespoons softened butter
2   cups shredded medium
      cheddar cheese
2   cups shredded Monterey
      Jack cheese
2   (4.5 ounce) cans green
      chiles
6   eggs
2   cups milk
1½ teaspoons *Tony Chachere's®*
      Creole Seasoning
1½ teaspoons paprika
1   teaspoon dried oregano
¼ teaspoon pepper
½ teaspoon garlic powder
4   tablespoons chopped yellow
      onion
¼ teaspoon dry mustard
      Fresh minced, seeded
      jalapeño (optional)

Slice bread ½ inch thick and trim off crusts. Spread softened butter on one side of bread. Arrange bread, buttered side down in 9 x 13 inch glass baking dish or 2-10 inch quiche dishes. Sprinkle cheeses evenly over bread. Distribute chiles over bread. In a bowl whisk the eggs together with the milk and add all seasonings, onion and dry mustard. Pour egg mixture over cheese. Cover and chill overnight or at least 4 hours. If you prefer a spicier version, remove seeds from a fresh jalapeño and finely mince. Sprinkle on top of strata before baking. Bake uncovered at 325 degrees for 50 minutes or until top is lightly browned. Let stand 10 minutes before serving.

Serve with warm flour tortillas, butter and salsa on the side. The idea for this dish came from a stay at the Briar Patch Inn in Sedona, Arizona. They served a homemade breakfast which was similar. We were seated for breakfast next to a babbling brook in beautiful surroundings.

For a variation add 8 ounces fried, drained chorizo sausage.

whisk
cheese grater

"One cannot think well, love well, or sleep well, if one has not dined well."

Virginia Woolf

Hashbrown Egg Pie

Serves: 8

7 slices bacon (preferably
   from the meat counter)
5 eggs
2½ cups frozen hash brown
   potatoes
1½ cups grated **Monterey Jack
   pepper cheese**
⅓ cup milk
2 green onions, chopped
1 medium tomato, seeded,
   chopped
½ teaspoon *Tony Chachere's®
   Creole Seasoning*

Grease a quiche pan or pie plate. Put the 2½ cups uncooked hash browns on bottom of pan. Fry bacon until crisp, drain and crumble. Set aside. In a bowl, beat eggs with hand mixer or whisk until fluffy. Stir in remaining ingredients. Pour over hash browns and refrigerate overnight. Bake at 325 degrees for 40 to 50 minutes. When knife is inserted it should come out clean and top of quiche should be slightly golden.

Monterey Jack pepper cheese has chunks of jalapeño peppers in the cheese.

glass pie plate or quiche pan
cheese grater
whisk

Fresh Strawberry Bread

Makes 2 loaves

2 cups washed and hulled
   whole strawberries
3 cups plus 2 tablespoons
   flour
2 cups sugar, plus extra to
   sprinkle on berries
1 tablespoon ground
   cinnamon
1 teaspoon salt
1 teaspoon baking soda
1¼ cups vegetable oil
4 eggs, beaten
1¼ cups chopped pecans

Slice strawberries and place in medium bowl. Sprinkle lightly with sugar and set aside while preparing batter. Grease and flour two loaf pans. Combine flour, 2 cups sugar, cinnamon, salt and baking soda in a large bowl. Mix well. Blend the oil and eggs into strawberries, add to flour mixture. Stir in pecans, blending until dry ingredients are just moistened. Divide batter into 2 pans. Preheat oven to 350 degrees. Bake for 45 to 50 minutes or until tester comes out clean. Cool 10 minutes before turning loaves out.

Raspberry Streusel Muffins   *Makes: 1 dozen*

Muffins

- 1½ **cups flour**
- ¼ **cup sugar**
- ¼ **cup packed brown sugar**
- 2 **teaspoons baking powder**
- ¼ **teaspoon salt**
- 1 **teaspoon ground cinnamon**
- 1 **egg lightly beaten**
- ½ **stick unsalted butter, melted**
- ½ **cup milk**
- 1¼ **cup fresh raspberries**
- 1 **teaspoon grated lemon zest**

Streusel Topping

- ½ **cup chopped pecans**
- ½ **cup packed brown sugar**
- ¼ **cup flour**
- 1 **teaspoon ground cinnamon**
- 1 **teaspoon grated lemon zest**
- 2 **tablespoons unsalted butter, melted**

Glaze

- ½ **cup powdered sugar**
- 1 **tablespoon fresh lemon juice**

Preheat oven to 350 degrees. Grease muffin tins. Sift the dry ingredients, then measure. Mix the flour, sugars, baking powder, salt and cinnamon together in a medium sized mixing bowl. Make a well in the center. Place egg, melted butter and milk in the well and stir with a wooden spoon just until ingredients are combined. Gently stir in raspberries and lemon zest. Fill each muffin cup ¾ full with batter. Combine the dry streusel ingredients and stir in the melted butter. Sprinkle this mixture over each muffin. Bake 20 to 25 minutes. While muffins are baking, make glaze by mixing lemon juice with the powered sugar. Drizzle glaze over warm muffins with spoon. Serve warm.

Mini muffin tins may be used instead of regular sized muffin tins.

wooden spoon
sifter
muffin tins
zester or cheese grater

Twila Baker: Dallas, Texas

Twila and I met at Kansas State University and we both ended up in Dallas. Our "Dinner Club" was started by a sorority sister of Twila's, Joan Lewis. Twila hosted a girls get together and made these for one of our brunches. They are mouth watering when served warm.

Sifting passes ingredients through fine mesh to remove large pieces. It incorporates air and will change measurements. Measure ingredients after they are sifted and that is the correct amount that should be added to the recipe, unless otherwise stated.

Baked Apple Doughnuts

Makes: 1 dozen

Doughnuts
1½ **cups sifted flour**
1¾ **teaspoons baking powder**
½ **teaspoon salt**
½ **teaspoon ground nutmeg**
½ **cup sugar**
⅓ **cup shortening**
1 **egg, beaten**
¼ **cup milk**
½ **cup peeled apple, grated**

Topping
½ **cup melted butter**
⅓ **cup sugar**
1 **teaspoon ground cinnamon**

Sift dry ingredients and mix together flour, baking powder, salt, nutmeg, and ½ cup sugar. Cut in shortening until mixture is fine. Mix together egg, milk and apple; add all at once to dry ingredients and mix quickly but thoroughly. Fill greased muffin pans ⅔ full. Bake in 350 degree oven 20 to 25 minutes or until golden brown. Remove from pans. Immediately roll top of doughnuts in melted butter then in cinnamon and sugar which have been mixed together. Serve warm.

muffin pan or mini muffin pan
cheese grater

Cream Cheese Brown Sugar Bites

Makes: 24

1 **egg yolk**
1 **(8 ounce) package cream cheese, softened**
¼ **cup sugar**
¾ **cup brown sugar**
1 **teaspoon ground cinnamon**
1 **(12 ounce) can refrigerated flaky biscuits**
6 **tablespoons butter, melted**
Cooking spray

Mix the softened cream cheese, egg yolk and ¼ cup sugar with a hand mixer. Mix together brown sugar and cinnamon. Set aside. Spray mini muffin tins with cooking spray. Split each biscuit into thirds by tearing into their natural layers. Spoon small amount of filling onto the split muffin. Pinch together forming a half moon. Roll in the melted butter, then in brown sugar and cinnamon mixture. Put one in each muffin cup with the rounded side up. Bake at 350 degrees 15 minutes. Serve warm.

Add 1 teaspoon orange zest to the cream cheese mixture for a different taste.

mini muffin pan
hand mixer

Sausage Crescents

Makes: 4 dozen

1   **pound seasoned sausage
    (spicy can be used)**
1   **(8 ounce) package cream
    cheese, softened**
2   **(8 ounce) packages
    refrigerated crescent rolls**
    Poppy seeds
1   **egg white, slightly beaten**

Preheat oven to 350 degrees. Lightly brown sausage and drain. While sausage is warm, add cream cheese and stir until cheese is melted and mixture is creamy. Cool completely. Separate crescent rolls into two rectangles. Form log of sausage mixture lengthwise down the center of each rectangle. Fold over the long sides of pastry to cover sausage log. Place on ungreased cookie sheet, seam side down. Brush with egg white. Sprinkle with poppy seeds. Bake 20 minutes until crust is golden. When completely cooled, slice into 1½ inch slices. These can be made ahead, frozen and reheated.

pastry brush

Melissa Ripley: Southlake, Texas

Melissa and I met through mutual friends and we hosted a spring brunch together. These were a hit and the kids and adults loved them. Make plenty, they go fast!

Cranberry Crunch Coffee Cake   *Serves: 10*

Cake
½   **cup butter, softened (1 stick)**
1   **cup sugar**
2   **eggs**
2   **cups flour**
1   **teaspoon baking powder**
1   **teaspoon baking soda**
½   **teaspoon salt**
1½ **teaspoons almond extract**
1   **cup sour cream**
1   **(16 ounce) can whole cranberry sauce**

Topping
¾   **cup almonds, chopped**
4   **teaspoons sugar**
½   **teaspoon cinnamon**

Preheat oven to 350 degrees. Grease and lightly flour a Bundt cake pan. Mix together topping ingredients and sprinkle over the bottom of the Bundt cake pan. Set aside. Cream sugar and butter with a hand mixer at medium speed until fluffy. Beat in the eggs one at a time. Mix together the flour, baking soda, baking powder and salt. Add the sour cream and extract to the dry ingredients and mix into butter, sugar mixture. Put half of the mixture in the pan, layer cranberries on top. Top with remaining batter. It is best to not get the cranberries all the way out to the edge of the pan or it will cause the cake to stick to the pan or separate. To avoid this, run a knife up and down the outside so there will be a layer of cake on the outside edge. Bake 55 minutes. Let cool 10 minutes. Use knife to loosen cake from the center of the pan. Invert onto cake plate.

hand mixer
Bundt cake pan or tube pan

Meta West: Abilene, Kansas

Meta is a Family and Consumer Science teacher in Abilene, Kansas and the sister of Marla Payne, a Dinner Club member. Meta got this recipe from the Windmill Inn Bed and Breakfast in Chapman, Kansas. Meta and I have enjoyed exchanging recipes and information over e-mail. This cake is delicious served slightly warm.

Sour Cream Coffee Cake

Serves: 8

Coffee Cake
1	**cup unsalted butter**
2	**cups sugar**
2	**large eggs**
1	**cup sour cream**
1	**teaspoon vanilla**
2	**cups flour**
1	**teaspoon baking powder**
¼	**teaspoon salt**

Topping
1	**cup chopped pecans**
1½	**tablespoons sugar**
1	**teaspoon cinnamon**

Use 10 inch springform pan, greased and lightly floured. Preheat oven to 350 degrees. Cream together butter and sugar. Beat in eggs and fold in sour cream. Add vanilla. Sift other ingredients, then measure and add to the creamed mixture. Mix together topping ingredients. Pour half of the batter in the pan and sprinkle with half of the topping. Repeat with remaining batter. Bake until toothpick comes out clean, approximately one hour. This freezes well.

To add color to your table, garnish top with fresh raspberries (approximately 1 cup). There is a cooking spray with flour in it that can be substituted for greasing and flouring pans. This coffee cake may be made in a Bundt cake pan as well. Layer small amount of topping, then half of the batter, another layer of topping (as a filling) and remaining batter. Bake approximately 50 minutes or until tester comes out clean.

hand mixer
springform pan
sifter

Lee Martell,
Murrysville, Pennsylvania

Laurie, Beth and Julie Martell are three of Lee's daughters that have recipes in the book. Lee gave Julie and I this recipe when we lived together in college. This is a delicious coffee cake recipe!

Spinach Spoon Bread

Serves: 6

½ **cup plus 2 tablespoons butter**
2 **tablespoons flour**
1 **cup milk**
½ **teaspoon salt**
¼ **teaspoon pepper**
½ **teaspoon paprika**
1 **cup sour cream**
1 **(10 ounce) package frozen chopped spinach**
1 **(8½ ounce) box "Jiffy®" Corn Muffin Mix**
2 **large eggs or 3 if small**

Thaw spinach and squeeze water out. Melt the 2 tablespoons butter over medium heat and add the flour and milk. Stir to slightly thicken for a white sauce. Add the salt, pepper and paprika to this. Mix together 1 stick melted butter, sour cream, chopped spinach, eggs and corn bread mix. Add this to the white sauce and bake at 350 degrees for one hour or just until set in a greased 7½ x 11 inch pan or pie plate. Spoon bread is ready when the top springs back at the touch of your finger.

Donna Edwards: Dallas, Texas

Donna and her husband Gaylon are members of the "Dinner Club" that started in 1989. They entertain by the pool when weather permits. This recipe is requested often. It is wonderful with grilled meats.

Spoon bread is a puddinglike bread that is baked in a casserole dish, just until set. It is served as a side dish and is generally soft enough to be eaten with a spoon or fork.

Best Rolls Ever

Serves: 12

¾ **cup margarine, divided use (1½ sticks total)**

2 **eggs**

2 **packages dry active yeast (rapid or regular)**

½ **cup lukewarm water**

½ **cup sugar**

1 **tablespoon salt**

1¾ **cups lukewarm milk (use dried skim mixed with water)**

5½ **cups flour**

Melt 1 stick margarine on low heat. Beat eggs in a small bowl. Add yeast to ½ cup lukewarm water to dissolve. Measure sugar and salt in a large bowl and add yeast mixture and lukewarm milk mixture. Stir until sugar is dissolved, then stir in about 3 cups flour. Beat in eggs and melted margarine. Beat thoroughly and add the rest of the flour in two additions. If making and baking immediately, let rise once until double in bulk, punch down and let rise again. Punch down again. Cut and prepare and let rise again before baking. No matter which preparation you choose, let rise a total of three times and punch down two times. If you are not ready to bake the rolls you may put dough in the refrigerator for up to four days. If this is done, put it in the refrigerator after it rises the first time. (They will rise once while in the refrigerator, punch down when pulled out.) When you are ready to bake (whether you have refrigerated or not,) melt ½ stick (¼ cup) margarine in a 9 x 13 inch cake pan. Let the margarine cool. Pull the dough out of refrigerator and punch down. Roll out dough on a floured surface to about a ⅜ inch thickness. Use a 2½ inch to 3 inch round biscuit cutter to cut out rolls. Coat the inside of the cut out dough with the extra stick melted margarine and fold in half. Cover and let rise until double in size. Bake at 350 degrees until golden. When Jane makes these for our dinner club she lets them rise two times, gets them cut and put into roll shape with margarine in between layers and puts them in the refrigerator. They will rise a little while in the refrigerator. Allow to sit approximately 2 hours at room temperature for them to completely rise before baking. This enables her to be with her guests instead of in the kitchen cutting out and preparing rolls.

Best Rolls Ever continued

Jane prefers to use Parkay margarine. She usually uses one half of the dough for these dinner rolls and the other half of the dough for her Sweet Rolls. Lukewarm water for activating yeast is 105 to 115 degrees.

Sweet Rolls

⅓	**cup margarine or butter**
1	**cup brown sugar**
2½	**tablespoons honey**
3	**tablespoons heavy cream or half-and-half**
1½	**cups pecans, coarsely chopped**
	Cinnamon and regular white sugar mixed together for sprinkling
	Extra melted butter for brushing on rolls

In a small saucepan or ovenproof 9 x 13 inch pan (which you can bake rolls in), melt margarine or butter over low heat and add brown sugar. (You do not want mixture to caramelize and get hard, just blend ingredients until sugar is no longer grainy.) Add honey, and cream to brown sugar/butter mixture and stir to blend. Stir in nuts. Pour this mixture into the bottom of a 9 x 13 inch pan. On a lightly floured surface, roll out ½ of the dough into a rectangle and spread with melted margarine or butter and sprinkle with cinnamon and sugar. Roll up and cut into 20 rolls. Lay the 20 rolls in the pan on top of the brown sugar/butter mixture and cover with a dishtowel. Let rise to double. Bake at 350 degrees until golden.

One 2½ inch to 3 inch round biscuit cutter
candy thermometer, if needed to test temperature of water

Jane Langlais: Southlake, Texas

Jane is one of the original members of the "Dinner Club" along with her husband Don. She makes these dinner rolls for all of our special occasions and we absolutely love them!

Jalapeño Cornbread

Serves: 12

½ cup butter plus 2 tablespoons for sautéing onion
1 red onion
2 (15.25 ounce) cans corn
2 (14¾ ounce) cans creamed corn
2 fresh jalapeños, seeded and chopped
1 (8 ounce) package cream cheese
1 (4 ounce) jar pimento, drained
6 eggs
3 (8½ ounce) boxes "Jiffy®" Corn Muffin Mix

Sauté the chopped red onion in the 2 tablespoons butter. Drain the regular corn. Remove seeds from jalapeños and finely chop. Soften the cream cheese in microwave 10 seconds. Mix all of the ingredients together. Grease 3 pie plates or a 9 x 13 inch pan and a pie plate. Bake at 400 degrees for 20 to 30 minutes.

Roasted red peppers from a jar, (drained) can be used instead of pimento.

Vince Martinez: Dallas, Texas

Vince Martinez, my friend and hair stylist gave me this recipe. He is a great cook and knows all his recipes by memory. Vince has fun and lives life to the fullest. He cooks the same way. He experiments by mixing unusual flavors and spices together.

Orange Pineapple Spice Tea

Serves: 4

4 **cups hot brewed tea**
⅓ **cup sugar**
3 **cups orange juice**
1 **cup unsweetened pineapple juice**
3 **(3 inch) sticks cinnamon, broken into pieces**
¾ **teaspoon whole cloves**
½ **teaspoon whole allspice**

Combine hot tea and sugar in a large pan. Stir in fruit juices. Add spices and bring to boil. Cover and reduce heat, simmering 30 minutes; strain tea to remove spices. This is wonderful served cold or hot!

Cranberry Tea

Makes: 5 servings

1 **quart water**
12 **whole cloves**
2 **cinnamon sticks**
⅓ **cup sugar**
4 **regular size tea bags**
1 **(12 ounce) can frozen cranberry juice, undiluted**

Bring the first four ingredients to boil. Pour over tea bags and steep 3 minutes. Remove tea bags, squeezing gently. Stir in cranberry concentrate and chill. Serve over ice. Ice may not dilute this as much as you would like. Taste and add more water if too sweet for your taste.

These teas make flavorful beverages for baby showers when made with decaffeinated tea. Flavored tea bags that have complimentary fruits and spices work well for these teas.

Pineapple Banana Punch

Serves: 40

1   **(12 ounce) can lemonade**
1   **(12 ounce) can orange juice**
1   **(46 ounce) can pineapple juice**
6   **bananas pureed**
½   **cup sugar**
1   **(2 liter) bottle of lemon-lime carbonated drink**

Prepare the lemonade and orange juice according to package directions. Puree bananas in blender or food processor. Mix the pineapple juice, pureed bananas and sugar into the lemonade/orange juice mixture. Freeze in containers overnight. Defrost two hours before serving and add the lemon/lime drink.

blender or food processor

Lisa McCain: Plano, Texas

Lisa hosted a baby shower for a mutual friend of ours. This is a refreshing punch and is not too sweet.

Sparkling Cranberry Tea

Serves: 4

8   **cups apple-cranberry drink (other cranberry combinations can be used)**
2   **cups double strength tea**
1   **(10 ounce) bottle or can of lemon/lime carbonated drink**
    Ice

In a pitcher mix first three ingredients together. Pour over ice. This is a nice alternative to iced tea. A flavored tea with orange and cinnamon spice can also be used.

Beach Buzzes

Makes: 8

6   **ounces 80 proof white rum**
4   **ounces vodka**
4   **ripe pitted peaches,**
      unpeeled
6   **ounces frozen pink**
      lemonade concentrate
I   **tray ice cubes or 12 cubes**

Put first four ingredients in blender and blend to chop peaches. Keep a pitcher close by in case blender gets too full. Pour half of blended mixture into a pitcher. Add ice to blender and blend to create a slushy frozen drink. More ice may be needed. Serve and repeat with the second half. These are not overly sweet and make a refreshing pool side drink! Store in freezer and blend again before serving.

blender

Ice that sits too long in the freezer takes on the flavor of what is being stored. When entertaining, be sure you have fresh ice or buy a bag to use for the party.

Spicy Bloody Mary Pitcher

Serves: 8

I   **(46 ounce) bottle chilled**
      spicy hot vegetable juice
2   **cups vodka**
I   **fresh lime, squeezed**
⅛   **teaspoon celery salt**
⅛   **teaspoon cayenne pepper**
1½ **teaspoons Worcestershire**
      sauce
I   **teaspoon bottled**
      horseradish
      Freshly ground pepper, to
      taste
      Tabasco® pepper sauce,
      optional
      Ice
      Small wedges of fresh lime
      for garnish, optional

In a 2 quart pitcher mix together first 7 ingredients. Add cracked black pepper so you can see the flecks floating in the pitcher when stirred (approximately 1 teaspoon). Pour over ice in individual glasses and garnish with a celery stalk or a spicy pickled green bean.

Spicy pickled green beans can be found in gourmet food stores. Beer Cookies are a great snack with Bloody Marys.

Rum Mint Coolers

Serves: 2

8	**teaspoons superfine sugar**
2	**limes, squeezed**
4	**ounces white rum**
24	**fresh mint leaves**
8	**ounces club soda**
	Crushed ice
	Additional limes for garnish

Shake sugar, lime juice and rum together until sugar dissolves. Fill a highball glass ⅓ full of crushed ice. Put 12 fresh mint leaves on top of ice. Layer with another ⅓ glass of ice. Pour the lime mixture on top. Pour club soda over this to the top of the glass. (You may not need this much club soda.) Stir with a fresh lime wedge.

If this is increased to pitcher size, add 1 or 2, (3 ounce) boxes of fresh mint leaves per pitcher rather than counting the leaves.

Susan and Russ Bee: Rockwall, Texas

My former boss, Susan, and her "Braumeister" husband Russ, gave me this wonderful cocktail recipe. The combination of lime and mint is very refreshing!

Smith and Kearns

Serves: 1

1	**ounce KAHLÚA®**
1	**ounce half-and-half**
	Club soda or carbonated water

Pour the KAHLÚA® and half-and-half over ice in a highball glass and fill with carbonated water or club soda. This drink was a favorite of my friend, Lee Martell. She is the mother of three dear friends of mine. She ordered this during mom's weekend in college and we all got to taste. Most places I've ordered it, I have had to tell them how to make the drink. It is delicious!

Margarita on the Rocks

Makes: 1 serving

1 (24 ounce) package True Crystals®, Lemon Sweet and Sour Cocktail Mixer
8 cups water
2 ounces gold tequila
1 ounce **GRAND MARNIER**® Fresh limes, sliced

Mix the crystals and 8 cups water in a gallon (4 quart) pitcher. For each margarita, shake together in a container with a lid, 4 ounces pre-mixed sweet and sour mix with the 2 ounces tequila and 1 ounce GRAND MARNIER®. Pour in short highball glass over ice and stir with a slice of lime. Add a squeeze of lime for a tart margarita.

This makes 32 drinks, but each will be hand mixed to maintain the correct proportion.

True Crystals® Cocktail Mixers can be found at some large liquor stores. The dry mix is what many restaurants use. To order call 1-800-237-7620 and speak to customer service. True Crystals® Cocktail Mixers, a division of Crystals International Foods will sell the mix in 6-1 gallon packages (24 ounces dry mix) or 12-1 quart packages. Split a case with a friend.

Chocolate Cognac Coffee

Serves: 6

6 ounces dark or milk chocolate
¼ cup sugar
¼ teaspoon salt
4 cups strong coffee
1 cup half-and-half
½ cup chocolate liqueur or brandy
½ cup whipped cream

In a saucepan, dissolve the chocolate, sugar and salt in one cup of hot coffee. Add the additional 3 cups coffee, half-and-half and liqueur. Heat until hot, but not boiling. Serve in regular or expresso cups. Top with whipped cream.

Snowbears

Serves: 2

1 **cup milk**
1 **cup crushed ice**
¼ **cup amaretto**
6 **heaping tablespoons vanilla ice cream**

Mix ingredients in blender until creamy smooth. Amaretto can be adjusted to your taste.

 blender

Tom Depperschmidt, Wichita, Kansas

Tom is a real estate agent and father of Brent, Brian and my Goddaughter Corinne. Tom makes this drink during the winter holidays. It is wonderful and not heavy like some ice cream drinks. Experiment with your favorite liqueurs. The ice cream base is versatile.

Soups, Salads & Sandwiches

Kitchen tools needed

May be prepared ahead

Fresh Tomato, Kalamata and Feta Salad with Herb Shallot Vinaigrette, page 120
Andouille Chowder, page 109

Andouille Chowder

Serves: 4

6	**tablespoons butter, melted**
2	**stalks chopped celery**
1	**chopped green pepper**
1	**chopped red pepper**
1	**chopped leek (white part only)**
3	**tablespoons flour**
4	**cups chicken stock**
1½	**teaspoons fresh thyme**
1½	**tablespoons fresh basil**
1	**tablespoon Tabasco® pepper sauce**
3	**links smoked andouille sausage, 6 inches long, sliced thin**
½	**cup heavy cream**

Peel casing off sausage. Slice and set aside. Melt butter. Add all vegetables and sauté until leek is translucent. Push vegetables to one side of pan and add the flour to the juices and blend with a whisk. Add chicken broth, spices, Tabasco® sauce and sausage. Simmer for 10 minutes and then add heavy cream. Simmer an additional 10 minutes or until slightly thickened. If it is too thick you can add more chicken broth. This can be refrigerated and gently reheated, do not boil.

A good chicken broth can be store bought. There are some chicken bases that are a paste that can be mixed with hot water to make a rich stock.

 whisk

Refrigerate fresh basil with a damp paper towel inside a plastic bag for up to 4 days. It will turn brown if you store it in the store container.

"Don't undermine your worth by comparing yourself with others. It is because we are different that each of us is special."

Nancye Sims

Corn Chowder

Serves: 6

3 ounces salt pork, diced
3 slices bacon, diced
1 yellow onion, diced
¼ cup flour
3 cups chicken stock
1 bay leaf
Black pepper, to taste
2 (14¾ ounce) cans creamed corn
2 potatoes, diced and cooked (½ pound)
3 ears fresh corn
1 red pepper, diced
1 leek, chopped (white part only)
½ cup heavy cream
¼ teaspoon *Tony Chachere's®* *Creole Seasoning*
Tabasco® pepper sauce, to taste

Sauté salt pork and bacon until lightly browned, add onions and diced red pepper. Sauté until tender. Add flour, blending with a whisk to make a roux. Cook 5 to 10 minutes over low heat. Do not brown. Blend in chicken stock. Add bay leaf and pepper. Bring to boil. Add creamed corn. Return to a boil. Reduce heat to simmer and simmer ten minutes. Add potatoes, fresh corn and leek. Simmer ten minutes longer. Stir in cream, *Tony Chachere's®* and Tabasco®. Heat but do not boil. This can be made a day ahead. Refrigerate. Reheat slowly.

Cooked shrimp or a kielbasa may be added for variety.

 whisk

"Happiness in the ancient, noble verse, means self-fulfillment and is given to those who use to the fullest whatever talents God or luck or fate bestowed upon them."

Arthur H. Prince

Ham and Bean Chowder

Serves: 6

1   (16 ounce) bag dried great Northern white beans or navy beans
2   quarts water
4   smoked ham hocks
1   (14.5 ounce) can chopped tomatoes
2   cups chopped yellow onion
½   cup chopped celery
2   teaspoons fresh minced garlic
2   whole cloves
1   bay leaf
¼   teaspoon pepper
3   (14½ ounce) cans chicken broth
2   cups shredded cheddar cheese

Wash beans. Cover beans with water in a 6 quart saucepot; bring to boil. Cover; boil two minutes. Remove from heat; let beans soak for one hour. Drain, reserving liquid. Return beans to saucepot; add 4 cups reserved liquid, meat, vegetables, seasonings and chicken broth combined with enough water to measure 6 cups. Bring to boil, lower heat and simmer 2 to 2½ hours or until meat is tender. Remove meat, bay leaf and cloves. Cut meat off ham hocks and return to soup. Skim off fat, add cheese and stir until melted. This is a good soup to make ahead and freeze for later.

Cheese that you shred yourself will melt better.

On our Spain excursion we tasted a similar soup, but thinly sliced chorizo sausage was added. It was delicious.

cheese grater

Brigitte Scherer;
Kansas City, Kansas

This is a wonderful soup and everyone has teased me that they would never get the recipe if it weren't for the publishing of Good Friends Great Tastes. *It is one of the most flavorful soups I have ever eaten.*

Wrap celery in foil before placing it in the refrigerator. It will stay fresh longer.

Lentil Soup

Serves: 8

1   (16 ounce) package dried
    lentils
3   **KNORR® Extra Large Beef
    Bouillon Cubes**
6   **cups water**
2   **slices raw bacon, diced**
1   **medium onion, finely
    chopped**
1   **carrot thinly sliced**
2   **stalks celery including tops,
    chopped**
1   **garlic clove, minced**
2   **teaspoons salt**
¼   **teaspoon pepper**
½   **teaspoon dried oregano**
1   **pound canned tomatoes
    (cut up in large chunks,
    with juice)**
1   **link good quality kielbasa or
    Polish sausage**
2   **teaspoons red wine vinegar**

Wash lentils. Cover and simmer all ingredients
excluding the sausage and vinegar in a large pot
until lentils are tender (approximately 1 hour).
Peel casing from kielbasa and cut into bite size
pieces. More than 1 link kielbasa may be added
if preferred. About 15 to 20 minutes before
serving add the kielbasa and the red wine vinegar.
Continue to simmer during the last 20 minutes
so the sausage warms. If the soup is too thick
for your liking, add a little more water. Stir to
let flavors blend.

*Crusty French bread from the refrigerator section
goes well with this soup. Serve the bread with softened butter.*

*Brigitte Scherer:
Kansas City, Kansas*

*My mother is the queen of good soups! In Kansas City the area of town
called Strawberry Hill has wonderful homemade Polish sausage that
enhances the flavor of this soup. Check your town for a similar ethnic
specialty.*

*A lentil is a tiny, lens-shaped dried seed that has long been used as a meat substitute.
The French or European lentil, sold with the seed coat on, has a grayish brown exterior
and a creamy yellow interior.*

Restaurant Style Baked Potato Soup

Serves: 10

8	**tablespoons butter**
4	**cups diced onions**
½	**cup flour**
¼	**cup chicken base mixed with 8 cups water**
1¼	**cups instant potato buds**
4	**cups half-and-half**
½	**teaspoon seasoned salt**
1	**teaspoon dried basil**
1	**dash Tabasco® pepper sauce**
2	**cups cooked diced potatoes or more if you prefer**
	Grated cheddar (grate your own)
4	**slices bacon, fried, drained and crumbled**
	Green onion tops or fresh chives

Sauté onions in butter 10 to 15 minutes. Do not brown. Add flour to onions and butter; cook 4 to 5 minutes. Do not brown. Mix chicken stock with the potato buds. Use a whisk to blend until smooth. Add stock mixture to roux, mixing slowly with whisk. Cook 15 to 20 minutes. Whisk in the half-and-half and cook for 10 more minutes. Do not boil. Add spices. Before serving, add the 2 cups baked, diced potatoes. Garnish with cheddar, chives and bacon.

whisk
cheese grater

Mary Pat Johnston:
Overland Park, Kansas

Mary Pat, my college "running buddy" gave me this recipe years ago when she lived in Cincinnati. It closely resembles the thick, restaurant style potato soup. Mary Pat likes to bake her potatoes with the skin on before adding the chunks to the soup.

Creamy Tomato Basil Soup

Serves: 8

1   **(28 ounce) can chopped, drained tomatoes, or 12 Roma tomatoes**
3   **cups tomato juice**
2   **cups chicken stock**
15 **fresh basil leaves**
1½ **cups heavy whipping cream**
1½ **sticks unsalted butter, cut in chunks**
½   **teaspoon salt**
½   **teaspoon freshly ground pepper**
    Freshly grated Parmesan cheese (optional)

If using Roma tomatoes, they must be peeled. Combine tomatoes, tomato juice and chicken stock in a large saucepan. Simmer 30 minutes. Add basil. Slightly cool and transfer in batches to food processor or blender and process until smooth. Do not get batch too large or the pressure will cause the processed soup to leak out the lid. Return to saucepan over low heat. Whisk in cream, butter, salt and pepper. Whisk until butter is melted and soup is thoroughly heated. Garnish with freshly grated Parmesan. This can be made 1 to 2 days ahead.

To peel tomatoes, drop them in water that has come to a boil. Remove from water after 2 to 3 minutes and they should peel easily.

 blender or food processor

Cynthia Granados: San Antonio, Texas

Cynthia was part of the original Single Girl's Dallas Dinner Club. Cynthia flies to Dallas for our special dinner club gatherings. We love this soup because it is similar to a soup we enjoy from a well known Dallas Bakery.

Pomi Tomatoes are shelf stable fresh tomatoes. They taste great in soups and sauces and one (26.55 ounce) package works well for this soup. They are found with the canned tomatoes but come in a shelf stable cardboard box.

Pesto Tortellini Soup

Serves: 4

1 **cup chopped green onion (2 bunches)**

3 **(14½) ounce cans vegetable or chicken broth**

1 **(9 ounce) package uncooked fresh or frozen cheese tortellini**

1 **(8 ounce) package washed, chopped portobello mushrooms**

⅓ **cup fresh, refrigerated pesto or pesto in a jar**
  Freshly grated Parmesan cheese

In a 5 quart saucepan combine vegetable or chicken broth and green onions. In order to get the right flavor this mixture must come to a boil. Add remaining ingredients and cook long enough that pasta cooks according to directions. Sprinkle with freshly grated Parmesan.

Pat Borkowski: Euless, Texas

Pat and I worked together at Caviar to Cabernet. She is a good cook and likes this because it is tasty, yet easy. Pat suggests serving this with bread that has been toasted with olive oil, crushed garlic, Parmesan and a little garlic salt. This soup has a wonderful flavor and takes only about 5 minutes from the point of adding tortellini.

Smoked Chicken Black Bean Soup

Serves: 6

½ **stick unsalted butter**
1 **cup peeled broccoli stems, chopped**
2 **cups broccoli tops, chopped**
½ **cup chopped carrot**
½ **cup chopped yellow onion**
½ **cup chopped celery**
1 **tablespoon fresh thyme, crumbled**
1 **teaspoon *Tony Chachere's*® *Creole Seasoning***
1 **tablespoon dried oregano**
1 **tablespoon dried basil**
½ **cup dry white wine**
4 **cups chicken broth**
1 **(15.5 ounce) can black beans, drained and rinsed**
1 **cup smoked chicken, chopped (one large boneless breast)**
1 **tablespoon Worcestershire sauce**
½ **teaspoon Tabasco® pepper sauce**
2 **cups heavy cream**
Liquid smoke

Brush chicken breast lightly with liquid smoke and either cook in microwave or on the grill. Liquid smoke is not needed if you grill the chicken in a smoker. In a sauté pan, melt butter over medium heat. Add peeled broccoli stems, carrots, onion and celery and sauté for 5 minutes. Add thyme, *Tony Chachere's*®, oregano and basil and sauté 5 more minutes. Pour in wine and bring to boil. Add stock and cook until reduced by half, stirring occasionally for about 15 minutes. Stir in broccoli tops, beans, chicken, Worcestershire and Tabasco®. Simmer 5 minutes. Add heavy cream and simmer but do not boil. Heat until warmed, 5 minutes. Salt and pepper if needed. You may choose to add more Tabasco® pepper sauce if a spicier flavor is preferred.

Steak Soup

Serves: 6

2½ pounds round steak cut into
   bite size pieces
1 pound ground beef
9 cups water, divided use
2 tablespoons beef flavor base
1 tablespoon coarse ground
   black pepper
1 (28 ounce) can sliced or
   chopped tomatoes
4 carrots, sliced
4 stalks celery, sliced
1 onion, chopped
1½ cups frozen mixed
   vegetables
1 stick butter
1 cup flour
2 teaspoons Kitchen
   Bouquet® Browning and
   Seasoning Sauce

Brown the round steak. Fry the ground beef and drain. Combine meats, 8 cups water, beef base and pepper. Add the tomatoes with juice, carrots, celery and onion. Bring to boil and simmer until steak is done. In the last 15 minutes before you are ready to serve, stir in 1½ cups frozen mixed vegetables. Melt 1 stick butter in saucepan and slowly whisk in 1 cup flour. Add 1 cup cold water to the butter/flour mixture and mix in some soup liquid. When smooth, add to soup. Add 2 teaspoons Kitchen Bouquet® to enhance color. This soup freezes well.

Beef flavor base is usually found in the spice section of the grocery store.

 whisk

Brigitte Scherer,
Kansas City, Kansas

My mother has made this delicious soup for many years. This is a hearty soup for a cold winter day. Serve with crusty French bread and butter.

Award Winning Chili with Red Wine and Steak Tips

Serves: 6

2	pounds steak tips
¼	pound bacon
1	large onion, chopped
6	cloves garlic, minced
1½	teaspoons *Tony Chachere's®* *Creole Seasoning*
1	green bell pepper, chopped
6	jalapeños, seeds removed and halved
4	tablespoons chili powder
1	tablespoon whole cumin seed
1	tablespoon oregano
1	(28 ounce) can tomatoes with juice
1	(8 ounce) can kidney beans or red beans, drained and rinsed
1	tablespoon Worcestershire sauce
1	cup dry red burgundy (such as a Beaujolais) Tabasco® pepper sauce, salt and pepper, to taste

Cut the beef against the grain in 1 inch strips. Sauté beef, bacon, onions and garlic. Add *Tony Chachere's®*, bell pepper, jalapeño pepper, spices, tomatoes, beans, Worcestershire sauce and wine. Crush tomatoes while stirring. Simmer for 2 hours on low heat. Add Tabasco® and salt and pepper to taste if needed. This is a good make ahead meal for a fall Bunco or Po-Keno party. Refrigerate and reheat when ready to serve so the flavors have a chance to blend. This was a winner for me at a chili cook off at work. The wine and bacon add interesting flavors to traditional chili.

Spray plastic storage dishes with cooking oil before pouring tomato-based sauces in them. It will keep them from staining.

Chicken Gumbo

Serves: 6

2	**large onions**
7	**stalks celery**
½	**green pepper**
1	**cup vegetable oil**
1¼	**cups flour**
2	**large ripe tomatoes, coarsely chopped**
5	**cups chicken stock**
1	**tablespoon cayenne pepper**
1	**bay leaf**
1	**tablespoon *Tony Chachere's*® *Creole Seasoning***
1	**(10 ounce) can Ro*Tel® Diced Tomatoes and Green Chiles**
1	**teaspoon coarse ground pepper**
1	**bulb garlic, peeled and cloves chopped**
1	**whole chicken for frying (approximately 3½ pounds)**
	Long grain white rice

Chop onions, celery and green pepper. Set aside. Take cast iron pot and heat oil on high. Oil should start to smoke. With a wire whisk, shake in flour while constantly stirring with the wire whisk. Continue whisking until this combination becomes the color of a brown paper bag or peanut butter, (may be as dark as milk chocolate) but be careful not to burn. Keep the stove fan on as you work. Add pepper, onion and celery immediately when the roux is the right color. Mixture will cool down and may splatter. Continue stirring using a wooden spoon. Stir until onions are translucent. You should still be cooking on high heat. Add the chopped tomatoes and 5 cups of chicken stock. Keep stirring to blend. Add cayenne, bay leaf, *Tony Chachere's*®, Ro*Tel®, pepper, garlic and 1 whole chicken. Continue to cook over medium high or roux will separate. Cook one hour until chicken falls off the bone. Skim off excess fat with a large spoon. Remove carcass and pull off the meat, return meat to pot. Cook rice according to package directions. Serve gumbo spooned over rice in individual bowls.

Thinly sliced kielbasa or Polish sausage may be added to gumbo.

large cast iron pot
whisk
wooden spoon

David Gore: Grapevine, Texas

Dave is my "soul" and "food" mate. We spend a couple nights a week in the kitchen cooking together. This is spicy and addicting! Serve with crusty French bread. Dave prefers to use a long grain rice from Texas or Louisiana.

Fresh Tomato, Kalamata and Feta Salad with Shallot Herb Vinaigrette

Serves: 8

Salad
4   **tomatoes, sliced**
⅓   **cup pitted kalamata olives**
⅓   **cup crumbled feta cheese**

Shallot Herb Vinaigrette
6   **tablespoons red wine vinegar**
2   **teaspoons dried oregano**
1   **tablespoon coarse grain Dijon mustard**
1   **shallot, minced**
1   **large garlic clove, minced**
1   **teaspoon minced fresh ginger**
1   **cup extra virgin olive oil**

For the Herb Vinaigrette, combine first six ingredients in bowl and whisk. While continuing to whisk, gradually add oil in a thin stream. It should be slightly thick. Season vinaigrette to taste with salt and pepper. Vinaigrette may be made ahead and refrigerated. Arrange tomatoes on either a large platter to pass or on individual salad plates. Sprinkle with olives and feta cheese. Drizzle with dressing.

The flavor of this dressing is wonderful on any salad combining lettuce, vegetables, olives and a sharp cheese. The combination of olives, cheese and tomatoes creates a colorful presentation and can be served for elegant occasions or casual meals. Substitute cooked and crumbled bacon in place of olives for a different flavor.

 whisk

Virgin olive oil and extra virgin olive oil have been cold pressed which is a chemical free process that involves only pressure and a lower level of acidity. The lower the acidity the higher the grade. Extra virgin olive oil is the finest and fruitiest of the olive oils and is less acidic. The deeper the color the more intense the flavor. Those olive oils that just state "olive oil" on the label are a combination of refined olive oil and virgin or extra virgin olive oil.

Fresh Tomato and Romaine Salad with Garlic Mint Dressing

Makes: ¼ cup

¼ teaspoon salt
1 clove garlic, crushed
1 tomato, chopped
3 leaves of fresh mint, chopped
¼ cup olive oil
½ lemon
 Salad greens such as romaine or leaf lettuce

Salt the bottom of a wooden bowl or glass bowl. Crush garlic in bottom of bowl with the salt to make a paste. Squeeze ½ lemon over this mixture. Add the oil and stir, then add the chopped tomato. Sprinkle with the mint. Let stand 15 minutes and toss the lettuce with this mixture. Allow about 1¼ to 1½ cups of greens per person. Double dressing if necessary.

Feta and kalamata olives would also be good in this salad.

Captain Terry Bennett,
Pilot Grove, Missouri

I met Terry flying into Dallas from Oklahoma City. He was sitting next to me as I proofed my recipes. He loves to cook and spent years perfecting this recipe. He got this from a Lebanese restaurant he frequented when he was a corporate pilot. It is a great combination with the hint of mint and lemon. I serve this with Lamb with Peppercorn Currant Glaze.

Chilled Asparagus Salad

Servings: 4

24	**asparagus spears, trimmed**
1	**teaspoon salt**
½	**teaspoon pepper**
½	**teaspoon garlic, minced**
¼	**teaspoon sugar**
½	**teaspoon dry mustard**
1	**teaspoon Creole mustard**
⅛	**teaspoon cayenne pepper**
	Dash Worcestershire sauce
	Dash Tabasco® pepper sauce
3	**tablespoons red wine vinegar**
5	**tablespoons olive oil**
5	**tablespoons vegetable oil**
2	**tablespoons heavy cream**
2	**teaspoons parsley, chopped**

Break asparagus where the tough stalk and the tender asparagus meet, by bending gently. Steam asparagus until tender-crisp. Mix all vinaigrette ingredients together in a jar. Shake to blend and chill. Shake before serving. Arrange on plates and drizzle over asparagus. If making several days ahead of time, do not add cream. Add cream to vinaigrette just before serving.

A dash is considered to be somewhere between ¹⁄₁₆ and ⅛ teaspoon and is accomplished by adding the ingredient (usually a liquid) to food with a quick, downward stroke of the hand. A pinch of dry ingredients is the amount you can pinch between two fingers, usually ¹⁄₁₆ of a teaspoon.

"*Know Your Passion, Show Your Passion*"
"*Your interests, wishes, and happiness determine what you actually do well, more than intelligence, aptitudes or skills do.*"

Richard Bolles

Hearts of Palm, Artichoke and Olive Salad

Serves: 6

Salad

1	**(14 ounce) can hearts of palm, drained and sliced**
1	**(14 ounce) can artichoke hearts, drained and sliced**
½	**cup chopped green pepper**
½	**cup chopped red pepper**
10	**pimento stuffed green olives, halved**
10	**black pitted olives, halved (not canned)**
1	**head Boston lettuce**
	Quartered hard boiled eggs and halved cherry tomatoes (optional)

Vinaigrette

3	**tablespoons red wine vinegar**
½	**teaspoon Dijon mustard**
½	**teaspoon salt**
½	**teaspoon pepper**
3	**tablespoons olive oil**
3	**tablespoons vegetable oil**

For Vinaigrette, whisk first four ingredients together. While continuing to whisk, add oils in a thin stream. Vinaigrette will thicken slightly. Toss salad ingredients with Vinaigrette. Chill one hour before serving. To serve, place salad on a leaf of Boston or Bibb lettuce. The Vinaigrette may be made ahead and refrigerated.

Crumbled blue cheese or feta is good sprinkled on top of this salad. For a unique presentation for a picnic, serve the salad in hollowed out red, green or yellow peppers. The Vinaigrette is delicious for marinating vegetables i.e., yellow squash, zucchini, carrots, broccoli and cauliflower. Create your own combination.

whisk

Donna Edwards: Dallas, Texas

Donna made this salad at one of the very first Dinner Club gatherings, and it has been a favorite ever since. It is elegant, colorful and simple. What more could a busy gourmet ask for?

Caesar Salad with Homemade Croutons

Serves: 4

Salad

1   head romaine lettuce, torn into bite size pieces
    Freshly cracked black pepper
½ cup freshly grated Parmigiano-Reggiano cheese

Dressing

1   tablespoon freshly squeezed lemon juice
½ teaspoon anchovy paste
2   large cloves garlic
1   teaspoon Worcestershire sauce
1   teaspoon Dijon mustard
1   fresh raw egg
1   tablespoon balsamic vinegar
1   cup extra virgin olive oil

Homemade Croutons

1   baguette, crust removed and cut into 1 inch cubes
3   tablespoons unsalted butter
3   tablespoons olive oil
2   cloves crushed garlic
1   teaspoon mixed Italian herbs (or mix together basil, parsley and oregano)
    Freshly cracked black pepper

Cut crust off bread and cube. For Dressing, put all ingredients excluding the oil in a blender or processor and blend until smooth. Add the oil through the top of the blender or food processor in a thin stream while the machine is running. Place blender on stir setting. Dressing should thicken if done this way. Refrigerate until ready to use. Wash romaine and wrap in paper towels. Refrigerate until ready to serve. Make croutons by heating oil and butter together in a skillet. Add garlic and spices. Add bread cubes and coat all sides. Cook over medium heat, tossing to coat. Heat oven to 350 degrees and put croutons on cookie sheet for 5 to 10 minutes or until crisp and slightly golden. Because oven temperatures vary, check after 5 minutes. If not serving immediately, store in an airtight container. May be made the day before. Tear lettuce into bite size pieces and toss with grated cheese, croutons and dressing to taste. Sprinkle with freshly cracked black pepper.

Add ½ cup crumbled blue cheese and fried crumbled bacon for a different version. This can also be served with a thin slice of a toasted baguette spread with pesto (omit croutons) and topped with thinly sliced roasted red pepper for a garnish.

blender or food processor

Eggs should be stored large end up in their original carton. The best flavor and cooking quality is obtained when eggs are used within one week. They can be refrigerated and used up to one month.

Southwest Caesar Salad with Homemade Croutons

Serves: 4

Salad

1	**large head romaine lettuce, torn into bite size pieces**
2	**medium tomatoes, seeded, diced**
½	**cup frozen corn kernels, thawed, drained**
4	**tablespoons freshly grated Parmesan cheese**

Dressing

½	**cup HELLMANN'S® Real Mayonnaise**
1½	**tablespoons chicken broth**
1	**tablespoon low sodium soy sauce**
1	**tablespoon fresh lemon or lime juice**
1½	**teaspoons Larry Fione's Adobo Sauce**
1	**teaspoon brown sugar**
	Salt and pepper, to taste

Homemade Croutons

1	**baguette, crust removed and cut in 1 inch cubes**
3	**tablespoons unsalted butter**
3	**tablespoons olive oil**
2	**cloves crushed garlic**
¼	**teaspoon *Tony Chachere's*® *Creole Seasoning***
¼	**teaspoon dried basil**

For Dressing, whisk mayonnaise, chicken broth, soy sauce, lemon juice, adobo sauce and brown sugar in medium bowl to blend. Can also be mixed in blender. Season dressing to taste with salt and pepper. Dressing may be prepared 1 day ahead. Cover and refrigerate. Mix lettuce, tomatoes and corn in large bowl. Add dressing and 2 tablespoons Parmesan cheese and toss to coat. Sprinkle with remaining 2 tablespoons Parmesan cheese and serve. Homemade croutons are optional. Make croutons by heating oil and butter together in a skillet. Add garlic and spices. Add bread cubes and coat all sides. Cook over medium heat, tossing to coat. Heat oven to 350 degrees and put croutons on cookie sheet for 5 to 10 minutes until lightly golden and crispy. Check after 5 minutes since oven temperatures vary slightly. Store in airtight container until ready to serve. May be made a day ahead.

To find Larry Fione's Adobo Sauce at a store nearest you, or to order call American Spoon Foods at 1-800-222-5886 or visit their web site at www.spoon.com

 whisk or blender
cheese grater

Adobo is a paste that is made from ground chiles, herbs and vinegar.

Romaine Salad with Pine Nut Vinaigrette

Serves: 6

Salad

1	**head romaine lettuce**
¼	**cup pine nuts, toasted**
¼	**cup coarsely shredded fresh Parmesan cheese**
	Freshly ground pepper

Pine Nut Vinaigrette

2	**cloves garlic**
1	**cup water**
¼	**teaspoon salt**
1	**teaspoon Dijon mustard**
2	**tablespoons white wine vinegar**
½	**cup virgin olive oil**

Toast pine nuts in oven on cookie sheet at 350 degrees, 3 to 4 minutes until slightly golden. Watch carefully, check after 2 minutes. Immediately remove from cookie sheet. Wash and tear romaine into bite size pieces. Shred Parmesan and set aside. Peel garlic. In a small saucepan, boil garlic in water for 10 minutes, drain. In small bowl, smash garlic and add salt to make a paste. Whisk in mustard and vinegar. Add oil in a stream while continuing to whisk, so mixture will emulsify. Dressing should thicken slightly. Add romaine, tossing well with desired amount of dressing and season with freshly ground pepper. Sprinkle Parmesan and pine nuts over salad and serve. Refrigerate leftover dressing.

whisk
cheese grater

There is little waste with romaine lettuce. Tear off any brown that may be found on the tip and cut off the root end in a v shape. Once washed in lukewarm water, dry off. Rather than serving immediately, this lettuce gets crisper if it is put in the refrigerator half an hour to an hour after washing. Refrigerate washed leaves in paper towels until ready to serve.

Romaine Salad with Fresh Basil Vinaigrette and Homemade Croutons

Serves: 4

Salad
6 cups romaine lettuce
¾ cup Parmigiano-Reggiano cheese
Freshly ground pepper

Fresh Basil Vinaigrette
1 teaspoon fresh minced garlic
2 teaspoons fresh basil leaves
1 teaspoon anchovy paste
¼ cup balsamic vinegar
½ cup olive oil

Homemade Croutons
1 cup French bread, without crust, cut in 1 inch cubes
2 tablespoons unsalted butter, melted
¼ teaspoon minced garlic
Freshly cracked black pepper

Wash and tear lettuce into bite size pieces. Preheat oven to 350 degrees. Mix the bread cubes with the melted butter and garlic and spread them on a baking sheet. Bake 5 to 10 minutes until they are golden and crisp. Cool. If not being served immediately, store in an airtight container. For Fresh Basil Vinaigrette, place the garlic, basil, anchovy paste and vinegar in a blender or food processor and process. Turn setting to stir and slowly add the oil in a thin stream through the feed tube or the hole in the top of blender. Blend until slightly thick. Toss lettuce, croutons and cheese with desired amount of vinaigrette. Refrigerate unused portion of vinaigrette. Sprinkle with freshly cracked black pepper.

 blender or food processor

Some vinaigrettes will solidify due to the temperature in the refrigerator and the type oil used. If this happens, run warm water over the jar to melt the build-up and re-whisk.

Baked Goat Cheese Salad with Herb Vinaigrette

Servings: 4

Salad

½ **head romaine lettuce**
  Spring mix or mesclun to make up enough for 4 salads
1 **(11 ounce) log goat cheese**
  Bread crumbs

Herb Vinaigrette

3 **sprigs fresh rosemary**
3 **sprigs fresh thyme**
3 **sprigs fresh oregano**
½ **cup extra virgin olive oil**
½ **teaspoon Creole mustard**
3 **tablespoons balsamic vinegar**
¼ **teaspoon salt**
¼ **teaspoon freshly ground pepper**

For Herb Vinaigrette, combine the first 4 ingredients in saucepan over medium-high heat. Bring to boil, remove from heat and let cool. This can be done earlier in the day. Cut cheese log into 8 rounds on a plate and drizzle with the seasoned oil mixture. Let stand 30 minutes. Pour oil from cheese into bowl and discard herbs. Chill cheese rounds 15 minutes until firm. Add mustard and next 3 ingredients to the seasoned oil, whisking with a wire whisk. Coat cheese with bread crumbs and place on baking sheet. Bake at 350 degrees 10 minutes and set aside. Combine both mesclun and romaine in a bowl, drizzle with oil mixture and toss to coat. Place evenly on four salad plates. Serve each with 2 goat cheese rounds, delicately placed on plates.

The goat cheese rounds are great in other salads with vinegar, oil and spice combinations. Olive oil may be used instead of seasoned oil and the goat cheese rounds can be rolled in pecans or walnuts and baked.

 whisk

Julie Lancaster: Grapevine, Texas

Julie and I met through our good friend Lynne. She invited us for a great dinner by her pool and made this salad from fresh herbs in her garden. Julie changed the mustard from Dijon to Creole and changed the greens from a mix of radicchio, Bibb and watercress to romaine and mesclun. This recipe came from Paula Lambert. Paula is the founder of the Mozzarella Company in Dallas. She approved of her recipe being used in Good Friends Great Tastes.

You can have wonderful cheese such as the goat cheese used in this salad shipped directly to you. Contact the Mozzarella Company at 1-800-798-2954 or visit their web site at www.mozzco.com.

Red Leaf Lettuce with Walnuts and Shallot Vinaigrette

Serves: 6

Salad

- ¾ **cup chopped walnuts**
- 1 **tablespoon vegetable oil**
  Salt, to taste
- 1 **head Red Leaf Lettuce**
- 4 **ounces grated Monterey Jack cheese**

Shallot Vinaigrette

- 2 **small shallots or 1 large, finely chopped**
- 2 **tablespoons red wine vinegar**
- 4 **teaspoons Dijon mustard**
- 1 **teaspoon sugar**
- ¼ **teaspoon salt**
  Pepper
- ⅔ **cup vegetable oil**
- 2 **tablespoons olive oil**

For Shallot Vinaigrette, chop shallots in blender or food processor. Add next 5 ingredients, blending after each addition. Oils should be added slowly in a thin stream through the feed tube or top of blender while machine is running. This allows mixture to emulsify or thicken. This can be made ahead. In a small pan over low heat, sauté nuts in oil 5 minutes. Lightly salt. Drain on paper towels and reserve. Tear lettuce into bite size pieces. Toss lettuce, walnuts and cheese in a large salad bowl and toss with vinaigrette.

Gruyère is a nice alternative to Monterey Jack and homemade croutons can be added.

cheese grater
blender or food processor

Warm English Salad with Bacon, Stilton and Mushrooms

Serves: 4

⅓ cup walnuts (optional)
6 slices bacon, cooked and crumbled (reserve 2 tablespoons grease)
¼ cup raspberry vinegar
1 cup Stilton cheese
6 slices red onion, separated into rings
1⅓ cup fresh mushrooms, sliced approximately ⅛ inch thin (12 mushrooms)
6 cups loosely packed curly endive
4 cherry tomatoes for garnish

Toast chopped walnuts on cookie sheet in a preheated oven at 350 degrees 2 to 3 minutes. Fry bacon until crisp, drain and reserve 2 tablespoons bacon grease. In a large skillet, warm the 2 tablespoons bacon grease and vinegar over medium heat until slightly bubbly. Add cheese and stir until it begins to melt. Add onions and mushrooms. Cook 1 minute to soften. Stir in walnuts, bacon and endive. Cook 1 to 2 minutes, tossing lightly until heated thoroughly. Serve immediately. Garnish with cherry tomatoes cut in half.

Regular or Cajun Pecans from the appetizer section change the flavor slightly, and are great in this! Jicama can be substituted for the nuts. Jicama is a root vegetable that is sweet, nutty and crunchy. It is good raw or cooked. Add this with the onions and mushrooms for another tasty combination of ingredients.

Curly endive grows in loose heads that have green outer leaves that curl at the edges. The leaves on the edge have a prickly texture and a slightly bitter taste.

Romaine and Red Leaf Lettuce with Caramelized Pecans and Gorgonzola

Serves: 6

Salad
1	**head romaine lettuce**
1	**head red leaf lettuce**
6	**ounces Gorgonzola cheese**
½	**red onion, thinly sliced (optional)**

Vinaigrette
4	**tablespoons flavored vinegar (champagne or raspberry preferably)**
½	**cup olive oil**
	Salt and pepper, to taste

Caramelized Pecans
1	**tablespoon sugar**
½	**teaspoon salt**
½	**teaspoon pepper**
1	**tablespoon water**
⅔	**cup pecan halves**

Wash lettuce and tear into bite size pieces. Set aside. Mix together vinaigrette ingredients. In a small saucepan heat the sugar, salt, pepper and water together until bubbly. Add pecans and stir to coat. They will be fragrant. Remove once sugar has caramelized. Cool on wax paper. Toss the lettuce with the pecans and Gorgonzola. Thinly sliced red onion adds slightly more color and additional depth of flavor. Thinly sliced red apples, pears or dried sour cherries are also a nice addition.

Lisa Taylor: Dallas, Texas

Lisa invited me to join a group of women entrepreneurs that meet once a week in her home. Lisa is an Etiquette Consultant and another member, Donna Collins, is a Feng Shui Educator and a Jewelry Designer. Through this weekly meeting, the three of us to have joined together to host dinners with guest speakers to educate and entertain women.

Spinach Salad with Balsamic Maple Vinaigrette and Sugared Pecans

Servings: 8

Salad
8   **cups fresh spinach, stems removed**
6   **slices bacon, fried, drained and crumbled**

Balsamic Maple Vinaigrette
⅓   **cup balsamic vinegar**
⅛   **cup pure maple syrup**
2   **tablespoons minced shallots**
1½   **cups olive oil**
¼   **teaspoon salt**
½   **teaspoon pepper**
    See variations for options

Sugared Pecans
¼   **cup pecans**
1½   **tablespoons sugar**
    Cooking spray

Mix vinaigrette ingredients in a jar with a tight fitting lid and shake vigorously. For pecans, spray a saucepan with cooking spray and cook sugar and pecans until crystallized. Remove pecans from pan and cool on wax paper. Toss the salad with the vinaigrette and pecans. Gently mix in fruit and onion if desired.

For color, add thin sliced red onion and mandarin oranges or unpeeled slices of Red Delicious apples.

Glass canning jars with lids are useful for storing your homemade vinaigrettes. Identify the vinaigrette or dressing by labeling the outside with a canning label.

 wax paper

"Cooking is like love. It should be entered into with abandon or not at all."

Harriet Van Horne

Frisée with Pistachios, Pears and Sherry Vinaigrette

Serves: 6

Salad
6 ounces frisée
½ cup shelled pistachios, toasted
¼ pound crumbled imported Roquefort
I large red skinned firm pear, unpeeled and cut into chunks

Sherry Vinaigrette
2 tablespoons sherry vinegar
I teaspoon Dijon mustard
¼ teaspoon salt
¼ cup cold pressed olive oil
Fresh ground pepper

Toast nuts at 350 degrees on cookie sheet in oven 2 to 3 minutes. For Sherry Vinaigrette, whisk together vinegar, mustard and salt. While continuing to whisk, add oil in a thin stream. Continue to whisk to help emulsify or thicken vinaigrette. You can make the vinaigrette ahead. Toss frisée with desired amount of dressing. Refrigerate unused portion. Divide salad among plates and sprinkle with nuts and cheese. Arrange pears on salad plate. Sprinkle with freshly cracked pepper.

whisk

Frisée is a member of the Chicory family and is a curly lettuce sometimes found in the mesclun mixture. Frisée should be crisp and stored in a sealed bag no longer than 5 days. It should be washed before using. Cold pressed olive oil is a chemical free process that creates a natural level of low acidity. (Cold pressed will be stated on the bottle.)

Bibb Lettuce with Maple Raspberry Vinaigrette

Serves: 6

Salad
2 heads Bibb lettuce
¼ cup toasted pine nuts
4 ounces crumbled blue cheese
1 small red onion, sliced and separated into rings

Raspberry Vinaigrette
¼ cup raspberry vinegar
2 tablespoons pure maple syrup
⅔ cup vegetable oil

For Raspberry Vinaigrette, combine vinegar and syrup. With a wire whisk slowly add oil in a thin stream while continuing to whisk. Tear lettuce into bite size pieces. Combine the lettuce and onion. Toast the pine nuts 3 minutes at 300 degrees until just lightly golden. Toss desired amount dressing with lettuce and arrange on plates. Sprinkle with toasted nuts and crumbled blue cheese.

whisk

Marla Payne: Coppell, Texas

Marla is one of our Dinner Club members along with her husband, Steve. She assigned this salad to me several years ago for one of our get togethers. It is a flavorful combination of ingredients, both sweet and tangy.

Bibb Lettuce with Feta, Sautéed Apples and Pears with Red Wine Vinaigrette

Serves: 6

Salad

¼	**cup toasted pecan pieces**
I	**mildly soft red pear with skin on**
I	**red skinned apple**
I	**tablespoon butter**
I	**head Bibb lettuce**
4	**ounces crumbled feta cheese**

Red Wine Vinaigrette

½	**cup sugar**
½	**cup red wine vinegar**
½	**teaspoon dry mustard**
½	**teaspoon salt**
½	**teaspoon paprika**
I ½	**cloves garlic, split**
½	**cup vegetable oil**

For Red Wine Vinaigrette, heat sugar and vinegar in saucepan until sugar is dissolved. Remove from heat and whisk in the next four ingredients. While continuing to whisk, slowly add oil in a thin stream. Continue to whisk to thicken slightly. Serve immediately or refrigerate until ready to serve. Toast pecans in 300 degree oven for 3 to 4 minutes. Cut apples and pears in ¼ inch slices. Do not peel. Sauté the pears and apples in melted butter. Wash lettuce and tear into bite size pieces. Toss lettuce with feta, fruits, nuts and as much vinaigrette as preferred. You will have leftover dressing that will keep nicely in any sealed jar in the refrigerator. The dressing can be used on any green salad.

Blue cheese can be substituted for feta.

 whisk

"We all take different paths in life, but no matter where we go, we take a little of each other everywhere."

Tim McGraw

Orange and Romaine Salad with Lime Vinaigrette and Sugared Pecans

Serves: 6

Salad
1	head romaine lettuce
1	large red onion, sliced
2	kiwis, peeled and sliced
1	star fruit or carambola (optional)
1	(11 ounce) can mandarin orange sections
3	ounces crumbled blue cheese

Lime Vinaigrette
¼	cup lime juice (juice of 2 limes)
1	tablespoon honey
3	tablespoons red wine vinegar
3	tablespoons orange marmalade
½	cup olive oil
	Salt and freshly ground pepper, to taste

Sugared Pecans
¼	cup pecans
1½	tablespoons sugar
	Cooking spray

Tear the lettuce into bite size pieces and place in a salad bowl with the onion. For Lime Vinaigrette combine the lime, honey, vinegar and marmalade with a whisk. Slowly add oil in a thin stream as you continue to whisk ingredients. Salt and pepper to taste. Refrigerate until ready to serve. Spray a saucepan with cooking spray and cook sugar and pecans until crystallized. Remove pecans from pan and cool on wax paper. Toss the salad with the vinaigrette and gently mix in the kiwi and oranges. Arrange the star fruit on plate or top of salad and top with blue cheese and sugared pecans. The vinaigrette can be made ahead and stored in a glass jar in the refrigerator.

whisk
wax paper

Carambola are available from summer's end to midwinter. They do not need to be peeled and once ripe can be stored in the refrigerator for up to a week. Star fruit or carambola is a wonderful garnish when cut crosswise ¼ inch thick. It is yellow and resembles a star. It tastes and looks great on cheese trays, desserts and in salads.

Strawberry Romaine Salad

Serves: 6

1 head romaine, Boston or
    other leaf lettuce
½ pint strawberries, sliced
½ cup shredded Monterey Jack
    cheese
¼ cup chopped walnuts or
    pecans
1 (12 ounce) bottle Briannas®
    Blush Wine Vinaigrette
    Dressing

Tear lettuce into bite size pieces. Toast the chopped nuts 3 to 4 minutes in a 300 degree oven. Combine the lettuce with cheese, nuts and strawberries. Shake dressing well. Add ¼ bottle of dressing. Taste to see if lettuce is coated enough for your taste. Add more if you prefer. This can be doubled and more than one type lettuce can be used. A handful of baby spinach and mesclun leaves added to the romaine and Boston lettuce adds depth of color. Briannas® is available in most major grocery stores.

If you would like a more exotic cheese, try crumbled Gorgonzola or traditional feta. For a more tropical flavor, kiwi can be added along with the strawberries. Top with chopped macadamia nuts instead of pecans or walnuts.

Joan Redhair: Leawood, Kansas

Joan and I lived on the same dorm floor in West Hall at Kansas State University. Our relationship has continued to grow since our college days. Melissa Weikel, another friend from the dorm days, comes to Dallas with Joan each year. We have lengthy conversations, drink wine and eat wonderful food. I always prepare a home cooked meal so we can relax and visit as I cook.

Spiced Peaches

Serves: 4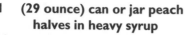

1 (29 ounce) can or jar peach
   halves in heavy syrup
½ cup sugar
½ cup white vinegar
1 stick cinnamon
   Whole cloves
   Bibb lettuce for garnish

Drain peaches and measure juice. It should be
1 cup. If not quite 1 cup, add water to bring
liquid to 1 cup. Add the sugar, vinegar and
cinnamon to the juice and bring to boil in a
saucepan for 5 minutes. Put 2 cloves in each
peach and let them sit in the spiced juice in the
refrigerator for 2 days. Serve 2 peach halves per
person on top of a piece of Bibb lettuce.

Trudy Brown: Paola, Kansas

*Trudy or "Putzi" as I know her, and Hannele her sister, are my mother's
best friends. The three of them get together and speak a combination of
German and English depending on what they want you to hear. These
peaches go well with Rouladen or any beef dish and kids love them too!*

Mesclun with Stilton, Grapes and Honey Vinaigrette

Serves: 6

Salad

½	**head red leaf lettuce or other variety lettuce other than iceberg**
¼	**cup toasted sliced or slivered almonds**
20	**seedless red grapes**
I	**Fiji apple**
4	**ounces mesclun**
⅓	**cup crumbled Stilton or blue cheese**

Honey Vinaigrette

¼	**cup chopped yellow onion**
¼	**cup honey**
¼	**cup white wine vinegar**
2	**teaspoons Tabasco® pepper sauce**
½	**cup vegetable oil**

Wash lettuce and wrap in paper towels in refrigerator until ready to use. Toast almonds on cookie sheet 3 to 4 minutes in 350 degree oven. For Honey Vinaigrette, put first four ingredients in a blender or food processor. Process until smooth. Slowly add oil in a thin stream while the blender or processor is running. Continue processing. Mixture will thicken slightly. Refrigerate until ready to serve. Shortly before you are ready to serve, halve the grapes and core the apple. Cut unpeeled apple into 16 wedges. Toss desired amount dressing with salad greens, grapes, cheese, apples and almonds.

blender or food processor

Allow approximately I ¼ to I ½ cups of slightly packed lettuce per person, per serving as a side dish.

"If one advances confidently in the direction of his dreams to live the life he imagined, he will meet with a success unexpected in common hours."

Henry David Thoreau

Cha Cha Chicken Salad

Serving: 6

4   **chicken breasts, grilled, sliced or cubed**

1   **(16 ounce) bag coleslaw that includes both red and green cabbage and carrots**

1½ **cups red seedless grapes, sliced in half**

1½ **cups celery, sliced thin**

1   **cup sliced walnuts, chopped medium (add before serving)**

1   **cup Asian pears, unpeeled (add before serving)**

1   **(12 ounce) bottle Briannas® Home Style Rich Poppy Seed Dressing**
   Tony Chachere's® Creole Seasoning
   Salt and pepper, to taste

Sprinkle chicken breasts with *Tony Chachere's®* Creole Seasoning before grilling. Mix cubed or sliced breasts with all other ingredients if serving immediately. Otherwise, add the pears and nuts when you are ready to serve. This will keep the pears from browning and walnuts from getting soggy. This is a fabulous salad for a light dinner or luncheon. Serve it on a leaf of red cabbage or leaf lettuce with a slice of fresh bakery bread on the side.

Briannas® is sold at most grocery stores.

Vince Martinez: Dallas, Texas

Vince is my hair stylist and colorist and is very colorful himself. He sings great cocktail music internationally. I enjoy my hair styling sessions with him because he's got his finger on the pulse of the trendiest of places to go in Dallas and usually has a wild story to go with it!

There are over 100 varieties of Asian pears and the most common is called the Twentieth Century. They are round and green to yellow in color. If you can't find an Asian pear then another variety can be substituted. The Asian pears are usually with specialty fruits in the grocery store and not with the other pears.

Oriental Cabbage Slaw

Serves: 10

Slaw

¼	**cup slivered almonds**
¼	**cup shelled sunflower seeds**
¼	**cup chopped, shelled cocktail peanuts**
2	**tablespoons sesame seeds**
2	**(3 ounce) packages oriental ramen noodles, uncooked (spice pack will be used)**
3	**tablespoons butter**
I	**head napa cabbage**
8	**green onions, use all but 4 inches of green onion**

Vinaigrette

½	**cup sesame oil**
¼	**cup white wine vinegar**
⅓	**cup sugar**
3	**tablespoons low sodium soy sauce**
I	**teaspoon crushed red pepper**
4	**cloves minced garlic**

Sauté the nuts and sesame seeds until lightly toasted and add crushed ramen noodles. Add the spice packets and toss to coat. Let mixture cool. The ramen and nut mixture may be made earlier in the day and stored in an airtight container. Cabbage may be cut up and mixed with onions and refrigerated until ready to serve. Mix Vinaigrette ingredients together in a glass jar. Shake vigorously and refrigerate. Mix together sliced cabbage, green onions and sautéed ramen and nut mixture in a large bowl. Shake vinaigrette. Toss the desired amount of dressing with the cabbage, nuts, seeds and noodles. Serve immediately.

Napa cabbage is cream colored with celadon tipped leaves. It is an elongated, not round head.

This Vinaigrette can be used on a green salad as well. Cashews may be substituted for cocktail peanuts. For those that like cilantro, ½ cup may be added. Add shredded chicken for a complete meal.

Vicki Morgan: Little Rock, Arkansas

When Vicki, a friend since junior high school, gave me this recipe it sent me on a quest for the best. I had variations of this recipe from Betty Krenger of Abilene, Kansas and Kathy Anderson of Kansas City, Missouri, so I took the best ingredients from them and created my own version. It is different and a tasty side dish with Asian spiced fish, chicken or grilled meats.

Broccoli Salad with Nuts and Raisins

Serves: 6

Salad
1 **head broccoli, chopped**
1 **cup raisins**
½ **cup chopped red onion**
¾ **cup shelled sunflower seeds**
8 **slices bacon, fried, drained and crumbled**

Dressing
2 **tablespoons red wine vinegar**
1 **cup HELLMANN'S® Real Mayonnaise**
½ **cup sugar**

Mix dressing ingredients together. Toss with the salad ingredients.

Carrie Hoffman, Olathe, Kansas, makes this and adds 1 cup chopped celery, for a little extra crunch. I have had this with salted peanuts instead of sunflower seeds and it was good!

Julie Martell, Denver, Colorado

Julie and I lived together for two years in college and had a blast. We arrange to go to Jimmy Buffett concerts together when possible and have had several reunions since college. Five out of the eight Martells have a recipe in the book. Julie said her recipe is a favorite barbecue side dish and it is always the first to go. I can attest to that!

Picnic Potato Salad

Serves: 12

Potato Salad

5 **pounds red skinned potatoes**

6 **tablespoons sweet pickle relish**

½ **large red onion**

3 **green onions**

7 **slices deli bacon cooked, drained and crumbled**

I **(8 ounce) can water chestnuts drained and chopped**

3 **hard boiled eggs peeled and chopped**

4 **tablespoons McCormick Salad Supreme (found in spice section)**

4 **teaspoons *Tony Chachere's®* *Creole Seasoning* (or more to taste)**

Dressing

3 **tablespoons Creole mustard**

I **cup HELLMANN'S® Real Mayonnaise**

I **tablespoon sugar**

2 **teaspoons red wine vinegar**

Dice potatoes very small and boil until tender, but not mushy consistency. Drain and cool slightly. Mix together the mayonnaise, mustard, vinegar and sugar. Set aside. Add all other ingredients to the potatoes and then stir in the dressing/mustard mixture. Mix gently. Refrigerate. This is best if it sits in the refrigerator 24 hours so flavors blend.

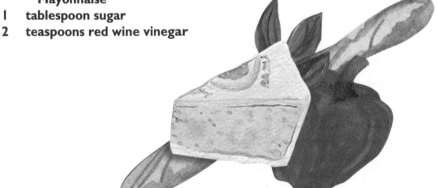

Warm German Potato Salad

Serves: 6

4	**slices bacon**
¾	**cup chopped onion**
1	**(10¾ ounce) can cream of celery soup**
¼	**cup water**
2	**tablespoons white vinegar**
½	**teaspoon sugar**
⅛	**teaspoon pepper**
2	**(14½ ounce) cans whole potatoes, drained and sliced**
¼	**cup chopped, fresh parsley**

Cook bacon until crisp; remove from skillet, reserve drippings. Crumble. Cook onion in bacon drippings. Blend in soup, water, vinegar, sugar and pepper. Heat, stirring occasionally. Add potatoes, parsley and crumbled bacon. Simmer 5 minutes. Can be made ahead. Serve warm.

Brigitte Scherer:
Kansas City, Kansas

This is my mother's recipe and is best with bratwurst or Reuben sandwiches that are made with deli pastrami, Swiss cheese, sauerkraut, Thousand Island dressing and grilled on rye bread.

"You pay for it whether you eat it or not."
Mom's lesson on not overeating and bringing home
the leftovers from restaurants.

Three Bean Salad

Serves: 6

Salad
2 cups yellow beans
2 cups kidney beans
2 cups canned green beans
(not French style)
½ cup chopped green pepper
½ cup chopped green onion or
½ cup white onion cut in
rings

Dressing
¾ cup sugar
⅔ cup vinegar
⅓ cup vegetable oil
1 teaspoon salt
1 teaspoon pepper

Drain and rinse beans. Pour dressing over beans, pepper and onion. Marinate overnight before serving.

Donna Gray: Kansas, City, Kansas

Donna, my friend Heather's mother, gave me this recipe in high school, and I have enjoyed it ever since. It is great for picnics with cold fried chicken or mixed in with a green salad.

Creamy Italian Ranch Dressing

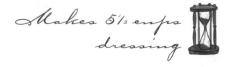

Makes 5½ cups dressing

3	**eggs**
¼	**teaspoon pepper**
¼	**teaspoon sugar**
¼	**teaspoon salt**
1	**teaspoon dry mustard**
½	**cup red wine vinegar**
1	**cup bottled Italian dressing**
2	**cups salad oil**
1	**cup mayonnaise**
1	**cup buttermilk**
1	**package Hidden Valley® Original Ranch® dry dressing mix**

Combine eggs, pepper, sugar, salt and dry mustard in blender, blend 2 minutes. Stop blender and add vinegar and Italian dressing, blend another minute. Very slowly add oil in a thin stream through the feeding tube or opening in the top of the blender and blend between each addition. Blend until the dressing is the thickness of mayonnaise. Transfer to a bowl and fold in mayonnaise, buttermilk and dry Ranch dressing. Recipe may be cut in half. Keep refrigerated.

This dressing can also be used on sandwiches and hamburgers, replacing mayonnaise.

blender or food processor

Balsamic Vinaigrette Dressing

Makes: ²/₃ of a cup

- ⅓ **cup vinegar, split equally between red wine and balsamic vinegar**
- 1 **teaspoon Dijon mustard**
- 1 **tablespoon sugar**
- ½ **teaspoon cracked black pepper to taste**
- ¼ **teaspoon salt**
- 2 **garlic cloves, split (optional)**
- ⅓ **cup oil, split equally between olive oil and vegetable oil**

Whisk first 6 ingredients together. While continuing to whisk, add oil in a thin stream. Continue to whisk to thicken. Refrigerate.

whisk

Balsamic vinegar is made from the Italian white Trebbiano grape and is aged in barrels to give it a dark color and pungent sweetness. Balsamic vinegar can also be used drizzled over mozzarella and tomatoes and sprinkled with fresh chopped basil and olive oil, for a delicious and colorful salad.

Linda Gore: Colleyville, Texas

Linda's son Dave passed this recipe on to me and we make it frequently. Linda and her husband David spend the hot summer months at a resort they own in Almont, Colorado. Besides guests of the resort they frequently entertain visitors, including their two daughters Peri and Susan that live nearby. They previously owned a gourmet store and have a great appreciation of food and wine.

Spicy Vinaigrette

Serves: 6

Spicy Vinaigrette

1   clove garlic, chopped or put
    in blender to chop
1   tablespoon orange juice
3   tablespoons red wine
    vinegar
½   teaspoon salt
½   teaspoon chili powder
1   tablespoon Dijon mustard
½   cup vegetable oil

Blend first six ingredients in blender or food processor. Blend on stir setting and slowly add oil through the top hole in blender or through the feed tube on the processor. Blend ingredients until they thicken slightly. Make ahead and keep for the following combinations.

Salad Variations:

Leaf Lettuce with Capers, Oranges and Red Onion

Serves: 4

1   head green or red leaf
    lettuce
1   tablespoon drained capers
    Sliced water chestnuts
    (to taste)
    Sliced red onion
    (leave in rings)
    Mandarin orange slices
    (¾ can)

Leaf Lettuce with Red Onion, Oranges and Avocado

Serves: 4

1   head red or green leaf
    lettuce
    Sliced red onion
    (leave in rings)
1   (11 ounce) can mandarin
    oranges
1   small avocado, sliced
    Croutons

Leaf Lettuce with Pecan Crunch and Blue Cheese

Serves: 4

1   head red or green leaf
    lettuce
¼   cup Pecan Crunch, chopped
    (see page 80)
½   cup crumbled blue cheese

148

Spicy Vinaigrette *continued*

Delicate ingredients, such as avocado and mandarin oranges should be used to garnish the salad so they don't break up when tossed in the salad.

blender or food processor

Mary Hutchinson: Topeka, Kansas

Mary was one of the original members of the "Single Girl's Dinner Club." We had this salad dressing at one of our first Dinner Club gatherings in Dallas. Mary cooked for us in her high rise apartment. Life has changed. She lives in Topeka with her husband, Steve, and has three children. In spite of a busy schedule, Mary still enjoys cooking and was recognized as "Cook of the Week" in the Topeka Capital Journal *Food Section several years ago.*

Oil is the last thing added to a salad dressing that you are trying to emulsify or thicken. Oil is added slowly in a thin stream at the same time as mixing rapidly either with a blender, processor or whisk. It is usually done with ingredients such as vinegar and oil that cannot normally combine smoothly. This process disperses and suspends minute droplets of one liquid throughout the other to create a thick and satiny texture.

Party Sandwiches

Servings: 8

1 **unsliced 8 to 10 inch long loaf pumpernickel bread or other dense specialty bread**
1 **bunch green onions, chopped**
1 **(8 ounce) package cream cheese, room temperature**
½ **teaspoon *Tony Chachere's® Creole Seasoning***
1½ **pounds thinly sliced rare roast beef, from the deli**
2 **tomatoes, thinly sliced**
1 **pound bacon, fried crisp and drained**
HELLMANN'S® Real Mayonnaise
Romaine lettuce leaves

Slice bread in half lengthwise and hollow out the top of the loaf about ½ inch deep. Bread loaf should be about 3½ inches wide. Mix green onion and *Tony Chachere's®* into the cream cheese. Fill cavity with the cream cheese mixture. Spread bottom half generously with mayonnaise. Cover to the edge of bread. Layer the lettuce on the bottom half, tomatoes, meat and top with the bacon slices. Top with the hollowed out bread filled with cream cheese. Slice sandwich diagonally at 2 inch intervals with a serrated knife.

The bread that is dense and large enough should come from a specialty baker and may need to be special ordered. Serve with soup for a complete meal.

sharp serrated knife
hand mixer

The Fresh Tomato, Kalamata and Feta Salad (p. 120) would be a great way to jazz up this sandwich by leaving the tomatoes in the sandwich and adding chopped feta and olives. Drizzle the tomatoes with the vinaigrette before putting in sandwich. Another yummy combination!

Jody Auerter:
Kansas City, Kansas

Jody, our next door neighbor in Kansas City, is a wonderful cook. When either of us need ideas for table settings or menus, we call each other. Jody suggested this sandwich for a couple's shower. It made a complete meal when served along with a few interesting appetizers. There were no leftovers!

Meats & Seafoods

Kitchen tools needed

May be prepared ahead

Beach Buzzes, page 105 ~ Orange and Romaine Salad
with Lime Vinaigrette and Sugared Pecans, page 136
Pineapple Shrimp Skewers with Honey Marinade, page 74 ~ Black Beans with Cilantro Pesto Rice, page 222
Tropical Fiesta Steak with Island Marinade and Caribbean Salsa, page 157

Beef Tenderloin with Red Zinfandel Sauce

Serves: 6

Beef

2	**tablespoons olive oil**
1	**(3 pound) beef tenderloin**
¾	**teaspoon salt**
3	**cloves garlic, minced**
1	**bay leaf, chopped**
1½	**teaspoons chopped fresh thyme**
½	**teaspoon black pepper**

Red Zinfandel Sauce

1½	**cups red Zinfandel wine**
1	**(14.5 ounce) can beef broth**
1½	**teaspoons tomato paste**
3	**tablespoons water**
2	**teaspoons arrowroot**
¼	**teaspoon salt**
¼	**teaspoon pepper**

Put oil in roasting pan and place over two burners. Add tenderloin and brown on all sides. Remove from heat and place meat on cutting board. Preheat oven to 450 degrees. Discard oil in pan. Crush salt, garlic, bay leaf, thyme and pepper into paste. Rub over the tenderloin. Return the roast to the roasting pan and roast 35 to 40 minutes at 450 degrees or until thermometer registers 145 degrees for medium rare or 140 degrees for rare. Once removed from oven it will continue to cook. Remove from roasting pan and put on platter. Tent with foil to keep warm. For sauce, heat wine to boiling. Add any bits from bottom of roasting pan. Boil until reduced to ½ cup. Pour into small saucepan. Add broth and tomato paste; boil 10 minutes or until reduced to 1½ cups. In a cup, mix the water and arrowroot; stir into wine mixture. Heat to boiling. Strain through fine mesh sieve into a measuring cup and add salt and pepper. Add any drippings from meat. To serve cut meat into ½ inch slices. Drizzle sauce over slices. Serve extra sauce on side. Sauce may be made ahead and drippings added when the meat is removed from the oven.

meat thermometer
fine mesh strainer

Arrowroot or arrowroot flour can be found in health food stores, Asian markets and some supermarkets. It is a rootstalk, dried and ground to a fine powder and has twice the thickening power of cornstarch. It should be mixed with a cold liquid and added to a hot mixture.

Beef Tenderloin with Bordelaise Sauce

Serves: 6

Beef Tenderloin
1 (3 pound) beef tenderloin
Salt and pepper

Bordelaise Sauce
¼ cup butter
2 shallots, chopped
2 cloves garlic, minced
2 slices onion
2 carrots, sliced
2 sprigs parsley
10 whole peppercorns
2 whole cloves
2 bay leaves
3 tablespoons flour
½ teaspoon beef base
1 (10.5 ounce) can beef broth
1 cup Burgundy wine (divided use)
⅛ teaspoon black pepper
¼ teaspoon salt
2 tablespoons finely chopped parsley (add at end)

Make sauce before preparing tenderloin. Keep the sauce warm or refrigerate until ready to use. To make sauce, melt the butter and sauté next 8 ingredients. Remove from heat and add 3 tablespoons flour. Cook until the flour is brown over low heat. Stir. Remove from heat and add beef base and the can of beef broth. Add ¾ cup Burgundy wine and bring to boil, stirring constantly. Reduce heat and simmer uncovered 10 minutes. Strain the sauce and throw away the vegetables and peppercorns. Add pepper, salt, parsley and remaining ¼ cup Burgundy. Warm sauce before serving; do not boil. To cook beef tenderloin, salt and pepper tenderloin. Broil in shallow metal roasting pan 45 minutes turning every 15 minutes. In an electric oven, door will need to be cracked while broiling. Once this process is done, cook 30 minutes at 300 degrees on middle rack with the meat thermometer inserted and the door closed. Cook to 140 degrees for rare and 145 degrees for medium rare.

roasting pan
meat thermometer
fine mesh strainer

Jody Huerter:
Kansas City, Kansas

Jody was my next door neighbor growing up and is the mother of five grown children. She has been a great inspiration to me in my own entertaining and has always encouraged high standards. This is one of her favorite recipes for guests. I am honored to have this special recipe.

Pepper Crusted Beef Tenderloin with Pinot Noir Sauce

Serves: 6

Beef
- 1 **(3 pound) beef tenderloin**
- 2 **tablespoons cracked black pepper**
- 1 **tablespoon olive oil**
  Fine sea salt

Pinot Noir Sauce
- ¼ **cup butter, softened (divided use)**
- 1 **tablespoon flour**
- 1 **cup finely chopped yellow onion**
- 1 **cup finely chopped carrots**
- 1 **cup finely chopped celery**
- 2 **tablespoons tomato paste**
- 1¼ **cups Pinot Noir wine**
- 1¼ **cups canned low salt chicken broth**
- 1¼ **cups canned beef broth**

Preheat oven to 500 degrees. Make sauce and keep warm or refrigerate until ready to prepare beef. For the sauce, mix together 2 tablespoons of the softened butter and flour. Set aside. Melt 1 tablespoon butter in skillet and add onion, celery and carrots. Sauté until tender about 10 minutes. Add tomato paste and stir until vegetables are coated. Add wine and boil until the liquid is reduced by half, approximately 3 minutes. Add both broths and boil until liquid is reduced to 1¼ cups, about 5 minutes. Strain liquid and discard solids. Return liquid to skillet. Add butter and flour mixture to sauce and whisk over medium heat until thickened, about one minute. Season to taste with salt and pepper. Sauce can be made one day ahead. Keep refrigerated. Warm sauce while beef is cooking. Mix any juices from the roasting pan into sauce once beef is removed from the oven. For beef, melt the remaining one tablespoon butter in large skillet and add one tablespoon olive oil. Sprinkle beef with sea salt and cracked black pepper. Add beef to skillet and cook until brown on all sides, about 5 minutes. Transfer to roasting pan. Roast beef approximately 25 minutes with meat thermometer inserted in thickest part of beef. Temperature should be 145 degrees for medium rare, 140 degrees for rare. Once removed from oven, meat will continue to cook slightly, so you do not want to overcook. Let rest 5 minutes once removed from oven. Cut in ½ inch slices and serve on plate with the slices slightly overlapping. Drizzle with sauce and pass extra sauce.

roasting pan
meat thermometer
whisk
fine mesh strainer

Stovetop Beef Tenderloin with Rosemary and Red Pepper

Serves: 4

1   **(2 pound) beef tenderloin**
1   **teaspoon celery salt**
1   **teaspoon coarsely crushed black pepper**
2   **slices bacon**
⅔   **cup red wine (Merlot)**
1½ **teaspoons minced rosemary leaves**
1   **red bell pepper**
1⅓ **cups veal or beef demi-glace**

Pat tenderloin dry and rub with celery salt and black pepper. Cut bacon into 1½ inch pieces. In a kettle large enough to hold beef tenderloin, cook bacon until crisp and transfer to a plate or bowl with a slotted spoon. Pour off all but 1 tablespoon fat and heat to high. Brown tenderloin on all sides, 5 minutes total. Take tenderloin out. To the kettle add wine, bacon and rosemary and boil 1 minute. Return the beef tenderloin to the kettle and simmer covered. Turn occasionally for 25 minutes or until the meat thermometer registers 145 degrees for medium rare when thermometer is diagonally inserted. Let meat stand 10 minutes before cutting. It will continue to cook while it rests. Make sauce while tenderloin is cooking. For sauce, dice bell pepper into ¼ inch cubes. With a slotted spoon remove bacon from cooking liquid. Add bell pepper and demi-glace to cooking liquid and boil over moderate heat until slightly thick and reduced to 1⅓ cups. To serve, cut the beef tenderloin into slices and arrange on platter. Spoon some of sauce over meat and garnish with rosemary. Pass additional sauce.

slotted spoon
meat thermometer
large kettle

Demi-glace is used in recipes when making a brown sauce. Most come as a concentrate and will need water added. In a store bought demi-glace, the complicated process has been done for you. A beef or veal reduction was made from boiling the bones for a 24 hour period to form a thick glaze. Vegetables and spices and a small addition of Madeira or sherry are added during the process to give the reduction a unique flavor.

Beef Tenderloin with Mustard Brown Sugar Glaze

Serves: 6

I **(3 pound) beef tenderloin**
Salt and pepper
Brown sugar
Yellow prepared mustard

Use mustard and brown sugar in equal parts and make a paste of the mustard brown sugar mixture. It will not be as thick as paste because of the moisture in the mustard. Salt and pepper the beef tenderloin and broil it in oven for 10 minutes on each side. Turn oven back to 350 degrees. Remove the tenderloin from oven and coat with the mustard and brown sugar mixture. Return to oven and bake at 350 degrees for 45 minutes. Turn off oven, leave door ajar and cook 45 minutes longer. If using a meat thermometer, the internal temperature should be 140 degrees for rare and 145 degrees for medium rare.

meat thermometer

This mustard and brown sugar rub, or the sauces from the previous tenderloin recipes (p. 151-154), will work with filet mignon as well. Filets may be cooked on the grill. If making one of the recipes with a sauce, you can drizzle the sauce over the meat or serve the meat on top of the sauce.

Joan Lewis: McKinney, Texas

Joan and Rick Lewis started our original "Dinner Club" in 1989. Originally we alternated houses and got together once a month. With busy schedules and longer distances between us, we try to gather quarterly. Joan held the annual holiday dinner club for the first few years. She made this special beef tenderloin and it is delicious.

Allow approximately a ½ pound of tenderloin per person.

Filet Mignon with Grilled Fennel and Red Onions

Filet Mignon

4   **filet mignons**
1   **bunch fresh rosemary**
       branches
2   **cloves garlic, thinly sliced**
½   **cup extra virgin olive oil**
       Freshly cracked black
       pepper

Grilled Fennel and Onions

2   **fennel bulbs, tops cut off,**
       washed, cut in half
2   **medium red onions, peeled,**
       cut in half
¼   **cup extra virgin olive oil,**
       plus extra for brushing
2   **tablespoons balsamic**
       vinegar
1½ **cups gourmet salad greens**
       (mesclun)
       Freshly cracked black
       pepper

Take the rosemary branch at the base and pierce it into the filet. Wrap it around the exterior and stick the tip of the stalk into the meat to hold it in place. Marinate the 4 filet mignons that have each been wrapped with a sprig of rosemary in the ½ cup olive oil, ¼ cup rosemary, 2 cloves garlic and freshly cracked pepper to taste, for one hour. While the steaks are marinating bring a pot of water to boil. Add the fennel bulbs and the onion and boil for one minute. Remove from water and plunge into ice water. Dry the vegetables with a dishtowel and brush with oil. Grill the vegetables until golden while grilling steaks to desired doneness. The stalk wrapped around the meat stays intact while grilling and makes a special presentation. Remove the vegetables once golden and coarsely chop. Mix the ¼ cup oil with the 2 tablespoons balsamic vinegar. Toss with the lettuce and oil and vinegar mixture. Sprinkle with freshly cracked black pepper. Serve steak on top of grilled fennel, red onion and lettuce mixture.

Tropical Fiesta Steak
with Island Marinade and Caribbean Salsa

Serves: 4

4 filet mignons, approximately
½ pound each

Marinade
½ **lemon or ⅛ cup lemon juice**
4 **cloves garlic, minced**
¼ **cup orange juice or juice**
    from one orange
3 **tablespoons olive oil**
1 **tablespoon Creole mustard**
3 **green onions, sliced**
¼ **teaspoon Tabasco® pepper**
    sauce
½ **teaspoon ground cumin**
1 **teaspoon chili powder**
1 **tablespoon dried oregano**

Caribbean Salsa
4 **Roma tomatoes, seeded**
1 **papaya, peeled, seeded and**
    diced
1 **cup red onion, diced**
2 **limes**
1 **tablespoon mint, diced**
2 **tablespoons brown sugar**
½ **teaspoon cumin**
1 **teaspoon chili powder**
1 **teaspoon crushed red**
    pepper flakes
½ **teaspoon salt**
1 **teaspoon Worcestershire**
    sauce
1 **avocado for garnish**

Mix marinade ingredients together. Add meat and toss to coat. Marinate meat 8 hours in the refrigerator, turning meat occasionally. Make salsa at least one hour ahead. If made a day ahead, refrigerate and let it come to room temperature before serving. To make salsa, combine tomato, onion and papaya in a bowl. Place this mixture in a blender and process until smooth. Return puree to the bowl. Add juice and zest of both limes. Add remaining ingredients, excluding avocado and stir to blend. For steaks, the approximate grilling time is 8 to 12 minutes for medium rare and 11 to 15 minutes for medium. Grill to desired doneness and serve with Caribbean Salsa. Spoon the salsa on top of the steak and garnish with chopped avocado. This salsa can also be made for other occasions and served as an appetizer with tortilla chips.

blender or food processor
zester or cheese grater

German Rouladen with Rich Brown Gravy

Serves: 6

12 pieces top round cut
 ⅛ to ¼ inch thick
 Yellow prepared mustard
 Salt and pepper to taste
1 onion, chopped
12 slices bacon, uncooked,
 diced
 Dill pickle spears or a
 quartered dill pickle for
 each individual Rouladen
 Butter, for browning
1 **KNORR® Extra Large Beef**
 Bouillon Cube
2 cups water

Rich Brown Gravy
 Juice from Rouladen
1 **(14½ ounce) can beef broth**
⅛ **cup Wondra flour**
½ **cup cold water**
1 **teaspoon KITCHEN**
 BOUQUET® Browning
 and Seasoning Sauce
 Salt and pepper, to taste

Potato Dumplings
1 **package potato dumpling**
 mix

Take a piece of top round for each person and salt and pepper, spread with mustard and sprinkle with diced bacon and onion. Put a quarter of a dill pickle on top of this. Roll it up and tie with thread tucking in the sides. Brown in butter. Dissolve the bouillon cube in the two cups water and add to Rouladen. Simmer 45 minutes. If you make these for 8 to 12 people you will need two bouillon cubes and 4 cups of water total. To make a paste of the Wondra flour, you will need an additional ½ cup water. You may refrigerate or freeze the Rouladen at this point. Leave string on until ready to serve. When ready to serve, reheat in broth. Remove the Rouladen from the broth and keep the Rouladen warm in oven while making gravy. For the gravy, use the juices from the Rouladen and the can of beef broth. If increasing to serve for a larger group or more gravy is preferred, add an additional extra large beef bouillon cube and 2 cups water. Heat until boiling. Mix the Wondra/water mixture with a fork until smooth. Add mixture slowly to gravy while stirring until thickened. Add one teaspoon of the KITCHEN BOUQUET®. The gravy should be a milk chocolate color. Depending on the increased amount of bouillon being used, more KITCHEN BOUQUET® and Wondra mixture may need to be added. The KITCHEN BOUQUET® will add flavor and color. Taste and add salt and pepper if needed. The Rouladen and the gravy can be reheated. This is best served with potato dumplings and a lot of Rich Brown Gravy. If freezing, defrost in the refrigerator and use juices to make gravy. Reheat the Rouladen in the juices with the string on. Keep warm on a platter while making gravy. Remove string before serving. Gently serve Rouladen with tongs. Spoon

German Rouladen continued

gravy over the top. Pass extra gravy separately. Dumplings should be made according to package mix. They are served by tearing open gently on your plate and topping generously with gravy.

Potato Dumplings are found in some grocery stores or German specialty food stores. Follow package directions for preparation. German butchers have sirloin already sliced to make a perfect Rouladen.

cooking string or unwaxed dental floss
whisk
tongs

Brigitte Scherer:
Kansas City, Kansas

My mother and father got married in Germany after World War II. My mother came over on a ship to America with the other war brides into Ellis Island. I remember a lot of newspaper articles written about my parents' story of how they met and of war times. I also remember taking my mother to show and tell during my grade school years. This is an authentic German dinner we have on special occasions. Serve Red Cabbage as a side dish.

Herb Crusted Prime Rib with Port Wine Sauce

Serves 6

Herb Crusted Prime Rib

1 **tablespoon coarsely ground black pepper**
1 **tablespoon chopped fresh parsley**
2 **teaspoons chopped fresh rosemary**
1 **teaspoon chopped fresh thyme**
2 **teaspoons minced garlic**
1 **teaspoon salt**
1 **(8 pound) prime rib roast (3 ribs)**

Port Wine Sauce

1 **(14½ ounce) can beef broth**
¾ **cup port wine**
2 **tablespoons chopped shallots**
1 **bay leaf**
3 **tablespoons melted butter**
2 **tablespoons flour**

Remove prime rib roast from the refrigerator 2 hours before roasting. In a bowl, combine pepper, parsley, rosemary, thyme, garlic and salt and rub mixture over entire surface of meat. Place meat on a rack in a roasting pan, fat side up. Preheat oven to 350 degrees. Insert a meat thermometer into the center of the meat so it does not touch the rib bones. Put roast in oven until internal temperature reaches 120 degrees to 125 degrees for rare to medium rare (2 to 2¼ hours), 130 degrees to 135 degrees for medium to medium well (2¼ to 2¾ hours). Let meat stand 15 minutes before carving. While meat is cooking, prepare sauce in a medium saucepan. Combine broth, port, shallots and bay leaf. Bring to boil. Reduce heat. Simmer uncovered 15 to 20 minutes. Remove bay leaf. Stir together butter and flour. Add ¼ of the butter and flour mixture to the port mixture. Cook and stir until slightly thickened. You want this to be a thin sauce you can drizzle, not a gravy. Cook and stir for one minute more. Use more of the flour and butter mixture if needed and more port if the sauce gets too thick. Make sauce ahead of time or during first hour of cooking. If making ahead and refrigerating, do not thicken. This can be done two days ahead. When ready to serve, return to medium saucepan and heat. Mix together the butter and flour and add ¼ of the mixture to the sauce. Cook until slightly thickened, and add more of the butter and flour mixture if needed for desired consistency.

Herb Crusted Prime Rib continued

If you prefer, purchase a package of Au Jus from the dry sauce section of the grocery store instead of making the sauce. This is a natural juice that will complement the meat. Serve sauce on the side. Cabernet Sauvignon may be used in place of port and demi-glace prepared according to package directions can be substituted for broth. Gorgonzola cheese (8 ounces) may be mixed into sauce as well. The cheese will change the consistency of the sauce. This addition may reduce the amount of flour and butter mixture needed for thickening the sauce to the desired consistency.

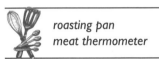

roasting pan
meat thermometer

"I've learned
The importance of chasing life's rainbows
And that the pot of gold may sometimes be a heart of gold
Found around the least expected corner."

Author Unknown

Brisket with Honey Barbecue Sauce

Serves: 8

Brisket

1	**(6 pound) brisket**
2	**tablespoons liquid smoke**
	Garlic salt
	Tony Chachere's® Creole Seasoning
1	**oven cooking bag**
1½	**cups water**

Barbecue Sauce

1½	**cups catsup**
½	**cup packed brown sugar**
¼	**cup Creole mustard**
¼	**cup apple cider vinegar**
1½	**teaspoons chili powder**
1½	**teaspoons pepper**
1	**teaspoon garlic powder**
1½	**teaspoons Worcestershire sauce**
½	**teaspoon celery salt**
1	**teaspoon Tabasco® pepper sauce**
½	**cup chopped onion**
½	**cup honey**

Season brisket on the meaty side with the liquid smoke and sprinkle generously with *Tony Chachere's®* and garlic salt. Shake 1 tablespoon flour (as directed on cooking bag directions) in the bag before adding beef. Put brisket fat side down in the oven bag and add 1½ cups water to the bag. Make 6 slits in the top of bag and close with the nylon tie provided. Lay in a baking dish fat side down. Do not let bag hang over side of the baking dish. Bake at 350 degrees for 3 hours until tender and a fork can be easily inserted. Remove from bag. Cool in refrigerator in a clean baking dish. Meat may be cooled overnight and reheated and served the next day. For sauce, combine all ingredients in saucepan and heat to boiling. Reduce heat. Cook covered for 30 minutes. Slice beef against the grain in ½ inch thick slices. Before serving, make the barbecue sauce above or use your favorite sauce and spread on top of sliced beef, heat covered in oven for 30 minutes at 350 degrees.

"With years richer life begins
The spirit mellows,
Ripe age gives tone to violins,
wine, and good fellows."

John Trowbridge

Garlic and Thyme Roasted Pork Loin with a Brandy Cream Sauce

Serves: 8

Roasted Pork Loin Roast

1	**(3½ pound) boneless pork loin roast, tied**
6	**large cloves garlic**
1	**teaspoon salt**
2	**teaspoons freshly ground pepper**
¼	**cup brandy**
4	**tablespoons fresh thyme**
¼	**cup olive oil**
1	**cup dry white wine**

Brandy Cream Sauce

4	**tablespoons butter**
½	**cup finely chopped yellow onion**
1	**cup dry white wine**
2	**cups heavy cream**
½	**cup brandy**
1	**teaspoon salt**
1	**teaspoon pepper**
1	**tablespoon cornstarch**
1	**tablespoon cold water**

Remove roast from refrigerator 30 minutes before preparing rub for meat. Preheat the oven to 350 degrees. In a blender or food processor, combine garlic cloves with salt, pepper, brandy and thyme. Add olive oil slowly in a thin stream through hole in top of blender or feeding tube of processor. Process to thicken slightly. Place pork roast in roasting pan; coat with the garlic and thyme mixture. Bake in oven with meat thermometer inserted, uncovered. Baste with a quarter cup of white wine every 15 minutes for one hour. Roast approximately 1½ hours or until internal temperature reaches 160 degrees. Make sauce while pork is roasting. For sauce, melt butter and sauté onion 3 to 5 minutes. Reduce heat and add wine and simmer 15 minutes. Gradually stir in cream. Add brandy, salt and pepper. Cook over moderately high heat, stirring to reduce liquid by ⅓, about 5 to 7 minutes. Mix together cold water and cornstarch. Add half of cornstarch mixture to sauce. Continue to simmer until slightly thickened. Use the remainder of thickening mixture if not to desired consistency. Once meat is removed from the oven, let rest 10 minutes. Slice in ¼ to ½ inch slices and serve. Pass sauce separately.

meat thermometer
roasting pan
blender or food processor

Garlic Marinated Pork Tenderloin

Serves: 4

2 **pork tenderloins**
    (**1 ½ pounds total**)
3 **cloves garlic, chopped**
⅓ **cup low sodium soy sauce**
⅓ **cup olive oil**

Marinate pork tenderloins overnight in garlic, soy sauce and olive oil mixture. Grill approximately 15 to 25 minutes or until 160 degrees in the center.

Add a tablespoon of cornstarch to the marinade and stir to dissolve. It will stick to the meat better.

Mary Hutchinson: Topeka, Kansas

Mary made this at one of the first Girl's Dinner Club gatherings she hosted. This marinade is one of the best for pork. Increase the marinade proportionately when marinating more than 2 tenderloins.

"To love and to be loved is to feel the sun from both sides."

David Viscott

Grilled Pork Tenderloin with Chili Maple Glaze

Serves: 4

Pork in Brine
2 **pork tenderloins**
   (1½ pounds total)
2 **cups water**
1½ **tablespoons sea salt**

Chili Maple Glaze
1½ **tablespoons pure maple**
   syrup
1 **tablespoon chili powder**

Dissolve sea salt in bowl with water. Marinate pork in the brine for 24 hours in the refrigerator. Next day, prepare grill. Mix together syrup and chili powder. Discard brine. Brush the chili maple glaze on all sides of meat. Grill meat approximately 15 to 25 minutes over hot grill or until internal temperature reaches 160 degrees.

meat thermometer
pastry brush

Maple-flavored syrup should not be substituted for pure maple syrup. Maple-flavored syrup is corn syrup with a small amount of pure maple syrup added and will not give foods the same flavor as pure maple syrup. Pure maple syrup must be refrigerated after opening.

Marinated Pork Tenderloin with Molasses Barbecue Sauce

Serves: 4

Marinated Pork

4	**cups water**
1½	**tablespoons sea salt**
1	**cup brown sugar**
1	**small onion, thinly sliced**
5	**cloves garlic, minced**
2	**teaspoons dried crushed red pepper flakes**
6	**large fresh thyme sprigs or 2 teaspoons dried thyme**
2	**pork tenderloins (1½ pounds total)**
2	**tablespoons olive oil (to brush on pork before grilling)**

Molasses Barbecue Sauce

3	**cups chicken broth**
1	**cup dry white wine**
¼	**cup apple cider vinegar**
¼	**cup molasses**
¼	**cup chopped tomato**
3	**tablespoons minced shallots**
2	**tablespoons chopped, pitted dates**
1	**tablespoon chopped garlic**
1	**teaspoon dried red pepper flakes**
1	**tablespoon cornstarch mixed with 1 tablespoon cold water**
	Salt and pepper, to taste

Dissolve sea salt in bowl with water. Add seasonings. Marinate pork in the bowl of salt water with seasonings for 24 hours in refrigerator. Next day, prepare grill. Drain pork and pat dry. Discard brine. Brush pork with oil. Make Molasses Barbecue Sauce. Grill meat approximately 15 to 25 minutes or until inside temperature reaches 160 degrees with meat thermometer. Check desired doneness after grilling 9 minutes on each side. Serve with Molasses Barbecue Sauce. For sauce, combine all ingredients excluding cornstarch/water mixture in heavy saucepan. Boil until reduced to 1½ cups, stirring occasionally for 20 minutes. Season with salt and pepper to taste. Use 1 tablespoon cornstarch with 1 tablespoon cold water to thicken. Heat until thickened. Serve warm. Sauce may be made 2 days ahead. Cover and chill until ready to serve. Heat before serving.

meat thermometer
pastry brush

Marinated Pork Tenderloin with Cumberland Sauce

Serves: 8

Marinade
½   **cup dry sherry**
½   **cup low sodium soy sauce**
2   **large cloves garlic, minced**
1   **tablespoon dry mustard**
1   **teaspoon dry, crushed thyme**
3¾ **pounds pork tenderloin**

Cumberland Sauce
2½ **cups tawny port, divided use**
1   **(10½ ounce) jar currant jelly**
⅔   **cup fresh orange juice**
3   **tablespoons brown sugar**
1½ **tablespoons fresh ginger, peeled and chopped**
2   **teaspoons dry mustard**
¼   **teaspoon salt**
¼   **teaspoon cayenne pepper**
2   **tablespoons cornstarch**

Combine the marinade ingredients and put in large plastic sealable bag. Add pork and marinade meat up to 24 hours in refrigerator. Cook on grill over hot coals 15 to 25 minutes, approximately 10 minutes per side. The internal temperature should be 160 degrees. If you are unable to cook outdoors, cook pork tenderloin in a skillet over medium high heat 5 minutes until browned. Place on a jelly-roll pan and bake with a meat thermometer inserted, 15 minutes at 375 degrees or until the meat thermometer reaches an internal temperature of 160 degrees. Make sauce while meat is cooking or up to 2 days ahead and reheat slowly. Bring 1½ cups port and next 7 ingredients to boil in a large saucepan. Reduce heat and simmer 20 minutes, stirring often. Stir together remaining 1 cup port and cornstarch until smooth. Stir into hot mixture. Bring to a boil over medium heat, and boil, stirring constantly, 1 minute. Slice meat in ½ to 1 inch thick slices and drizzle sauce over the meat. Serve additional sauce on the side.

Cumberland sauce is popular with the English and is excellent with venison, duck or other game.

---

jelly-roll pan
meat thermometer
vegetable peeler (to peel fresh ginger)

Tiger's Pork Tenderloin Stuffed with Andouille and Greens

Serves: 4

Stuffed Pork Tenderloin

2   **pork tenderloins (1½ pounds total)**
½   **pound andouille sausage, casings removed**
½   **cup fresh chopped collard greens**
1   **cup fresh chopped spinach**
½   **cup fresh chopped turnip greens**
1   **cup fresh mustard greens**
2   **large garlic cloves, minced**
½   **teaspoon fresh lemon juice**
½   **cup grated Gouda cheese**
    Salt and pepper, to taste

Sauce

2   **cups demi-glace**
1   **tablespoon chopped fresh parsley**
2   **tablespoons butter, cut in cubes**
¼   **cup water**
2   **tablespoons cornstarch**
    Salt and pepper, to taste

Pound pork with the flat side of a meat mallet to ¼ to ½ inch thickness. Steam greens for 12 to 15 minutes. Cook the sausage over medium heat, until no pink remains. Drain sausage and mix greens, garlic, lemon juice and cheese. Stir until cheese melts. Salt and pepper pork. Spread the sausage mixture over the pork and roll from the long side to form a tubular roast. Salt and pepper outside and tie every two inches with cooking twine. You may make ahead and refrigerate. Preheat oven to 350 degrees and place pork on a rack in a roasting pan. Cook until a meat thermometer reaches 160 to 165 degrees for medium, about 45 minutes. For Sauce, heat demi-glace in saucepan over medium high heat. Add parsley. Gradually add butter, reducing heat to medium to maintain boiling for about 10 minutes. Once Sauce is reduced to half, but no less than 1 cup, lower heat. Mix together cornstarch and water. Add a little at a time until sauce begins to thicken. You may only need ½ of the cornstarch mixture to get desired consistency. Salt and pepper to taste. Cut the string and slice into medallions. Spoon Sauce onto plate and lay medallions on top of Sauce. Drizzle with additional Sauce.

roasting pan with rack
cheese grater
meat thermometer
meat mallet
cooking twine

Tiger's Pork Tenderloin continued

Joe Graber: Arlington, Texas

Joe, my friend and photographer for Good Friends Great Tastes *has a genuine appreciation for good food. He was at the Master's Golf Tournament in Augusta, Georgia the year Tiger Woods won the tournament, thus the name Tiger's Tenderloin. He won the trip to the Master's for outstanding sales accomplishments. During his stay, the chef at his accommodations cooked this wonderful dish. Joe went home with knowledge of the general ingredients and was able to duplicate this great entrée.*

Pork Chops with Peppers and Basil

Servings: 4

4 **pork chops, cut ¾ inch thick**
3 **tablespoons olive oil, divided use**
2 **teaspoons lemon pepper**
2 **teaspoons garlic powder**
2 **teaspoons fresh rosemary leaves, chopped**
  Tony Chachere's® Creole Seasoning
¼ **cup sliced toasted almonds, chopped**
½ **red bell pepper, chopped**
½ **green bell pepper, chopped**
½ **cup chopped onion**
1 **tablespoon garlic, finely chopped**
¼ **cup fresh basil, chopped**
1 **tablespoon red wine vinegar**

Rub pork chops with 2 tablespoons oil and season chops with lemon pepper, garlic powder and rosemary. Sprinkle generously with *Tony Chachere's®*. Refrigerate 4 hours. Make topping while the chops are being grilled. Toast almonds in 300 degree oven 3 to 4 minutes. In a saucepan, heat one tablespoon oil and add the chopped peppers, onion and garlic. Cook 3 to 4 minutes over medium heat. Add toasted almonds, basil and vinegar. Stir-fry an additional 1 to 3 minutes. Keep warm. Grill pork chops approximately 6 to 11 minutes or until internal temperature is 160 degrees. Top with the pepper, basil, almond mixture.

Lamb shoulder chops may be substituted.

Do not use the same platter for raw and cooked meats.

Honey Marinated Pork

Servings: 4

4 butterfly pork chops

Marinade
1 teaspoon chopped garlic
½ teaspoon dry mustard
¼ teaspoon black pepper
**3 tablespoons Worcestershire
   sauce**
1½ tablespoons Creole mustard
½ cup honey

Mix all marinade ingredients together and pour over pork chops. Marinate at least 4 hours. Grill over moderate heat 6 to 11 minutes, basting as you cook. These are delicious and easy. Serve with Corn Maque Choux and Spinach Spoon Bread.

This same marinade may also be used on 2 (¾ pound) pork tenderloins. Grill 15 to 25 minutes or until center reaches 160 degrees with a meat thermometer.

To butterfly meat, split lengthwise down the middle, cutting almost but not completely through. The two halves are then opened flat to resemble a butterfly shape. Butterflied pork chops are available at the meat counter.

"*Work like you don't need money,
Love like you've never been hurt,
And dance like no one's watching.*"

Author Unknown

Basil Pesto Stuffed Chicken Breasts with Sun-Dried Tomato Cream

Serves: 4

Chicken

4 **boneless skinless chicken breasts**
4 **slices prosciutto**
¼ **cup pesto**
2 **tablespoons lemon juice**
1½ **cloves garlic, chopped**
 Freshly ground pepper, to taste
⅛ **cup olive oil**

Basil Pesto

½ **cup fresh basil with stems removed**
I **clove garlic**
¼ **cup pine nuts, toasted**
⅛ **teaspoon ground black pepper**
½ **cup freshly grated Parmesan cheese**
⅛ **cup olive oil**

Sun-Dried Tomato Cream

¼ **cup chopped shallots**
2 **tablespoons butter**
⅓ **cup dry white wine**
1½ **cups heavy cream**
⅛ **cup oil packed sun-dried tomatoes, drained**
¼ **cup fresh shredded basil**
2 **tablespoons lemon juice**
I **tablespoon cornstarch mixed with equal amount cold water, optional**

For pesto, wash basil and remove stems. In blender mix basil, garlic, pine nuts, pepper and Parmesan. Blend until smooth and add the oil slowly to mixture. (Purchased pesto may replace homemade.) Pound chicken breasts to ¼ inch thickness. Place one slice prosciutto and one tablespoon pesto on each chicken breast. Tuck in ends and roll jelly roll style. Secure with toothpicks or skewers. Place chicken breasts in glass dish. Drizzle with 2 tablespoons lemon juice. At this point the breasts may be chilled overnight. Before baking or grilling chicken, mix chopped garlic with pepper and olive oil. Drizzle over chicken. Bake at 350 degrees for 25 to 35 minutes. Juices should run clear when pierced with a fork. If grilling the breasts and they have been chilled overnight, let them stand at room temperature 30 minutes before grilling. Grill over medium coals, 20 minutes. While breasts are cooking, make basil cream. Sauté shallots in butter. Add wine and bring to boil. Cook until liquid is reduced to ¼ cup. Add cream and return to boil. Cook 8 to 10 minutes or until sauce is reduced to 1 cup. Whisk continually, add tomatoes and cook 2 minutes. Whisk in basil and lemon. Cook until heated through. If you need to thicken sauce use 1 to 1½ tablespoons cornstarch mixed with an equal amount cold water until smooth. Add slowly to hot liquid, stirring to get desired consistency, you may not need the entire amount. Remove toothpicks and cut the chicken breasts in slices to show off the center. Drizzle the chicken breasts with sauce and pass additional sauce.

blender
toothpicks or wooden skewers
whisk

Baked Sour Cream Marinated Chicken

Serves: 6

6 chicken breasts, boneless and skinless
2 cups sour cream
¼ cup lemon juice
4 teaspoons Worcestershire sauce
4 teaspoons celery salt
2 teaspoons paprika
4 cloves garlic, finely chopped
2 teaspoons salt
½ teaspoon pepper
1¾ cups bread crumbs
½ cup butter
½ cup shortening

Defrost chicken breasts if they are frozen. Combine sour cream, lemon juice, Worcestershire, celery salt, paprika, garlic, salt and pepper. Add chicken to mixture. Coat well. Refrigerate overnight. Preheat oven to 350 degrees. Remove chicken from sour cream mixture; roll in bread crumbs, coating evenly. Arrange in a single layer in large shallow pan. Melt butter and shortening in small saucepan. Spoon half over chicken. Bake chicken, uncovered, 45 minutes. Spoon the remaining butter mixture over chicken. Bake 10 to 15 minutes longer until chicken is tender and browned. Keep warm until ready to serve.

A portable egg timer allows you to time things that are in the oven when you need to go to another room in the house where the timer cannot be heard. The extra timer and the oven timer can both be used when you are timing more than one recipe.

Chicken Saltimbocca

Serves: 6

Chicken

6	**chicken breasts boned and skinned**
	Salt and pepper, to taste
6	**slices prosciutto**
3	**ounces Monterey Jack or Gruyère cheese, cut into 6 bars**
⅓	**cup flour**
2	**tablespoons butter**
1	**tablespoon oil**

Sauce

3	**tablespoons butter**
½	**pound mushrooms, sliced**
3	**cloves garlic, chopped**
¼	**cup shallots, chopped**
1	**cup chicken broth**
½	**cup white wine**
½	**cup sherry**
½	**cup heavy cream**
½	**teaspoon thyme**
½	**teaspoon oregano**
	Salt and pepper, to taste
1	**tablespoon cornstarch**
1	**tablespoon cold water**

Flatten chicken breast with a meat mallet. Sprinkle lightly with salt and pepper. Top with one slice of prosciutto and cheese. Tuck in ends and roll jelly roll style. To hold each chicken roll, fasten with wooden toothpicks or short bamboo sticks. Put flour onto platter and lightly coat the chicken breasts. Brown in 2 tablespoons butter mixed with 1 tablespoon oil over medium heat. Remove chicken breasts to baking dish and wipe out the pan if butter browned. At this point, you may refrigerate browned breasts and continue the next day. Melt the 3 tablespoons butter and sauté the garlic and shallots until soft. Add the mushrooms, broth, wine, sherry and herbs. Simmer until mushrooms are tender, 10 minutes. Add the heavy cream and stir to blend ingredients. Pour sauce over the chicken and bake at 325 degrees 25 to 35 minutes. Remove chicken breasts and put on serving platter. Keep warm. Whisk together the cold water and cornstarch until all lumps disappear. Pour sauce into saucepan and thicken with half of cornstarch mixture. Simmer to thicken, add more if needed. Salt and pepper to taste. Do not over salt. To serve, remove skewers and drizzle breasts with sauce. Pass additional sauce.

meat mallet
toothpicks or short wooden skewers
whisk

Chicken Saltimbocca continued

Carrie Hoffman:
Overland Park, Kansas

Carrie and I became friends in high school and later shared an apartment off campus at Kansas State University. Carrie got this wonderful recipe from a former business partner. The combination of shallots, sherry, thyme and heavy cream is delicious!

I recommend cooking with moderately priced wines you enjoy. An inexpensive Merlot can be used for red wine sauces unless a certain grape variety or region (i.e. Burgundy) is specified. A Sauvignon Blanc is a nice dry white wine for cooking. Sauternes is a nice sweet white wine that can be used in recipes. It is best to cook with a wine that you would drink and that complements the food with which it's paired. I do not recommended using cooking wines sold in grocery stores because they contain salt and will alter the flavor of the recipe.

Chicken Cordon Bleu

Serves: 4

Chicken
4 **chicken breasts boned and skinned**
4 **slices boiled ham**
2 **ounces Swiss cheese, cut into 4 bars**
½ **cup flour**
½ **cup bread crumbs**
I **egg, beaten**
2 **tablespoons butter**
I **tablespoon oil**
 Salt and pepper, to taste

Sauce
2 **tablespoons butter**
¼ **pound sliced mushrooms**
I **medium yellow onion, chopped**
¾ **cup water**
I **teaspoon chicken base to be mixed with the ¾ cup water**
I **tablespoon chopped fresh parsley**
I **teaspoon fresh chives, chopped**
¼ **cup heavy cream**
 Salt and white pepper, to taste
I **tablespoon cornstarch**
I **tablespoon cold water**

Flatten chicken breast with a meat mallet. Sprinkle with salt and pepper, top with slice of ham and cheese. Tuck in ends and roll jelly roll style. To hold each chicken roll, fasten with wooden toothpicks or short bamboo sticks. Put flour onto platter and lightly coat the four chicken breasts with flour. Roll in egg and then in bread crumbs. Melt 2 tablespoons butter and add I tablespoon oil. Brown chicken breasts over medium heat. Put in baking dish and bake at 350 degrees or approximately 25 to 35 minutes or until juices run clear. Melt two tablespoons butter in skillet and sauté onion and mushrooms until onions are translucent. Add more butter if necessary. Add water, chicken base, parsley and chives. Bring to a boil. Lower heat, add cream and simmer 10 minutes until sauce thickens slightly. If sauce is too thin, thicken with I tablespoon cornstarch mixed with I tablespoon cold water. Mix until smooth and add to the hot liquid and simmer until thickened. Not all of the mixture must be used. Cornstarch is twice the strength of flour but allows mild thickening so you don't turn your sauce into a gravy. Taste and season with salt and white pepper. Remember the ham has some salt in it so don't over salt. Remove skewers and drizzle sauce over chicken breasts. Pass additional sauce. Serve with rice. If you are making ahead, brown the breasts and refrigerate. Make sauce up to the point of adding cream and refrigerate. Continue with additional steps when ready to serve. Guests will need to be advised to remove toothpicks.

meat mallet
whisk
short bamboo sticks or toothpicks

Chicken Breasts
with Sour Cream Almond Sauce

Serves: 4

4   **boneless, skinless chicken breasts**
3   **tablespoons butter**
2   **tablespoons chopped onion**
1   **clove garlic, minced**
1   **tablespoon tomato paste**
2   **tablespoons flour**
1½ **cups chicken stock**
2   **tablespoons dry sherry**
3   **tablespoons sliced almonds, chopped**
¼   **teaspoon dried tarragon (optional)**
   Salt and pepper, to taste
¾   **cup sour cream at room temperature**
½   **cup grated Gruyère cheese**

Sauté the chicken on both sides in butter. Remove breasts from skillet while making sauce. Add the onion and garlic, stir for 2 to 3 minutes. Add the tomato paste and flour to skillet, stir until blended and smooth. Gradually add the chicken stock and sherry. Cook and stir until slightly thickened. Return the chicken to the skillet. Add the almonds, tarragon, salt and pepper. Cover and simmer on low for 30 minutes or until breasts are tender. Arrange the chicken in a shallow baking dish. Stir the sour cream into sauce and pour over chicken. Sprinkle with grated cheese and broil until cheese melts. Serve with rice.

cheese grater

Chicken Kiev

Serves: 4

Chicken

4   chicken breasts, skinned
        and boned
4   tablespoons butter
I   clove garlic, chopped
2   teaspoons fresh chives,
        chopped
I   tablespoon oil
     Salt, to taste
     White pepper, to taste
½   cup flour
I   egg, beaten
½   cup bread crumbs

Sauce

2   tablespoons flour
4   tablespoons butter, divided
        use
I   cup chicken broth
½   cup fresh mushrooms, sliced
¼   cup heavy cream
I   tablespoon cornstarch
I   tablespoon cold water
     Salt and white pepper, to
        taste

Pound the chicken breasts with a meat mallet until ¼ inch thick. Cut 2 tablespoons of the cold butter into individual tablespoons and then in half. Place a piece of firm, cold butter in the middle of each breast with a little garlic and ½ teaspoon of chopped chives. Salt and pepper breasts and roll them up, tucking ends and securing with short bamboo skewers. Roll chicken breasts in flour on plate, then in beaten egg and bread crumbs. Melt 2 tablespoons butter in a frying pan. Add I tablespoon oil. Brown chicken in frying pan until golden and then place on baking dish in preheated 350 degree oven to cook 25 to 35 minutes, until juices run clear. If you want to make ahead, brown the breasts and refrigerate until you are ready to bake. They may need a few extra minutes to heat thoroughly through. While the chicken breasts are baking, make sauce. Melt 2 tablespoons butter and sauté mushrooms. Set mushrooms aside. In the same pan, melt the remaining 2 tablespoons of butter and add 2 tablespoons flour. Whisk over medium low 3 minutes until it bubbles and thickens slightly. Add the chicken broth and whisk until lumps disappear. Add heavy cream. Heat until desired consistency. Add mushrooms and season with salt and white pepper. For thicker sauce, mix I tablespoon cornstarch with I tablespoon cold water until smooth. Add mixture to sauce. Simmer until mixture is desired consistency. When serving, remove skewers and drizzle sauce over the chicken. Pass additional sauce. This is wonderful served with a white or wild rice.

whisk
meat mallet
short bamboo skewers

Pollo Maria

Serves: 4

Chicken

4	**(8 ounce) chicken breasts, skinned and boned**
⅓	**cup flour**
2	**tablespoons vegetable oil**
½	**ounce tequila**

Sauce

½	**cup fresh mushrooms, thinly sliced**
I	**cup half-and-half**
I	**teaspoon chicken base, undiluted**
5	**dashes MAGGI® Seasoning**
	Salt and white or black pepper, to taste

Coat the chicken breasts in flour and fry in 2 tablespoons of hot oil until lightly brown. Drain excess oil. While continuing to sauté breasts on low approximately 4 minutes per side, add the ½ ounce tequila to the pan and light or flambé. The flame should die down quickly on its own. Add the ½ cup mushrooms and gradually stir in the half-and-half and chicken base. Simmer until sauce starts to thicken. Add 5 dashes MAGGI® Seasoning. Serve with herbed rice and squash.

MAGGI® is a seasoning sauce and can be found in your grocery store usually where liquid smoke is found. Chicken soup base is the consistency of a paste. It is a chicken stock that when mixed with water makes a great rich stock and can be used in recipes in place of broth. Flambé safety: To extinguish the flame after you flambé, keep the skillet lid in close proximity to the stove. Immediately place lid over the skillet if necessary. Without oxygen, the flame cannot burn. Alcohol ignites easily, so keep your face and clothing at a distance.

La Margarita: Irving, Texas

This is our getaway once a week when we need to be waited on and have a margarita on the rocks and great food. Joel is our bartender, and we usually say "Let's go visit Joel" instead of "Let's go to dinner." Gabriel and the staff are family and give Dave and I incredible service. La Margarita's food is inventive, reasonable and wonderful! What a great local hangout! I was thrilled they shared their delicious Pollo Maria recipe with me.

For those in the Dallas area, Bar Fresh Lemon Sweet and Sour Mixer from Sigel's is similar to Joel's margarita. Use 2 ounces gold tequila with 1 ounce GRAND MARNIER® and 4 ounces Bar Fresh (mix according to directions.) Shake together and pour over ice in a 12 ounce mug.

Garlic Rosemary Chicken

Serves: 4

Chicken

1	**whole chicken (3 to 5 pounds)**
2	**tablespoons chopped garlic**
6	**sprigs fresh rosemary**
1/8	**teaspoon olive oil**
2	**teaspoons spice rub**

Spice Rub

2	**teaspoons sea salt**
1	**teaspoon white pepper**
1	**teaspoon onion powder**
1	**teaspoon garlic powder**
1	**teaspoon dried basil leaves**
1	**teaspoon black pepper**

Have butcher cut chicken in half. Remove insides and discard. Lift chicken skin and season each half with the garlic, pushing it under the skin. Do the same with the rosemary sprigs. Rub the outside of the chicken with the olive oil and sprinkle with the spice mixture. Grill outdoors 40 to 50 minutes over medium, bone side up. Juices should run clear and no pink should remain. If roasting chicken in the oven, preheat oven to 425 degrees with the rack in the middle of the oven. Put the whole chicken (breast side up) on the rack inside the roasting pan. Place the flap of neck skin underneath. Tie the legs together with cooking twine. Put the roasting pan in the oven. After 15 minutes reduce the heat to 350 degrees. When the chicken starts to brown, baste with the pan juices. Roast for one hour. To check for doneness, look for clear juices and easy movement of the leg joint. No pink should remain. (A smaller chicken will roast about 1¼ hours and a larger one about 1½ hours or more.) Internal temperature should be between 175 to 180 degrees. Let chicken rest for 15 minutes before carving.

meat thermometer
If cooking indoors, a roasting pan with rack and cooking twine is needed

Do not use forks for turning meat on a grill. Forks pierce the meat and allow juices to escape. Instead, use tongs or a spatula.

If you don't have time to make the spice mixture sprinkle the chicken generously with Tony Chachere's® Creole Seasoning.

Cajun Chicken à la King

Serves: 6

Seasoning Mix
1	tablespoon salt
1½	teaspoons dried basil leaves
1	teaspoon garlic powder
1	teaspoon onion powder
1	teaspoon white pepper
1	teaspoon paprika
1	teaspoon dry mustard
½	teaspoon dried summer savory, not ground
¼	teaspoon nutmeg

Chicken
2	pounds boneless, skinless chicken breasts
½	cup softened, unsalted butter plus 5 tablespoons unsalted butter
¼	cup flour
¼	cup white wine
1	cup chopped onion
2	cups thinly sliced fresh mushrooms
1	cup chopped red bell pepper
1	cup chopped green pepper
2½	cups heavy cream
2	tablespoons dry sherry
1	(10 ounce) package frozen puffed pastry shells

Mix together seasoning and chop all vegetables. Measure out all other ingredients before starting. Sprinkle 1 tablespoon plus one teaspoon seasoning over chicken and rub in with your hands. Cut the chicken breasts into strips. Combine the ½ cup softened stick of butter with the flour to make a paste. Cut the other 5 tablespoons into pats. Heat a large skillet over high heat. When the pot is hot add seasoned chicken and the 5 tablespoons butter. Cover and do not stir for approximately 4 minutes. Uncover and stir, recover and cook an additional 4 minutes. (Be sure vent is on entire time because you are cooking at such a high heat.) Add the wine (reserving the sherry), onions, mushrooms and peppers and remaining seasoning. Stir well, cover and cook 5 minutes. Turn heat down to medium. Uncover and add the butter-flour mixture a spoonful at a time. Stir as you add, until mixture dissolves and sauce thickens. Stir in 2 cups of the cream and heat until small volcanoes erupt. Do not let boil. Let the volcanoes erupt 3 times and stir after each eruption. Add the remaining ½ cup cream and heat again until another group of small volcanoes erupt. Remove from heat and stir in sherry. Keep on low heat until ready to serve, stirring occasionally so it doesn't stick to the bottom of pan. The puffed pastry shells should be cooked according to the package directions. Remove the top of the puffed pastry shells after they are baked. The sauce can be made ahead on the day you are serving and kept on a very low heat until you are ready to serve. Make the puffed pastry shells just before serving. Turn the heat up on the sauce to get the desired temperature for serving and spoon a generous amount of the chicken mixture inside the baked puff pastry shells. Top each with the baked pastry shell top.

Cornish Game Hens with Honey Glaze and Caramelized Onions

Serves: 2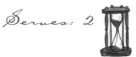

Cornish Hens
2   **Rock Cornish game hens (2.5 pounds total,) defrosted**
    Salt and pepper

Honey Glaze
½   **cup plus 2 tablespoons unsalted butter (one tablespoon reserved for spinach)**
¼   **cup plus 2 tablespoons honey**
1½ **cups Muscat wine or other sweet wine**
1   **cup chicken broth**
2   **tablespoons low sodium soy sauce**

Onions
1   **(10 ounce) basket of pearl onions**
2   **tablespoons unsalted butter**
¼   **cup water**
1   **tablespoon honey**

Spinach
1   **bunch (10 ounces) fresh spinach, washed and tough stems removed**

Rice
1   **box wild rice medley, cooked according to directions**

For sauce, heat honey in small heavy skillet over medium heat until honey darkens and becomes fragrant, swirling pan occasionally, about 3 minutes. Carefully add the wine and chicken broth. Boil mixture until reduced to one cup, about 20 minutes. Add soy sauce and boil 3 minutes longer. When you are ready to serve hens, bring sauce to boil and add ½ cup plus 1 tablespoon butter. This can be made a day ahead, refrigerated and butter can be whisked in when reheating. For the onions, bring a medium saucepan of water to boil. Add onions and blanch 2 minutes. Drain. Rinse onions under cool water. Cut off end of each onion and peel. Melt butter in heavy skillet over medium heat. Add onions to skillet and sauté until golden brown and tender, almost 10 minutes. Add ¼ cup water and honey. Cover and simmer until onions are tender, about 5 minutes. Uncover and continue cooking until onions are caramelized, about 2 to 5 minutes. Keep warm. These can be made 8 hours ahead. Let stand covered at room temperature. Reheat over medium heat, stirring constantly. Cook rice according to package directions and clean and trim spinach while hens are cooking. For game hens, preheat oven to 425 degrees and season hens with salt and pepper. Arrange hens breast side up on baking sheet. Bake until juices run clear when thighs are pierced with a fork, about 30 to 45 minutes. Keep warm. Melt the one tablespoon of remaining butter over medium high heat and add the fresh spinach. Cover and cook until spinach is wilted, about 2 minutes. Drain. Salt and pepper to taste. Divide spinach among

Cornish Game Hens *continued*

plates and place 1 hen on top of spinach. Line rice underneath the hen on both sides. Drizzle lightly with sauce. Place caramelized onions down wing area or outside edge of plate and drizzle hen generously with sauce (pictured on back cover).

For extra color add ½ cup fresh corn kernels to the rice.

The Muscat grape has a sweet, musky flavor. It is a white or black grape and is typically grown in Italy, France, Greece, Spain and California.

Chicken Stroganoff

Serves: 4

I	(3.5 pound) chicken
I	stalk celery
I	large carrot
I	large **KNORR®** Chicken Bouillon Cube
4	tablespoons butter
I	yellow onion, chopped
I	(8 ounce) package sliced mushrooms
I	clove garlic, minced
I	**KNORR®** Extra Large Beef Bouillon Cube
1½	cups hot water
½	cup half-and-half
I	tablespoon **A.I.®** STEAK SAUCE
4	tablespoons flour (divided use)
¾	cup sour cream
¼	teaspoon black pepper
⅛	teaspoon cayenne pepper (or to taste)
⅛	teaspoon white pepper
¼	teaspoon onion powder
⅛	teaspoon garlic powder
¼	teaspoon dry mustard
I	teaspoon *Tony Chachere's®* Creole Seasoning
I	tablespoon fresh parsley, minced

Mix dry spices together and set aside. Rinse mushrooms. Boil chicken in chicken bouillon cube with carrot and celery added to water. Drain off broth and freeze broth for another dish. Let chicken cool and debone, discarding bones and skin. Sauté onion, mushrooms and garlic in the butter until onion is translucent. Dissolve the beef bouillon cube in the hot water. Mix the 3 tablespoons flour with 4 tablespoons water. Add to the vegetable mixture. Add broth and chicken. Boil until slightly thickened (mixture should be close to desired consistency before adding half and half and sour cream). Reduce heat, add half and half. Add the spices and the A.I.® STEAK SAUCE to the mixture. Over low heat, gently stir in the sour cream mixed with I tablespoon flour. Whisk to desired consistency. Do not boil once sour cream has been added. Serve over rice or noodles and sprinkle with fresh parsley.

Four boneless, skinless chicken breasts may be substituted for whole chicken. Sprinkle lightly with Tony Chachere's® and pan sauté in oil or butter, approximately 4 minutes per side. Leave whole or cut into strips. If chicken breasts are left whole, spoon sauce over breast otherwise, mix cooked chicken strips into sauce. This sauce is good for a beef stroganoff or to top a pork chop or steak as well.

whisk

Southern Fried Chicken

Serves: 4

1	**whole frying chicken cut up or 8 pieces chicken**
1	**(12 ounce) can evaporated milk**
1½	**cups flour**
2	**cups shortening**
1	**teaspoon salt**
2	**teaspoons pepper**
¾	**teaspoon cayenne pepper**

Wash and dry chicken. Mix spices with the flour. Roll chicken in the evaporated milk and in the flour. Repeat. Melt oil over medium high heat. The temperature should be approximately 375 degrees for frying, so that the chicken doesn't soak up the oil. Fry chicken in oil turning once, until crisp and golden (approximately 10 to 14 minutes). Do not crowd chicken. Keep chicken warm in a 200 degree oven on a baking sheet, until ready to serve.

Buttermilk may be substituted for evaporated milk and self-rising flour may also be used in place of all-purpose flour. Tony Chachere's® Creole Seasoning or McCormick Old Bay Seasoning may be substituted for salt if more spice is preferred. Olive oil may also be used to fry chicken instead of shortening. Boneless, skinless breasts or chicken tenders may be substituted for the whole chicken. The Sun-Dried Tomato Cream (p. 172) is tasty drizzled over a boneless chicken breast that has been coated and fried in olive oil.

Melissa Brown: DeSoto, Texas

Melissa and I worked together and we had many conversations about decorating and cooking. The double dipping of the chicken has to be what makes Melissa's chicken so crispy. Try fried chicken with honey on the side for dipping. It is wonderful!

If you feel you must drain chicken, brown paper bags will absorb the most oil. You can use a plastic or paper bag to shake the chicken in flour before frying.

Empress Stir-Fry Chicken

Serves: 4

¼ **cup soy sauce**
2 **tablespoons honey**
2 **tablespoons ketchup**
2 **tablespoons cider vinegar**
1 **clove garlic, minced**
½ **teaspoon ginger**
1 **tablespoon cornstarch**
2 **cups onion, cut in chunks**
2 **cups sliced celery**
1 **(8½ ounce) can water chestnuts, drained and sliced**
2 **whole chicken breasts, boned and skinned**
1 **tablespoon peanut oil, if necessary add a little more when sautéing**

Combine soy sauce, honey, ketchup, vinegar, garlic and ginger. Dissolve cornstarch in mixture, set aside. Prepare vegetables. Cut chicken into chunks. Heat oil over high heat in skillet or wok. Add onion, celery and chestnuts. Stir-fry about 4 minutes or until vegetables are tender crisp. Remove from skillet. Stir-fry chicken until lightly brown. Add sauce, cook, stir until thick. Add vegetables, heat through. This is good over white rice. You may add cashews or peanuts and substitute your favorite vegetables if others are preferred.

A boxed Chinese rice from the grocery store adds additional oriental flavor.

Robin Murphy:
North Richland Hills, Texas

Robin made this recipe years ago when we were getting together with the "group" to watch Knots Landing. We still get together often, but wonder how we ever made a commitment to a weekly gathering. This can be a complete family meal since the starch, vegetables and meat are all part of the dish.

Chicken Enchiladas

Serves: 6

2   grilled chicken breasts,
     chopped
½   teaspoon *Tony Chachere's*®
     Creole Seasoning
½   teaspoon lemon pepper
1   tablespoon butter
1   small yellow onion
1   clove garlic
1   (4.5 ounce) can chopped
     green chiles
1   (7 ounce) jar green
     chile/tomatillo salsa
2   cups Monterey Jack cheese
2   cups heavy cream
½   teaspoon salt
12   corn tortillas
     Vegetable oil for softening
     tortillas
1   chopped tomato
1   bunch green onion tops for
     garnish

Before grilling, sprinkle chicken breasts with *Tony Chachere's*® and lemon pepper. Grill 6 to 7 minutes per side, 15 minutes total, over moderate heat. Sauté onion in 1 tablespoon butter until translucent. Add garlic just before onion is totally sautéed. Combine 2 cups chopped chicken, onion, garlic, green salsa, chiles and one cup cheese in a bowl. Mix heavy cream and salt together in a bowl. Heat ½ inch oil in a skillet. Dip each tortilla in a skillet about 5 seconds to soften. Dip each tortilla into bowl containing cream and salt, coating each side. Fill each tortilla with chicken mixture. Roll seam side down and place in ungreased 9 x 13 inch baking dish. Pour remaining cream over enchiladas and sprinkle with cheese. Bake at 350 degrees for 20 to 25 minutes. Garnish before serving with tomato and green onion tops.

If you choose not to grill the chicken, then heat skillet over high with 5 tablespoons butter and sauté chicken cubes or strips for 4 minutes, covered. Uncover, stir and cook an additional 4 minutes. Frozen corn can be added to the mixture for a variation.

When grilling, grill extra chicken breasts and freeze them. You can defrost them later and add them to a casserole. The fresh grilled flavor tastes better than boiled or microwaved chicken.

Chicken Chalupas

Serves: 20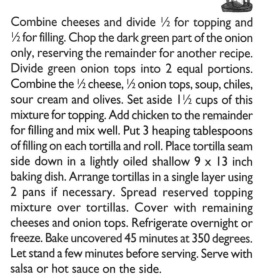

12 ounces Monterey Jack
    cheese, grated
12 ounces cheddar cheese,
    grated
1 (10¾ ounce) can cream of
    mushroom soup
1 (10¾ ounce) can cream of
    chicken soup
1 (4.5 ounce) can chopped
    green chiles
1 (16 ounce) container sour
    cream
2 bunches green onion tops
1 (4.25 ounce) can sliced
    black ripe olives
20 (6 inch) flour tortillas
4 cups cooked chicken breasts
    cut in 1 inch pieces
    Bottled salsa or hot sauce

Combine cheeses and divide ½ for topping and ½ for filling. Chop the dark green part of the onion only, reserving the remainder for another recipe. Divide green onion tops into 2 equal portions. Combine the ½ cheese, ½ onion tops, soup, chiles, sour cream and olives. Set aside 1½ cups of this mixture for topping. Add chicken to the remainder for filling and mix well. Put 3 heaping tablespoons of filling on each tortilla and roll. Place tortilla seam side down in a lightly oiled shallow 9 x 13 inch baking dish. Arrange tortillas in a single layer using 2 pans if necessary. Spread reserved topping mixture over tortillas. Cover with remaining cheeses and onion tops. Refrigerate overnight or freeze. Bake uncovered 45 minutes at 350 degrees. Let stand a few minutes before serving. Serve with salsa or hot sauce on the side.

One chicken breast equals approximately one cup.

 cheese grater

Kathryn Farr,
Morgantown, West Virginia

Kathryn contributed this recipe because when she entertains it is usually a large group and children are included. She prefers to prepare meals a day ahead because they have three young daughters that keep them very busy. My memories of Kathryn include sharing chili dogs, ice cream sandwiches, corn nuts and Swannie's Yum Yums rather than gourmet meals, as we have known each other since Kindergarten and roomed together our first year of college.

Green onions are often called scallions. When a recipe calls for the tops, use only the dark green portion.

Mexican Chicken Delight

Serves: 6

3 cups cooked chicken
1 onion, chopped
3 tablespoons butter
1 (10¾ ounce) can cream of mushroom soup
1 (10¾ ounce) can cream of chicken soup
1 cup chicken broth
1 (7 ounce) can chopped green chiles, drained
1 (10 ounce) can Ro*Tel® Diced Tomatoes and Green Chiles
1 small package corn tortillas (12 to 15 tortillas)
2 cups cheddar cheese, grated

Cut tortillas into 1 inch strips. Boil chicken and clean from bone or use boneless chicken breasts that have been grilled, boiled or microwaved. Approximately 3 breasts are needed for 3 cups meat. Sauté onion in butter. Add soups, broth, Ro*Tel®, chopped onion and green chiles to the chicken. In a 9 x 13 inch casserole dish, layer tortillas, chicken mixture and cheese. Bake at 325 degrees for 40 minutes covered and an additional 15 minutes uncovered. Let cool slightly before serving. Serve this with a salad and chips and hot sauce on the side.

This casserole is a great thing to make ahead and refrigerate until ready to bake and serve. The refrigeration helps it to set up better. You may need to heat slightly longer so the center gets warm.

cheese grater

Debbie Smith, Lawrence, Kansas

Debbie says "Eat this until you speak fluent Spanish." Debbie lived with my family for a year while she finished high school because her parents moved out of the district. We enjoyed some of my mother's terrific meals together.

Spice Cured Turkey

Serves: 12

Brine Soaked Turkey

1   **(14 pound) turkey, defrosted**
1   **cup coarse sea salt**
½ **cup plus 2 tablespoons sugar**
2   **bay leaves**
1   **tablespoon dried or fresh thyme**
7   **whole cloves**
½ **tablespoon whole allspice berries**
½ **teaspoon whole juniper berries**
1   **teaspoon freshly cracked black pepper**
8   **quarts water (32 cups)**

Sage Butter

1   **cup unsalted butter (2 sticks)**
20 **fresh sage leaves**

Spice Rub

1½ **tablespoons whole fennel seeds**
1   **large dried red chile**
½ **tablespoon whole allspice berries**
½ **tablespoon whole black peppercorns**

Vegetable Stuffing

24 **garlic cloves, mashed**
3   **medium onions, coarsely chopped**
1   **large rib celery, chopped**
½ **cup celery leaves, chopped**
2   **cups chicken stock or low sodium broth**

In a very large stockpot, combine the coarse salt, sugar, bay leaves, thyme, cloves, allspice, juniper berries and water. Bring to boil over high heat. Remove from heat and bring to room temperature. Add turkey to the brine, breast side down, cover and let stand overnight in the refrigerator. Prepare the Spice Rub, place measured spices in small pan and toast until fragrant about 3 minutes. Once cool, transfer to blender and grind. Set aside. To make Sage Butter, melt the butter in a saucepan and simmer until butter turns brown. Stir occasionally so solids do not stick to pan. Do not let butter burn. Remove from heat and add sage leaves. Let the leaves steep in the butter 5 minutes. Remove the sage leaves with a fork and pour the butter in a glass or ceramic dish. Refrigerate overnight. Make the Vegetable Stuffing. Preheat the oven to 500 degrees and in a large bowl toss the chopped vegetables with the mashed garlic and ½ tablespoon of the spice rub. Spoon all but 2 cups of the stuffing into the chest and neck cavities.

Using your fingers loosen the skin from the breast without tearing it. Evenly spread the Sage Butter under the skin. Close the neck with toothpicks. Set the turkey breast side up in a roasting pan on top of a rack. Sprinkle the remaining spice over the bird and tie the legs together with kitchen string. Scatter the remaining 2 cups stuffing around the turkey and pour the stock over the stuffing. Roast the turkey for 20 minutes. Cover the turkey loosely with foil and adjust the oven temperature to 350 degrees. Continue roasting for about 4 hours, basting frequently. The turkey can be removed from the oven when the internal temperature of the thigh is 165 to 170 degrees. Add water to the pan during cooking if the juices evaporate.

Spice Cured Turkey continued

Transfer the turkey to a carving board and let rest 15 to 20 minutes before slicing. Serve the stuffing alongside the turkey. Serve with Turkey Gravy.

blender or food processor
large roasting pan
large kettle
meat thermometer

Louella Arndt, Houston, Texas

I was a sportswear buyer for Louella several years ago. When we traveled to New York and Los Angeles as a group, she selected the restaurants where we would have dinner. She chose some of the best and most interesting places I have dined. She loves great atmosphere as much as the food. Her recipe requires soaking the turkey in brine, which makes the turkey extremely tender. This process and the unusual spice combination creates a gourmet meal.

Turkey Gravy

Serves: 8

4¼ cups water, divided use
1 chicken bouillon cube or one teaspoon chicken base
3 medium onions, coarsely chopped
1½ carrots, washed and coarsely chopped
1½ stalks celery, coarsely chopped
  Rinsed neck, gizzard and liver from inside turkey
  Pinch dried thyme
1½ tablespoons cornstarch
¼ cup cool chicken broth
1 teaspoon KITCHEN BOUQUET® Browning and Seasoning Sauce
  Salt and pepper, to taste

Bring 4¼ cups water to boil with chicken base. Once dissolved, reserve ¼ cup stock. Add next 5 ingredients. Reduce heat and cook until meat is done. Strain all ingredients out, reserve neck and return broth to pan. Cut off as much neck meat as possible and add to broth. Mix together 1½ tablespoons cornstarch and ¼ cup cool chicken broth until smooth. Continue to simmer the gravy and add ½ of the cornstarch mixture. Continue to cook until thickened to desired consistency. If not thick enough, add the remaining cornstarch mixture. Add 1 teaspoon KITCHEN BOUQUET® or enough to get a caramel colored gravy. Salt and pepper to taste. Heat thoroughly, serve with turkey and dressing.

I included this recipe because when I was in the retail world, I never went home for Thanksgiving. Over the years, I spent a lot of time on the phone with my mother walking me through the steps of this gravy making process.

"*Friendship is the only cement
that will ever hold the world together.*"

Woodrow Wilson

Grilled Lamb Chops
with Peppercorn Currant Glaze

Serves: 6

Lamb Rib Chops

12 lamb rib chops
1 tablespoon olive oil

Peppercorn Currant Glaze

4 tablespoons olive oil
2 onions, diced
4 carrots, diced
4 stalks celery, diced
2 bay leaves
2 sprigs fresh thyme
2 cups red wine vinegar
1 cup red wine
2 teaspoons crushed black peppercorns
2 cups demi-glace
4 tablespoons red currant jelly
2 teaspoons cornstarch mixed with 2 teaspoons cold water

Heat 4 tablespoons oil in skillet over medium-high heat and add onion, carrots and celery. Sauté until soft. Add bay leaf, thyme, vinegar and wine, simmer until reduced by half. Add peppercorns and demi-glace and simmer 30 minutes. Strain sauce through fine mesh strainer and reserve. Brush both sides of lamb rib chops lightly with remaining oil and place on a hot grill. When meat is cooked halfway and 1 side is brown (approximately 4 minutes), use tongs to turn chops over. Cook second side to desired doneness. For medium doneness grill chops over moderate heat 4 inches from grill, 9 to 11 minutes. If you would rather do as a rack, place in the oven at 375 degrees for 25 to 27 minutes for rare or 28 to 30 minutes for medium. To grill, cook to an internal temperature of 145 degrees for medium rare and 160 degrees for medium.

Meanwhile, bring sauce to a simmer and stir in currant jelly. Add cornstarch mixture and allow the mixture to thicken slightly. Using small ladle, pour sauce onto each plate. Arrange your favorite sautéed vegetables on plate and place 2 to 3 lamb chops alongside. Garnish with sprigs of fresh thyme.

Demi-glace can be found at gourmet stores and must be diluted according to directions.

fine mesh strainer
meat thermometer

Stuffed Veal Scaloppine with Red Wine Shallot Sauce

Serves: 6

Veal Rolls

4	**tablespoons butter, divided use**
¼	**cup white or yellow onion, chopped**
¼	**cup carrots, finely chopped**
¼	**cup celery, finely chopped**
¼	**cup mushrooms, finely chopped**
¼	**teaspoon dried or fresh thyme**
12	**thin slices veal (scaloppine)**
⅓	**cup flour plus additional for dusting, divided use**
2	**tablespoons olive oil** **Tony Chachere's® Creole Seasoning**

Red Wine Shallot Sauce

1	**tablespoon butter**
1	**shallot, minced**
¼	**cup mushrooms, chopped**
¼	**cup red wine (Merlot)**
1½	**cups brown sauce (see below)**
1	**tablespoon cornstarch**
1	**tablespoon cold water** **Salt and pepper, to taste**

To make the Brown Sauce needed for the Red Wine Shallot Sauce, melt butter and sauté onions, carrots and celery until celery is translucent. Add flour and cook until it browns. Gradually stir in red wine, both broths and tomato paste. Stir mixture until it boils. Reduce heat and add Worcestershire, Tabasco®, and pepper. Strain out vegetables, salt to taste. Freeze what you don't use. Be sure that you stir sauce before using, otherwise you will use the richer portion and what you freeze will seem diluted. Start Red Wine Shallot Sauce before assembling the veal. To make sauce, melt butter and sauté shallots and mushrooms. Stir in wine. Boil until reduced by half. Stir in prepared brown sauce. Season with salt and pepper to taste. Continue to simmer, adding cornstarch mixture until thickened to desired consistency. For veal filling, melt 2 tablespoons butter in saucepan and sauté onion, carrots, celery and mushrooms over medium heat until onion and celery are translucent and vegetables are tender. Stir in thyme. On a piece of wax paper lay out veal scaloppine and sprinkle with *Tony Chachere's®* and dust with flour. Put 2 teaspoons of the filling in each scaloppine and secure with a toothpick. Coat again with flour. In an ovenproof skillet, melt 2 tablespoons butter and 2 tablespoons oil on medium-high, sauté the scaloppine rolls until browned on all sides. If you prefer well-done meat, place skillet, covered, in oven 5 to 7 minutes at 400 degrees. Serve 2 veal rolls with sauce, per person. Remove toothpicks before serving.

toothpicks or unwaxed dental floss to tie up veal rolls

Stuffed Veal Scaloppine continued

Brown Sauce

1	tablespoon butter
2	tablespoons white or yellow onion
2	tablespoons carrot, finely chopped
2	tablespoons celery, finely chopped
1	tablespoon flour
½	cup red wine (Merlot)
1	cup beef broth
1	cup chicken broth
3	tablespoons tomato paste
1	teaspoon Worcestershire sauce
¼	teaspoon Tabasco® pepper sauce
¼	teaspoon pepper
	Salt, to taste

Tomato and anchovy paste come in resealable tubes that are great because recipes generally only call for small amounts. The tomato paste can be found with the canned tomato products and the anchovy paste is usually with the fish products.

Wiener Schnitzel

Serves: 4

1	pound pork or veal cutlets
	Salt and pepper
½	cup flour
2	eggs, beaten
1¼	cups dry bread crumbs
	Vegetable oil
1	lemon, cut in wedges
	Chopped fresh parsley for garnish

Pound cutlets as thin as possible. Sprinkle with salt and pepper. Set up assembly line with flour on one plate, beaten eggs on another and bread crumbs on a third. Coat cutlet in flour, shake off excess. Dip cutlet in egg, making sure meat is completely coated. Cover with bread crumbs. Heat ¼ inch oil in a large frying pan over medium high heat. Add as many cutlets as possible to fit without crowding. Cook until golden brown on each side, 1½ minutes total. Drain cutlets on paper towels. Serve with lemon wedges. (Let each guest squeeze desired amount over cutlet.) Garnish with chopped parsley.

meat mallet

Rosemary Grilled Lamb with Port Wine Sauce

Serves: 6

Rosemary Rack of Lamb

2 **racks of lamb
   (1½ pounds each)**
⅓ **cup oil**
3 **garlic cloves, finely chopped**
2 **teaspoons chopped fresh
   rosemary**
¼ **cup coarse-grain Dijon
   mustard (no extra spices)**

Port Wine Sauce

1 **(14.5 ounce) can beef broth**
¾ **cup port wine**
2 **tablespoons chopped
   shallots**
1 **bay leaf**
3 **tablespoons melted butter**
2 **tablespoons flour**

Combine marinade ingredients and pour into large sealable plastic bag or marinade dish. Add lamb and turn to coat. Refrigerate for 24 hours. Make Port Wine Sauce. In a medium saucepan combine broth, port, shallot and bay leaf. Heat over medium until mixture boils, reduce heat. Simmer uncovered 15 to 20 minutes. Remove bay leaf. Stir together butter and flour. Add ¼ of the butter and flour mixture to the port mixture. Cook and stir until slightly thickened and bubbly. This sauce should be a consistency to drizzle over meat, not a gravy. Add more of the butter and flour mixture if necessary, to get desired consistency. Simmer and stir for one minute more. To cook lamb outdoors, cook over moderate coals. Grill about 4 inches from heat for approximately 9 to 11 minutes. Desired doneness is 140 degrees for rare, 150 degrees for medium and 160 degrees for well done. If using a meat thermometer, the tip of thermometer should be in center of meat not touching bone, fat or grill. To cook in the oven, place rack meaty side up and roast at 375 degrees using meat thermometer and temperatures listed above for desired doneness. Serve with the Port Wine Sauce.

meat thermometer

Horseradish Sauce for Steaks

Serves: 8

1 **cup heavy cream**
½ **cup prepared horseradish, drained**
⅓ **cup mayonnaise**
1 **teaspoon dry mustard**
 Generous dash of cayenne pepper
 Tony Chachere's® Creole Seasoning and lemon pepper for steaks, if desired

Whip cream with a mixer until it forms peaks. Gently fold in remaining ingredients.

hand mixer

David Gore: Grapevine, Texas

This is a delectable sauce Dave served with a grilled filet mignon topped with Gruyère cheese. Lightly broil steak in oven after grilling to melt the Gruyère before serving. Serve the sauce alongside the beef with Garlic Chive Mashed Potatoes (p. 228). Steaks can be seasoned with lemon pepper and Tony Chachere's® Creole Seasoning *before grilling.*

Mushroom Red Onion Steak Topping

Serves: 4

1	cup ruby port
2	cups beef broth
4	cloves garlic
½	cup butter
1	pound mushrooms
1	red onion sliced into thin rings
2	teaspoons fresh thyme
2	teaspoons fresh oregano
2	teaspoons fresh rosemary
½	teaspoon fine sea salt
4	teaspoons cornstarch
4	teaspoons cold water
8	tablespoons French goat cheese (keep cool until ready to crumble)

Mix together the beef broth and the port over medium heat. Reduce to 1½ cups. Add garlic. In an additional skillet, sauté mushrooms and onion in the butter, until onions are translucent and mushrooms are cooked but not soggy. Add the spices and salt. When liquid is reduced, add the liquid to the mushroom mixture. Mix together the cornstarch and cold water. Add only half to mixture and cook over medium to medium-high heat, stirring constantly. If desired thickening occurs, do not add additional cornstarch mixture. If you prefer a thicker topping, use additional cornstarch mixture. Pour over grilled steaks that have been seasoned before cooking with fresh cracked pepper and lemon pepper. Crumble the French goat cheese on top.

This topping is also good served as an appetizer with warmed pita bread triangles.

Shallot Cream Steak Sauce

Serves: 4

2   **tablespoons butter**
2   **tablespoons minced garlic**
¼   **cup minced shallots**
½   **cup dry white wine such as Sauvignon Blanc**
2   **tablespoons Dijon mustard**
1   **cup heavy cream**
⅔   **cup canned beef broth**
1   **tablespoon cornstarch**
1   **tablespoon cold water**

Melt butter in a heavy skillet over medium heat. Add garlic and shallots and sauté until shallots are translucent, 3 minutes. Add wine. Increase heat to high and boil until the liquid is reduced to half, 4 minutes. Whisk in mustard, cream and broth. Boil until reduced to 1¼ cups, 7 minutes. If sauce is too thin, mix together the cornstarch and water. Add half of mixture and continue to cook over medium to desired consistency. If not thick enough, add the remaining thickener. You may mix in extra juices from steaks when they are taken off the grill. Roll steaks in cracked black pepper, to add extra flavor. If you are serving a sliced tenderloin or filet mignon, you may fan slices out and slightly overlap them. Drizzle the sauce over the steak. Pass extra sauce. This can be made ahead and reheated slowly.

To crack peppercorns, put them inside a sturdy self-sealing plastic bag and crush with a meat mallet or rolling pin.

Black Pepper Steak Sauce

Serves: 2

¼   **cup minced shallots**
2   **tablespoons butter**
1   **tablespoon cracked black pepper**
¼   **teaspoon dried or fresh oregano**
¼   **teaspoon dried or fresh basil**
½   **cup red wine (Merlot)**
1¾   **cups demi-glace**
2   **teaspoons cornstarch mixed with 2 teaspoons cold water**
¼   **cup fresh chopped parsley**

Sauté shallots in butter for 2 minutes. Add pepper, oregano, basil and red wine. Reduce liquid (approximately 3 minutes). Add good quality demi-glace and simmer approximately 5 to 6 minutes. Thicken with 2 teaspoons cornstarch mixed with 2 teaspoons cold water, if necessary. Blend in parsley and serve over steaks.

Demi-glace is a reduction made from beef or veal bones. It is sold at gourmet stores and should be mixed according to package directions before using.

Balsamic Sauce for Steaks

Serves: 4

¼ **cup dry red wine**
¼ **cup dry sherry**
3 **tablespoons balsamic vinegar**
1 **shallot, chopped**
2 **garlic cloves, chopped**
5⅓ **tablespoons butter**
2 **egg yolks**
KITCHEN BOUQUET®
Browning and Seasoning Sauce (optional)

Bring the first 6 ingredients to boil in a saucepan. Cool. Whisk in egg yolks over low heat, whisking constantly until thickened. A few drops of KITCHEN BOUQUET® may be added to create a slightly brown sauce, otherwise, the sauce is slightly pink. Pass sauce separately.

Julie Lancaster: Grapevine, Texas

Julie, my accountant made this for grilled steaks. It is very flavorful. She and her husband Joe, recommend rubbing steaks with olive oil and sprinkling with coarse ground black peppercorns and coarse sea salt before grilling. Pass sauce separately.

KITCHEN BOUQUET® Browning and Seasoning Sauce adds color to your sauce. You only need a few drops for brown gravy or a balsamic sauce.

Sautéed Salmon with a Champagne Macadamia Cream Sauce

Serves: 4

4 (8 ounce) skinless salmon
   fillets
5 tablespoons butter, divided
   use
1 cup lightly salted
   macadamia nuts
   (1½ 3.5-ounce jars)
2 tablespoons flour
1 cup whole milk
½ cup fish or lobster stock
¼ cup cream
½ cup pink sparkling wine or
   champagne
   Salt, to taste

Coarsely chop macadamia nuts. Sprinkle fillets with salt. In a saucepan sauté 1 cup macadamia nuts over medium heat in 1 tablespoon butter until lightly golden. Remove from heat and set aside ¼ cup for garnish. Add champagne to the ¾ cup macadamia nuts. Cook mixture until it boils 5 minutes. Set aside. In another skillet, melt 2 tablespoons butter and add 2 tablespoons flour. Whisk to blend. Cook until bubbles begin to form and stir in milk. Continue to whisk as sauce thickens. Add the ½ cup fish or lobster stock. Simmer an additional 5 minutes. Add cream. Simmer until thickened to desired consistency. Add roux to macadamias, butter and champagne mixture. Stir to blend and keep warm. Salt to taste if needed. Sauté salmon in 2 tablespoons butter until opaque in center, 4 minutes per side. Place on plate. Serve sauce over salmon and sprinkle with reserved salted macadamia nuts.

Mumm makes a pink sparkling wine called Mumm Cuvée Napa, Blanc de Noirs. This sparkling wine is made from 85% Pinot Noir grape and 15% Chardonnay grape. It is a great accompaniment to this entrée.

nut chopper
whisk

Jane Langlais: Southlake, Texas

Jane and her husband Don moved to Australia with their son Reid for Don's work assignment. They have been part of the Dinner Club that started in 1989 and we missed them while they were away. They returned with this wonderful recipe, a knowledge and supply of great Australian wines and a new son, Luke!

Béchamel Sauce is made by stirring milk into a butter flour mixture called a roux. The thickness depends on the portion of butter and flour to the milk. If a few teaspoons of heavy cream are added with the milk, it tastes as though the whole sauce was made from cream.

Grilled Salmon with Spinach and Gorgonzola Cream

Serves: 4

Salmon
4 (8 ounce) skinless salmon fillets
2 tablespoons olive oil

Gorgonzola Cream Sauce
2 tablespoons butter
I tablespoon chopped fresh dill
½ cup dry white wine
I cup low salt chicken broth
½ cup +/- heavy cream
¼ cup Gorgonzola cheese
¼ teaspoon ground white peppercorns

Red Pepper Garnish
I red bell pepper
2 tablespoons olive oil
Black pepper

Spinach
2 cups vegetable oil
I package frozen whole leaf spinach
Chopped fresh parsley for garnish

Thaw the spinach. Prepare fillets by removing any remaining bones or skin. Brush with 2 tablespoons oil. Measure all ingredients and put in small bowls. Cut up peppers and toss with the olive oil and sprinkle with black pepper. Set aside. Prepare and light the grill if using charcoal. Prepare sauce. Melt butter over medium heat and add dill. Stir for one minute and add the wine. Stir the sauce 1 to 2 minutes and add the chicken broth and pepper. Cook over medium heat until sauce is reduced to ¾ cup. Gradually add the heavy cream, stirring until the sauce begins to thicken. Do not boil. Slowly add the Gorgonzola and stir to get a smooth, creamy consistency. Keep the sauce warm until fish is cooked. Grill salmon, arranging peppers on the outside of the fire. Cook salmon on outside of fire, approximately 4 to 5 minutes per side, turning with a spatula only once, as the salmon will come apart. Remove peppers as they begin to blacken. In a medium saucepan, heat 2 cups cooking oil to a temperature suitable for frying. Fry spinach until it darkens and gets crispy. Transfer to paper towels with slotted spoon. Serve salmon over the spinach with the sauce poured on top. Arrange the grilled peppers around the salmon.

pastry brush
slotted spoon

Grilled Salmon *continued*

Sauces can be thickened with a mixture of cornstarch and cold water added to a hot liquid. Gravies are typically thickened with flour.

Joe and Jeanne Graber:
Arlington, Texas

Joe and Jeanne are dear friends and made this for me on my birthday several years ago. Joe is a great cook and Jeanne helps with the preparation. Jeanne recommends getting everything chopped and measured ahead of time. It definitely helps organize the process and leaves less room for error. The combination of ingredients in this dish is mouth watering.

To test if oil is hot enough for frying, put the thin end of a wooden spoon to the bottom of the pan with oil. If bubbles rise briskly to the end of the wooden spoon, your oil is ready.

Salmon Sautéed with Shallots on a Bed of Spinach

Serves: 4

4	**(8 ounce) skinless salmon fillets**
4	**tablespoons butter**
6	**large shallots, sliced**
3	**tablespoons chopped fresh tarragon**
6	**ounces fresh spinach**
⅔	**cup dry white wine**
½	**cup whipping cream**
	Salt and pepper, to taste

Sprinkle fillets with salt and pepper. Melt 2 tablespoons butter in skillet. Sauté salmon until opaque in center, 4 minutes per side. Place on plate. Melt 1 tablespoon butter in the same skillet. Add half of the shallots and half of the tarragon. Sauté 1 minute. Increase heat to high. Add the spinach. Toss until wilted and divide between plates. Melt the remaining tablespoon butter in the skillet over medium high. Add remaining shallots and tarragon. Sauté 1 minute. Add wine and cream. Boil until sauce is thick enough to coat the spoon, 3 minutes. Season with salt and pepper. Return salmon to the skillet and simmer about 1 minute. Place salmon on top of spinach and top with sauce.

Becky Loboda: Mission, Kansas

Becky and I have been friends since high school and have always loved to go to good restaurants and try new foods. Drew, her husband, told her this was "restaurant quality." The tarragon is not overpowering and the balance of the ingredients is very appetizing.

Red Snapper
with Garlic Lime Butter

Serves: 2

6   **tablespoons clarified butter**
1   **teaspoon olive oil**
3   **cloves garlic, chopped**
2   **fillets skinless red snapper**
    Flour
    Tony Chachere's® Creole
    ***Seasoning*, to taste**
1   **lime**

Ask the butcher to remove the skin from fish when purchasing. Melt butter in a saucepan. Turn off heat and take spoon and scrape the white foam off the top. Leaving the solids behind, pour the melted butter in a skillet large enough to fry fish. Sprinkle fillets with *Tony Chachere's®* seasoning. Dust fillet with flour. Heat chopped garlic in butter and oil mixture until garlic is slightly brown. The teaspoon of oil keeps butter from browning. Add fish to butter, garlic, oil mixture. It will take approximately 10 minutes total to sauté the fish until flaky. Remove fillets from butter, squeeze lime into butter. Pour the lime butter over the fish.

Serve with Bacon-Brown Sugar Carrots and Steakhouse Creamed Spinach. Because of the duplication of bacon in these two recipes, omit bacon from spinach if serving paired with carrots.

Meta West, a Family and Consumer Science teacher from Abilene, Kansas, passed on this tip for cleaning up after cooking. It is best to use cold water to wash dishes that held eggs, flour, starch, cream and milk. Hot water is best for those dishes that have contained oils, butter, sugar and syrup. Meta suggests using a paper towel to wipe away excess butter and oil prior to washing. After dishes are soaked, all dishes should be washed with soap in hot water for sanitary purposes.

Orange Roughy with Parmesan and Green Onion Topping

Serves: 2

1½ **pounds skinless orange roughy**
Fresh lemon juice
½ **cup freshly grated Parmesan cheese**
¼ **cup butter**
3 **tablespoons HELLMANN'S® Real Mayonnaise**
3 **tablespoons green onion, chopped**
Dash of Tabasco® pepper sauce

Place fillets in greased glass baking dish; brush with lemon and let sit 10 minutes. Broil 4 inches from heat until they almost flake. Combine remaining ingredients. Spread mixture on fish. Broil 2 to 3 minutes longer until topping is golden.

cheese grater

Becky Loboda: Mission, Kansas

Becky and I have been friends since 1976. We have always enjoyed deep discussions over dinner in restaurants with cozy atmospheres and innovative food. Becky gave me this recipe over 10 years ago, and it is still a favorite. The topping can be used on any fish.

Easy Shrimp Creole

Serves: 4

½ **pound small, uncooked, peeled and deveined shrimp**
1 **medium onion, chopped**
1 **green pepper, sliced**
2 **cloves garlic, chopped**
2 **tablespoons vegetable oil**
1 **(14.5 ounce) can tomatoes, chopped (reserve liquid)**
1 **small bay leaf**
¼ **teaspoon sugar**
½ **teaspoon basil**
½ **teaspoon paprika**

Sauté onion, green pepper and garlic in a skillet with 2 tablespoons vegetable oil until tender. Add chopped tomatoes and liquid, bay leaf, sugar, basil and paprika. Simmer 20 to 25 minutes until tomatoes fall apart. Add raw shrimp and cook 5 minutes longer. Do not over cook or shrimp will get tough. Serve over white rice or in a puffed pastry shell.

Renée Griffin Scherer; Lenexa, Kansas

Renée was my boss and then became a dear friend. She is also the mother of my sweet niece Audrey. We always get together when I go back to Kansas City and try a trendy new restaurant. Renée enjoys great food, but has little time for cooking. She loves this dish because it is easy, good and low in fat!

When shrimp curl to a semicircle they are done. When they are tightly coiled, they are overdone.

Chicken Breasts Stuffed with Shrimp in Puffed Pastry

Serves: 6

Stuffed Chicken Breasts

1 **pound raw shrimp, cooked, peeled, deveined**
10 **tablespoons butter, divided use**
½ **bunch green onions, chopped**
1 **clove garlic, minced**
2 **tablespoons brandy**
1 **tablespoon flour**
2 **tablespoons dry vermouth**
½ **cup heavy cream**
6 **boneless, skinless chicken breasts**
 Fine sea salt and freshly ground pepper, to taste
 Extra flour to dust chicken
12 **sheets phyllo pastry**
1 **egg, beaten**

Shrimp Sauce

½ **pound cooked, peeled, deveined shrimp**
1 **(3 ounce) package crab boil**
6 **tablespoons butter**
6 **tablespoons flour**
1½ **cups half-and-half**
1 **cup lobster stock, fish stock or clam juice**
¼ **cup dry vermouth**
½ **cup shredded Gruyère cheese**
½ **cup freshly grated Parmesan cheese**
 Dash of Tabasco® pepper sauce or white pepper optional for extra seasoning

You may make the filling and get the chicken assembled up to the point of wrapping it in the dough the day before. Peel and devein 1½ pounds shrimp. Cook ½ pound shrimp in crab boil. Chop shrimp and reserve for the sauce. Remove the tails and chop the remaining 1 pound shrimp. Melt 4 tablespoons butter. Add the green onions and garlic and cook gently for 1 minute. Add the one pound shrimp and cook for 30 seconds. Pour brandy in skillet. Mix the flour, vermouth and cream together and stir into the shrimp mixture to thicken. Season with salt and pepper and cool. Flatten each breast slightly with the side of a mallet. Divide the mixture among the chicken breasts and fold over. If necessary, secure with a toothpick. Season each breast with salt and pepper and lightly dust the outside with flour. Fry chicken until three quarters of the way cooked in 3 tablespoons butter. If necessary, add a tablespoon of oil to keep butter from browning. Brush 2 sheets of phyllo with the remaining 3 tablespoons melted butter. Butter and wrap each chicken breast like a parcel in 2 buttered and stacked sheets of phyllo dough. Glaze with beaten egg. Place on buttered baking sheet. Cook in preheated 350 degree oven for 15 minutes. Pastry should be golden. While breasts are baking, make sauce. The sauce may be made a day ahead and reheated. Melt butter and sprinkle with flour, cook and stir 3 minutes. Gradually add half-and-half, stock and vermouth. Cook and stir until well blended and thickened. Stir in Gruyère and Parmesan cheese. Cook until cheeses are melted. Adjust seasonings if needed. Add the ½ pound chopped shrimp and keep warm until chicken is ready to serve. A drop of

Chicken Breast Stuffed with Shrimp *continued*

Tabasco® pepper sauce or white pepper may be added to sauce if needed. Top each chicken breast with Shrimp Sauce and serve.

Clam juice is usually found with the nonalcoholic drink mixers.

meat mallet
toothpicks
pastry brush

Vermouth is a white wine that has been fortified and flavored with herbs and spices.

Shrimp with Cilantro Pesto Cream Sauce

Serves: 4

Pesto
1	**bunch fresh cilantro**
1½	**teaspoons garlic, minced**
¼	**cup raw pumpkin seeds**
⅛	**teaspoon ground black pepper**
¼	**cup freshly grated Parmesan cheese**
¼	**cup olive oil**

Shrimp
24	**large shrimp, peeled and deveined**
2	**tablespoons olive oil**

Pesto Cream Sauce
1	**cup heavy cream**
¼	**cup white wine**
3	**tablespoons prepared Pesto**
1	**tablespoon cornstarch**
1	**tablespoon cold water**
	Salt and pepper, to taste

Prepare Pesto. Wash cilantro and remove stems. In blender or processor chop pumpkin seeds. Add cilantro, garlic, pepper and Parmesan. Blend until smooth and add the oil slowly to mixture. Set aside. For shrimp, heat 2 tablespoons oil and sauté shrimp until pink. They should be shaped in a semicircle when done but not tightly coiled. Remove from the pan and keep warm. Deglaze the pan with the white wine. Add the 3 tablespoons Pesto and the heavy cream. Mix together the cold water and cornstarch until blended. If cream and Pesto are heated thoroughly add a small amount of the cornstarch mixture. Stir until thickened, add slowly to get desired consistency. You may not need entire amount. Add the shrimp back to the sauce and warm thoroughly. Season with salt and pepper. Serve with rice or angel hair pasta.

cheese grater
blender or food processor

Chicken Breasts Stuffed with Lobster in a Garlic Cream Sauce

Serves: 4

Stuffed Chicken Breasts

2   tablespoons butter
¼   cup chopped yellow onion
¼   cup chopped celery
I   cup crushed buttery
    crackers
2   tablespoons sherry
½   teaspoon garlic powder
½   teaspoon Worcestershire
    sauce
I   tablespoon chopped fresh
    parsley
I   tablespoon chopped green
    onion
    Salt and pepper, to taste
4   boneless, skinless chicken
    breasts
8   ounces lobster meat,
    divided and steamed
½   cup dry white wine

Garlic Cream Sauce

2   tablespoons shallots
I   tablespoon butter
I   cup heavy cream
5   ounces garlic herb Boursin
    cheese

Melt butter in skillet. Sauté onions and celery in butter, until celery is soft and onion is transparent. Remove from heat and add crackers, sherry, garlic powder, Worcestershire, parsley, green onions, salt and pepper to taste. Pound each breast to same thickness. Divide lobster among the 4 breasts, then divide cracker mixture among the 4 breasts. Roll up, tucking ends in and fastening with a toothpick or short bamboo skewers. Place breasts in baking dish and pour wine over. Bake at 350 degrees for 25 to 35 minutes or until juices run clear when pierced with a fork. Filling may be made a day ahead and breasts filled. Refrigerate until ready to bake. To make sauce, sauté shallots in butter until soft. Add heavy cream, cook over medium heat until liquid is reduced and slightly thickened. Cut cheese into cubes and add. When mixture is thickened and cheese is melted, remove from heat. Serve chicken breasts with sauce.

Lobster tail can be steamed at your local grocer and is not too expensive. One tail should be enough lobster meat. Boursin cheese typically comes in a small box and is displayed with specialty cheeses in the grocery store.

meat mallet
short bamboo skewers or toothpicks

Cajun Spiced Shrimp with Mushrooms

Serves: 2

1	**pound, uncooked shrimp**
½	**lemon**
½	**teaspoon salt**
¾	**teaspoon ground cayenne**
¼	**teaspoon white pepper**
¼	**teaspoon black pepper**
¼	**teaspoon dried basil**
½	**teaspoon dried thyme**
½	**teaspoon rosemary**
⅛	**teaspoon dried oregano**
¾	**cup unsalted butter, divided use (12 tablespoons total)**
¼	**cup green onions, finely chopped**
1	**teaspoon garlic, chopped**
½	**pound mushrooms, sliced into ¼ inch slices, portobello, white or mixed**
6	**tablespoons lobster or shrimp stock (chicken stock may be substituted)**
3	**tablespoons chopped fresh parsley**
¼	**cup beer at room temperature**
	Long grain white rice

If you purchase lobster or shrimp stock, dilute according to directions. Otherwise, peel and devein shrimp and reserve shells. Squeeze lemon over peeled shrimp. Boil shells in 2 cups water for 20 minutes. Remove shells and reserve 6 tablespoons stock. For extra flavor, the remainder of stock may be used instead of plain water to cook rice. Cook rice according to package directions and keep warm. Measure salt and next 7 ingredients in small bowl before starting. Chop and measure all ingredients, put in individual bowls. In a large skillet melt one stick of butter over high heat. When almost melted, add the green onions, garlic and dried spices. Add the shrimp and sauté until they turn pink. Shake the pan rather than stirring. Flip the shrimp with spatula if necessary. Add mushrooms and ¼ cup stock. Add the remaining 4 tablespoons butter cut into tablespoons and continue shaking the pan. Before the butter is completely melted, add the chopped parsley and remaining 2 tablespoons stock. Then add warm beer. Continue cooking until butter thickens slightly. Pour over hot cooked rice.

This is outstanding and it can be served to a large group if measured ahead of time. Peel and devein the amount of shrimp needed. Divide the shrimp into one pound per two people. Squeeze with lemon. Use plastic cups for each ingredient and measure the spices into one cup, (for two people) mushrooms into another and green onions, butter, beer and parsley. Set up an assembly line and appoint a helper. Serve with Hurricanes and listen to some good Cajun music!

Good stocks are always needed. Keep a good chicken and lobster base for making stock on hand. Each must have water added according to the directions. If you can't find a good one in your grocery store ask a local restaurant or specialty store if they can order them for you in a size manageable for the home.

Pasta, Rice
&
Vegetables

Pasta, Rice & Vegetables

Kitchen tools needed

May be prepared ahead

Orange Pineapple Spice Tea, page 103 ~ Hearts of Palm, Artichoke and Olive Salad, page 123
Jalapeño Cornbread, page 245 ~ Tomato Pie, page 238
Coconut Cherry Bars, page 291

Pasta with Olive Oil, Garlic and Pine Nuts

Serves: 2

¼ **cup butter**
2 **tablespoons extra virgin olive oil**
¼ **cup chopped garlic cloves**
⅓ **cup pine nuts**
1 **(9 ounce) package fresh pasta (any shape)**
1 **cup halved cherry tomatoes (optional)**
Freshly grated Parmesan cheese (optional)

Heat butter and olive oil in a medium size skillet. Add garlic and pine nuts and cook several minutes until pine nuts are slightly golden. Add tomatoes and cook 2 additional minutes. Set aside. Cook pasta according to package directions, drain but do not rinse. Toss pine nuts, garlic and tomatoes with pasta. Can be served warm or cold.

Cheese tortellini makes this dish more filling and spinach pasta adds color.

Emery and Laurie Pino:
Denver, Colorado

Laurie and I found out our senior year of college, that we both had jobs in Fort Worth, Texas. We lived together until my transfer to Dallas. Laurie is one of the Martell sisters and we take every opportunity to get together when our paths cross in business or pleasure. Laurie and Emery whipped this up for a picnic and received rave reviews. It is excellent and makes a complete meal for me when I need something quick.

Pine nuts are also called piñon nuts or pignoli. They come from inside a pinecone, which generally must be heated to facilitate their removal. This labor-intensive process makes them expensive. They are torpedo shaped and have a delicate flavor. They should be stored in an airtight container in the refrigerator. They will keep this way for about 3 months; frozen for up to 9 months.

Creamy Chicken Tetrazzini
Serves: 6

3	**boneless, skinless chicken breasts, boiled with a carrot and a piece of celery**
8	**ounces uncooked spaghetti**
3	**tablespoons butter, divided use**
I	**cup sliced, fresh mushrooms**
I	**clove garlic, minced**
¼	**cup flour**
I	**teaspoon salt**
½	**teaspoon celery salt**
½	**teaspoon paprika**
⅛	**teaspoon pepper**
2	**cups whole milk**
I	**cup chicken stock**
¼	**cup roasted red peppers from a jar, drained**
¾	**cup freshly grated Parmesan cheese**
	Cooking spray

Boil chicken breasts in enough water to cover. Peel the carrot and cut in half. Add the celery and the carrot to the water for extra seasoning. While breasts are cooking, grate cheese and measure the other ingredients. When breasts are tender, remove them and the carrot and celery from water and add enough water to remaining broth to boil 8 ounces spaghetti according to package directions. Reserve I cup stock. Chop breasts into bite size pieces and set aside. Melt I tablespoon butter and add minced garlic and I cup sliced mushrooms. Sauté until tender and set aside. Melt the remaining 2 tablespoons butter and stir in flour, salt, celery salt, paprika and pepper. Cook for 2 minutes over low heat, remove from heat and whisk in the milk and chicken stock. Whisk to blend and cook over medium heat, stirring constantly until thickened. Add chicken, mushrooms, red peppers, cooked spaghetti and ¼ cup of Parmesan cheese, heat thoroughly. Spray a 9 x 13 inch glass dish or casserole dish with cooking spray. Place chicken mixture in dish and sprinkle the remaining ½ cup Parmesan over the top. Broil about 3 inches from heat, approximately 3 minutes, until top is lightly browned. May be made ahead, refrigerated and reheated. Serve with a salad and bread.

Pimento may be substituted for roasted red pepper and a (2 ounce) can of mushrooms (drained) may be substituted for the fresh mushrooms.

Pasta with Fresh Tomato Sauce with Asparagus and Shrimp

Serves: 6

12	medium fresh tomatoes
2	teaspoons lemon juice
1	cup red wine (Chianti)
1	teaspoon fresh basil
1	bay leaf
1¼	teaspoons salt
1½	teaspoons freshly ground pepper
½	cup virgin olive oil, divided use
3	bunches green onions, chopped
4	cloves garlic, minced
1	medium green pepper, chopped
1	pound medium shrimp (30 count total) **Tony Chachere's® Creole Seasoning**
2	bunches fresh asparagus (2 to 2½ pounds)
2	cups freshly grated Parmigiano-Reggiano cheese
2	(9 ounce) packages fresh angel hair pasta

Cut off the end of the tomatoes where the stem was. Grate the tomatoes; discard skin. Add the lemon juice, Chianti, basil, bay leaf, salt and pepper to the tomatoes. In a saucepan, bring to boil, lower heat and simmer 45 to 60 minutes, stirring occasionally. Remove bay leaf. In a separate pan, heat ¼ cup olive oil and sauté the chopped green onions, minced garlic and chopped green pepper. When cooked to medium softness, set aside. While sauce is cooking, peel and devein shrimp. Sprinkle with *Tony Chachere's® Creole Seasoning*. Trim the asparagus and cut in 1 inch pieces on the diagonal. Heat ¼ cup olive oil and sauté the shrimp with the asparagus until the shrimp turns pink and asparagus is crisp-tender. Cook fresh angel hair pasta in boiling water according to package directions. Drain, but do not rinse. Sprinkle with *Tony Chachere's®*. To serve, pour a generous amount of sauce over each serving of pasta and top with onion, garlic, pepper mixture, shrimp and asparagus mixture and grated Parmesan cheese.

cheese grater

John Martell: Topeka, Kansas

John is the father of three dear friends, Beth and Julie Martell and Laurie Martell Pino. We have remained in contact over the years, often meeting in different cities to attend Jimmy Buffett concerts. John is a sailor and enjoys life. I was happy to receive this recipe from him that he calls "Molto Bene Pasta," which means "Top Choice Pasta."

Carbonara

Serves: 6

1 **pound good quality bacon from the butcher**
1 **stick unsalted butter**
2 **tablespoons olive oil**
1 **medium onion, chopped fine**
3 **cloves garlic, chopped**
1 **(16 ounce) package good quality rigatoni pasta**
2 **eggs, room temperature, beaten**
1 **cup heavy cream, room temperature**
  Salt and freshly cracked black pepper
1 **cup freshly grated Parmigiano-Reggiano cheese**
  Extra Parmigiano-Reggiano freshly grated, optional

Chop and fry bacon until brown. Drain bacon on paper towels, but do not wash out skillet. Add butter to skillet plus 2 tablespoons olive oil. Add onion and garlic to this butter, oil mixture. Sauté until onion is translucent. In the meantime, boil pasta and drain, but do not rinse. Add the room temperature heavy cream, beaten eggs, bacon, onion, garlic, Parmesan, salt and pepper to the hot pasta. This must be tossed as you add the eggs so they do not cook unevenly on pasta.

A good quality Italian pasta should be used for this recipe. It is found with other dried pasta.

Pancetta (an Italian bacon that is not smoked) may be substituted for bacon.

Zyliss cheese grater

Visit their web site at www.zylissusa.com or call customer service toll free at 1-888-794-7623 to find a store near you that carries them. Their grater makes Parmigiano-Reggiano easy to grate!

Jim Johnston
Overland Park, Kansas

Jim studied in Rome and received this recipe from a friend. It is delicious! He made this for a dinner party and after dinner we enjoyed a great drink with equal parts of amaretto and Irish cream shaken together and served in chilled vodka glasses...wow.

The name Parmigiano-Reggiano is stenciled on the rind of the cheese. If you grate it yourself, you can be sure you are not getting an imitation. Nothing compares to this Parmesan from Italy, found at cheese shops and some grocery stores.

Spaghetti with Meat Sauce

Serves: 4

1½ **pounds ground beef**
2 **onions, chopped**
8 **ounces fresh mushrooms,**
   sliced
1 **(1.37 ounce) package**
   McCormick Thick and
   Zesty Spaghetti Sauce
1 **(6 ounce) can tomato paste**
2 **cups water**
1½ **teaspoons *Tony Chachere's*®**
   Creole Seasoning
1 **teaspoon coarse ground**
   pepper
½ **teaspoon dried basil**
½ **teaspoon oregano**
1 **clove elephant garlic,**
   chopped
⅔ **cup red wine**
   (Merlot or Cabernet)
½ **teaspoon salt**
½ **teaspoon additional salt or**
   ***Tony Chachere's*®**
   (for more spice), optional
1 **(16 ounce) box spaghetti**
   Freshly grated Parmesan
   cheese

Fry the ground beef until almost all red is gone. Break apart large chunks with a spoon. Do not drain. Add the onion and sauté until almost translucent and add mushrooms. Continue to sauté until translucent and stir in the dry spaghetti sauce mix. Add the can of tomato paste and slowly add 2 cups of water. Stir to blend. Bring to boil and add remaining ingredients. Stir to blend and reduce heat to low. Simmer one hour or until ready to serve. Taste, if you prefer more salt, add additional ½ teaspoon or for salt and spice, add additional *Tony Chachere's*® if needed.

Elephant garlic is the mildest garlic and the bulbs are large. If substituting regular garlic use 2 large cloves.

One pound of Italian sausage links (sliced) and 1 (2.25 ounce) can of sliced black olives can be substituted for ground beef. Serve with penne pasta and freshly grated Parmesan for a tasty Italian meal.

David Gore: Grapevine, Texas

David is the Texan who taught me the "spice of life." He got me hooked on Tony Chachere's® *and he puts it in everything he makes. Dave's son Ryan challenges his dad to make sauce as good as his grandmother Gunny's. This sauce is hard to beat!*

Pasta with Chicken, Cream and Creole Spice

Serves: 6

Creole Spice

8	tablespoons paprika
2	tablespoons onion powder
1½	teaspoons dried thyme
1	tablespoon oregano
3½	tablespoons salt
1½	tablespoons cracked black pepper
1½	tablespoons white pepper
1	tablespoon cayenne
1	tablespoon dried basil

Pasta

4	boneless, skinless chicken breasts
4	tablespoons butter
4	teaspoons minced garlic cloves
½	cup green onions, finely minced
¾	pound sausage (bulk pork sausage-not spicy)
2	cups chicken stock
1	cup heavy cream, room temperature
2	(9 ounce) packages fresh angel hair pasta

Mix dry spices together before starting and set aside (2½ to 3½ tablespoons of spice mixture will be used depending on your preference). Boil water for pasta. Measure out spice and roll chicken in spice. In a large skillet, melt butter and sauté garlic and green onions for one minute. Turn burner up to medium to medium high and add chicken. Cook until chicken breasts turn white, and no pink remains in center. Remove from heat and reserve onions and garlic. Cut chicken into bite size pieces. Return chicken to pan with onions and garlic and keep warm. Cook sausage in another pan and drain. Add the sausage to the chicken. Add chicken broth to the meats and simmer. Cook pasta and drain, but do not rinse. Add the cream to the pasta and mix with the meat and broth mixture. Simmer for 1 minute and mix in the remaining spice used for coating the chicken breasts. You may want to add additional spice, but taste before adding. Serve immediately.

This Creole Spice mix can be used for fish, eggs or for grilling meat. Mix together ahead of time to quicken preparation time.

For a different version, make the chicken breasts as directed and leave them whole. In a separate pan from the chicken breasts, sauté in 3 tablespoons butter and 1 tablespoon spice, ⅔ cup each of julienned carrots, zucchini and yellow squash. Add ⅔ cup sliced mushrooms. When vegetables are tender, add one cup of heavy cream. Boil until slightly thick. Pour the sauce over

Pasta with Chicken, Cream and Creole Spice *continued*

the breasts that have been cooked with the spice, garlic and green onion. It is excellent!

Joan Redhair: Leawood, Kansas

Joan and I have been separated by distance since our college days, but continue to get together in Kansas City and Dallas whenever possible. This recipe has a flavor so unique that I crave it! Because of the spice, it pairs well with a slightly sweet white wine such as Gewürtztraminer.

Julienne is to cut into thin, matchstick strips. When boiling pasta, cover pot after putting pasta in so it will quickly return to a boil and pasta won't stick together.

Spinach and Sausage Lasagne with Fresh Mozzarella

Serves: 8

Sauce

1	**tablespoon olive oil**
1	**cup onion, chopped**
¾	**cup peeled carrots, finely chopped**
2	**tablespoons minced garlic**
8	**ounces lean ground beef**
6	**ounces spicy Italian sausages, casings removed**
1	**(28 ounce) can crushed tomatoes with added puree**
¼	**cup tomato paste**
⅓	**cup fresh basil, chopped**
1	**tablespoon brown sugar**
1	**tablespoon dried oregano**
1	**bay leaf**
½	**teaspoon dried, crushed red pepper**

Lasagne

15	**lasagna noodles**
2	**(15 ounce) containers ricotta**
1	**cup grated Parmesan cheese**
1	**(10 ounce) package frozen, chopped spinach, thawed, drained, squeezed dry**
2	**large eggs**
4¾	**cups sliced or grated fresh mozzarella cheese (about 1½ pounds)**

For Sauce, heat oil in heavy saucepan over medium heat. Add onion, carrots and garlic; sauté until tender, about 12 minutes. Add beef and sausages to pan and cook, breaking up meat with spoon. Drain only if grease is excessive. Add remaining ingredients. Cover and simmer until mixture measures about 5 cups. Discard bay leaf. Cool. For lasagna, preheat oven to 350 degrees. Cook noodles in large pot of boiling water about 7 minutes. The noodles should be almost tender but firm. Combine ricotta and ¾ cup Parmesan in bowl. Mix in spinach. Season to taste with salt and pepper. Mix in eggs. Drain pasta and pat dry. Spread ½ cup sauce over bottom of 9 x 13 inch glass baking dish. Place 5 noodles over sauce. Spread ½ of the ricotta and spinach mixture over noodles. Sprinkle 2 cups grated (or sliced if using fresh) mozzarella over ricotta-spinach mixture. Spoon 1½ cups sauce over mozzarella and spread with spoon. Repeat. Arrange remaining noodles on top of second layer and spread remaining sauce over this. Sprinkle with the remaining Parmesan. You can make this one day ahead and cover with plastic wrap until you are ready to bake the next day. To bake: Cover the plastic wrap with foil and bake at 350 degrees 40 minutes. This will seal in moisture. Uncover and continue baking an additional 40 minutes. Let lasagna stand 15 minutes before serving.

To make soft cheeses easier to grate, place in freezer 20 minutes.

For extra special lasagna, use fresh mozzarella and ricotta from a specialty food store or visit the Mozzarella Company web site @www.mozzco.com or call 1-800-798-2954 to have fresh mozzarella shipped directly to you.

Lemon Rice Pilaf

Serves: 6

2½ teaspoons freshly grated
    lemon peel
1 tablespoon plus 1 teaspoon
    fresh lemon juice
2 extra large egg yolks
¼ cup heavy cream
2 tablespoons butter
1½ cups uncooked long grain
    white rice
3 cups low salt chicken broth
3 tablespoons freshly grated
    Parmesan cheese
3 tablespoons minced fresh
    parsley
    Salt and pepper, to taste

In a small bowl, combine lemon peel, lemon juice, egg yolks and heavy cream. Whisk until blended and set aside. In a small saucepan, melt butter and add rice. Stir and cook briefly, until rice turns opaque. Pour in chicken broth and sprinkle with salt. Heat to boiling and reduce heat to simmer. Cover and cook for 20 to 25 minutes. Just before serving, fold lemon-cream sauce into rice. Stir in Parmesan and parsley. Season with salt and pepper. Serve immediately.

whisk
cheese grater

Wild Rice with Fresh Corn and Shallots

Serves: 6

2 shallots, chopped
2 tablespoons olive oil
1 cup wild rice or
    combination of white and
    wild rice
2¼ cups chicken stock or broth
3 ears corn, cut from cob
    (or substitute frozen)
1 bunch cilantro or parsley,
    chopped
    Cooking spray

Wash and drain rice. Sauté shallots in olive oil in a saucepan over medium heat until soft. Add wild rice, cook 2 to 3 minutes. Add stock and bring to boil and cover. Transfer to 9 x 13 inch casserole dish that has been sprayed with cooking spray. Bake 45 minutes at 350 degrees. Check after 30 minutes to see if more stock is needed. Cut kernels from cob. Add uncooked corn (defrosted if frozen) to rice during the last 10 minutes of cooking. Stir in cilantro or parsley. Serve shortly after baking or rice will dry out.

Wild rice is really a marsh grass native to the northern Great Lakes area. It must be soaked in cold water before cooking so debris can float to the top. Once this step is taken it can be prepared according to package directions.

Black Beans with Cilantro Pesto Rice

Serves: 12

Cilantro Pesto

⅓ **cup pine nuts**
½ **cup freshly grated Parmesan cheese**
2 **large garlic cloves**
1½ **cups packed fresh basil leaves**
1½ **cups packed fresh cilantro leaves**
1 **cup packed fresh parsley leaves**
2 **tablespoons lime juice**
¾ **cup olive oil**

Beans and Rice

1 **pound dried black beans**
1 **ham hock**
4 **cups water**
2 **cups long grain rice**
¼ **cup butter, softened**
2½ **teaspoons** *Tony Chachere's®* **Creole Seasoning, divided use**
⅛ **teaspoon cayenne**

Beans must be soaked overnight in water 2 inches higher than the beans, or use the quick soak method on package. Preheat oven to 350 degrees and toast pine nuts 3 minutes or until very lightly toasted. Cool completely. In a blender, mix cooled pine nuts with remaining pesto ingredients. The following day when ready to prepare, drain beans. In a covered kettle, add 2 inches of cold water to drained beans and ham hock. Simmer beans until tender, about 1 to 1¼ hours. Drain beans, discard ham hock and keep beans warm. While beans are simmering, in a large heavy skillet bring 4 cups of water to a boil and stir in rice and ½ teaspoon Tony's seasoning. Cook rice covered over low heat, undisturbed 18 to 20 minutes or until water is absorbed and rice is tender. Fluff rice with fork and add to beans. Stir in butter, pesto, *Tony Chachere's® Creole Seasoning* and cayenne. Serves 12 as a side dish. Add a little more *Tony Chachere's®* if more salt is needed, more cayenne if you want a spicier dish.

This dish looks great when served in a hollowed out pineapple. Do not use canned black beans.

This recipe can be cut in half to serve with the Chili Maple Glazed Pork or Tropical Fiesta Steak.

blender or food processor to make pesto

To clean the blender after making pesto, squirt in a little dishwasher soap and fill half way with water. Blend and rinse out.

Potatoes Gruyère

Serves: 8

3½ **pounds russet potatoes, peeled and thinly sliced**
2 **large garlic cloves**
3 **cups whipping cream**
1⅓ **cups Gruyère cheese, grated**
Salt and pepper, to taste

Preheat oven to 400 degrees. Butter a 9 x 13 inch baking dish. Bring cream and garlic to boil over medium heat. Gently mix in the potatoes. Reduce heat to medium, cover and cook until the liquid returns to a boil, about 4 minutes. Transfer ½ of the potatoes to a prepared dish and season generously with salt and pepper. Sprinkle with ½ of the cheese. Top with the remaining potatoes, sprinkle with salt and pepper. Cover and bake 45 minutes. Uncover casserole and top with remaining cheese until potatoes are tender, cheese melts and sauce bubbles, about 15 minutes. Let stand 10 minutes and serve.

To create a variation of this, add 1 chopped shallot and ½ teaspoon crushed red pepper to the chopped garlic and sauté in 2 tablespoons butter before adding to cream. Combine ⅓ cup Parmesan with the 1 cup Gruyère cheese for a slightly different taste.

potato peeler
cheese grater

Lynn Holcomb
Raleigh, North Carolina

Lynn and I worked together years ago and we exchanged recipes often. We keep in touch at holiday time. She suggested adding a combination of shallots and red pepper to this dish.

Potato Mushroom and Spinach Tart   *Serves: 6*

2   **sticks (1 cup) unsalted butter**
2   **medium Yukon gold potatoes**
10 **ounces fresh spinach, washed and tough stems removed**
16 **ounces portobello or Italian mushrooms or your preference**
5   **shallots, finely chopped**
¼   **cup chopped parsley leaves**
2   **tablespoons fresh chopped thyme leaves**
2   **cups chicken broth**
6   **phyllo dough sheets**
    Salt and pepper, to taste

Defrost phyllo dough according to package directions. Preheat oven to 350 degrees. Clarify butter. To do this, slowly melt butter. Once melted, skim foam off top and slowly pour into another pan, leaving the white solids in bottom of pan. Leave the clarified butter (the butter free from foam and solids) on low heat. Brush unpeeled whole potatoes with the clarified butter. Roast potatoes at 350 degrees one hour, until soft when pierced with a fork. Cool before peeling. Discard stems from spinach and coarsely chop. Discard stems from mushrooms and thinly slice. Finely chop shallots. Keep all of these vegetables separate. In a large skillet add one tablespoon clarified butter. Heat until foam subsides. Add chopped spinach, cook one minute or until just wilted. Drain on paper towels and sprinkle with salt and pepper. Add another tablespoon of butter to skillet and cook one third of the mushrooms over moderate heat, stir until browned. Remove from pan. Cook in 3 batches, adding one tablespoon butter each time. To skillet, add one tablespoon butter and chopped shallots, stir until translucent. Remove from heat and combine parsley, shallots, 1½ tablespoons thyme and mushrooms. Add broth to skillet and deglaze over moderate heat, stirring in brown bits from pan. Reduce to one cup. Whisk in 3 tablespoons of the clarified butter. Keep covered and warm. Keep phyllo dough covered with damp kitchen towel while you are working. On a baking sheet, lay 1 sheet phyllo dough and brush with clarified butter. Sprinkle this with about ¼ of the remaining thyme, sprinkle lightly with salt and pepper. Repeat this process with 2 additional layers brushing with butter, sprinkling with salt and pepper. Cover this with plastic wrap and a damp cloth. Make another stack in the same

Potato Mushroom and Spinach Tart *continued*

manner, this will be the top sheet. Be careful not to over salt. Arrange potatoes down the middle of the first stack of phyllo that is on the baking sheet. Top potatoes with the mushroom mixture and spinach. Brush edges with butter. Carefully drape remaining phyllo stack over filling and roll edges to seal. Bake at 350 degrees for 20 to 25 minutes. Cut in slices, drizzle with sauce and serve.

pastry brush

Deglazing is done by heating a small amount of liquid in a pan that has been used in cooking and stirring to loosen brown bits of food on the bottom. This flavored liquid then becomes the base for a sauce.

"*I am the master of my fate; I am the captain of my soul.*"

W.E. Henley

Rosemary Potato Squash Gratin

Serves: 8

1 tablespoon cornstarch
1½ cups heavy cream
3 pounds baking potatoes, peeled, thinly sliced, boiled 5 minutes, drained
2 pounds butternut squash, halved lengthwise, seeded, peeled and sliced ¼ inch thick
1 teaspoon fresh thyme, chopped
1 teaspoon fresh rosemary, chopped
1½ teaspoons salt
¼ teaspoon white pepper
1 cup shredded Gruyère cheese
2 tablespoons grated Parmesan cheese

Preheat oven to 400 degrees. Butter 9 x 13 inch glass baking dish. Whisk cornstarch into cream and bring to boil in large pan over medium heat. Gently mix in potatoes and squash, and add thyme and rosemary. Reduce heat to medium, cover and cook until liquid returns to boil, about 4 minutes. Transfer half of potatoes to prepared dish. Season with salt and white pepper and sprinkle with ½ of the Gruyère cheese. Top with remaining potato mixture. Cover and bake 45 minutes. Uncover casserole and sprinkle with remainder of Gruyère and the 2 tablespoons Parmesan. Continue baking until potatoes are tender, cheese melts and sauce bubbles, about 15 minutes. Let stand 10 minutes and serve.

whisk
vegetable peeler

Cambozola Mashed Potatoes

Serves: 6

3 pounds Yukon gold potatoes, peeled and quartered
2 tablespoons butter
¼ cup half-and-half, warmed to room temperature
4 ounces Cambozola cheese, warmed to room temperature
Salt and pepper, to taste

Peel and quarter potatoes and cover in large pot with cold water and 1 teaspoon salt. Boil potatoes, removing when tender and drain. Using a hand mixer whip potatoes slowly adding butter and half-and-half. Add the Cambozola cheese and continue to whip until blended. These should be like a mashed potato, so add slightly more butter and half-and-half if necessary for desired consistency. Add salt and pepper to taste.

Yukon gold potatoes have a golden skin and flesh and make excellent mashed potatoes.

hand mixer
vegetable peeler

Baked Mashed Potatoes Supreme   *Serves 12*

18 small to medium sized red skinned new potatoes, unpeeled
8   slices good quality bacon from the deli
½   teaspoon pepper
1½ teaspoons *Tony Chachere's®* *Creole Seasoning*
6   tablespoons unsalted butter
¾   cup whole milk (you want mashed potato consistency)
5   green onions, chopped
1   cup sour cream
1½ cups grated cheddar cheese

Preheat oven to 300 degrees. In a large pot, boil potatoes with the skin on until tender. If you are using the larger potatoes, cut into smaller pieces to boil. Boil until tender, about 30 minutes. While potatoes are cooking, fry bacon until crisp in a large skillet. Drain well and lay on paper towels. Crumble when cool. When potatoes are tender, drain well and add pepper, *Tony Chachere's®* and butter. With a hand mixer, mash potatoes, slowly adding enough milk to get mashed potato consistency. The amount of milk used will vary due to the potatoes holding some water. Add ½ cup sour cream and half of the onions and bacon. Spoon mixture into a 9 x 13 inch glass baking dish. Cover with remaining sour cream, cheese and bacon. Bake 20 minutes or until cheese melts. Garnish with remaining onions.

This is an excellent dish for a large group and can be made ahead. This recipe is similar in taste to twice baked potatoes and makes great leftovers.

hand mixer
cheese grater

Garlic Chive Mashed Potatoes

Serves: 8

4   **pounds russet potatoes,
     peeled and cut into
     quarters**
1   **(8 ounce) package cream
     cheese**
4   **tablespoons butter**
3   **cloves fresh, chopped garlic**
1   **cup sour cream**
2   **tablespoons fresh chives,
     chopped**
     **White pepper and salt, to
     taste**
     **Whole milk or half-and-half,
     at room temperature**

Put potatoes in large pot with enough cold water to cover. Bring to boil. Add a pinch of salt and boil until tender when pierced with a fork. Drain well. Soften the cream cheese in microwave 10 to 20 seconds. Add cream cheese, 2 tablespoons butter and garlic and whip with hand mixer. Add sour cream and chives. Gradually add half-and-half, adding only enough half-and-half to get the desired mashed potato consistency. Taste and season with salt and white pepper. Spread potatoes in buttered 9 x 13 inch pan. These can be made ahead of time and refrigerated. Bring to room temperature before reheating. Dot with remaining butter and bake at 350 degrees for 30 minutes.

Roasted garlic may be substituted for the chopped garlic. Cut ¼ inch off a head of garlic and place in baking dish. Drizzle with ⅛ cup olive oil and toss to coat. Bake at 350 degrees for 55 minutes. Squeeze garlic from cloves and add to potatoes. Use as many cloves as preferred.

*hand mixer
vegetable peeler*

Nancy Wilson: Lee Summit, Missouri

Nancy and I met years ago in Kansas. She and her husband Jeff, moved to Texas around the same time I did. Nancy cut my hair while she lived here and I got this from her on one of my visits. I changed it over the years, adding fresh garlic, herbs and half-and-half.

Mashed Potatoes with Caramelized Onions

Serves: 6

4	**tablespoons butter**
2	**tablespoons olive oil**
2	**red onions, thinly sliced**
4	**pounds Yukon gold potatoes, unpeeled**
1½	**cups half-and-half, at room temperature**
	White pepper and salt, to taste

In a sauté pan over medium heat, melt butter and olive oil. Add onion and cook until translucent. Reduce heat to low and let cook until caramelized, about ½ hour. Remove from heat. Wash potatoes and put in large pot with enough cold water to cover. Bring to boil. Add a pinch of salt and boil until tender when pierced with a fork. Drain well. Add half-and-half and onions and whip with your hand mixer until smooth. Season with salt and white pepper to taste. If you are making these ahead, put them in a buttered 9 x 13 inch pan and refrigerate. Bring to room temperature before heating at 350 degrees for 30 minutes.

hand mixer

When storing potatoes, place an apple in with the potatoes to keep them from budding.

"Minds are like parachutes-they only function when open."

Thomas Dewar

Spinach Stuffed Twice Baked Potatoes

Serves: 8

4	**large russet potatoes**
1	**(10 ounce) package frozen creamed spinach**
2	**egg yolks**
1	**teaspoon salt**
¼	**teaspoon pepper**
¼	**teaspoon garlic powder**
1¼	**cups grated cheddar cheese Paprika**

Preheat oven to 450 degrees. Prick the potatoes with a fork and bake 50 minutes until fork tender. Cook spinach according to package directions until just thawed, about 8 minutes. Cut potatoes in half lengthwise. Scoop out the meat of the potato, leaving the shell intact. Combine the potatoes with the egg yolks, salt, pepper and garlic powder until smooth, beating with an electric mixer on medium speed. Stir in the defrosted spinach. Place the mixture back into the shells. Top with the grated cheese and sprinkle with paprika. Place in a baking dish and heat at 450 degrees for 10 minutes or until the cheese melts and potatoes are heated thoroughly. These can be prepared earlier in the day then heated at 450 degrees for 15 to 20 minutes.

For a buffet where there may be several potato choices, the potato halves can be cut into quarters.

hand mixer
cheese grater

Feta Potatoes

Serves: 6

3	large russet potatoes or 2½ pounds potatoes
1	teaspoon *Tony Chachere's® Creole Seasoning*
½	teaspoon coarse ground pepper
1	large clove garlic, minced
4	tablespoons chopped onion
3	ounces grated longhorn Colby cheese
3	ounces grated Swiss cheese
3	ounces crumbled traditional feta
3	tablespoons chopped fresh parsley
½	cup butter, melted
½	cup bread crumbs

Peel potatoes and boil until tender. Drain and refrigerate until cool. Grate the potatoes once cool and mix with onion, seasoning, cheeses and parsley. Pour the melted butter on top and sprinkle with bread crumbs. Bake at 350 degrees for 45 minutes in a buttered 9 x 13 inch glass baking dish or refrigerate until ready to bake. Let warm to room temperature before baking.

cheese grater
vegetable peeler

Lynne Borkowski, Julie Lancaster:
Grapevine, Texas

Lynne and Julie try and get together at least once a month to catch up on each other's lives. I join them occasionally and I always have a great time. They exchange a lot of recipes and they gave me this one to pair with the lamb dishes in Good Friends Great Tastes.

Colby cheese is a mild, whole milk cheddar cheese. It has a higher moisture content and it does not keep as long as other cheddar cheeses.

Simple Garlic Potatoes

Serves: 6

3 **baking potatoes, skins on,
washed and cut into
¼ inch slices**
⅓ **cup melted butter**
2 **cloves garlic, chopped
Seasoned salt**
⅓ **cup freshly grated
Parmesan cheese**

Slightly overlap potatoes in 9 x 13 inch glass baking dish. Pour melted butter over potatoes. Sprinkle finely chopped garlic over potatoes. Sprinkle with seasoned salt and Parmesan. Cover with foil and bake at 350 degrees for 1 hour.

Jean Neill: Bella Vista, Arkansas

I got this recipe when I was around 10 years old, from Jean, a family friend. They lived two doors down from us when I was born. We then moved, and they moved into our new neighborhood a few years later. Jean's husband Bill, was the principal at my high school, and a good friend of my father's.

Julienne Vegetable Medley

Serves: 6

¾ **pound unpeeled zucchini, cut
in ¼ inch julienne strips**
¾ **pound carrots, peeled and cut
in ¼ inch julienne strips**
¾ **pound unpeeled yellow
squash, cut in ¼ inch
julienne strips**
½ **cup butter, room
temperature**
**Salt and pepper to taste
(*Tony Chachere's® Creole
Seasoning* may be
substituted for salt and
pepper)**

Arrange vegetables in vegetable steamer over 1 inch boiling water and steam until tender-crisp. Drain off water and toss with butter and salt and pepper to taste. This is easy and colorful.

Rosemary Potatoes

Serves: 6

2½ **pounds small red skinned**
 potatoes, unpeeled
2 **tablespoons olive oil**
 Salt and pepper, to taste
1 **teaspoon dried rosemary**
4 **sprigs fresh rosemary**

Wash and cut potatoes in quarters. Toss with olive oil and put on lightly oiled jelly-roll pan. Sprinkle with salt and pepper (I prefer sea salt). Sprinkle dried rosemary over tops of potatoes. Put 1 sprig of fresh rosemary on each side of pan. Do not stir. Bake at 350 degrees for 15 minutes and remove from oven. Stir. Bake an additional 30 minutes or until you can easily pierce the potatoes with a fork. Crumble the fresh rosemary over potatoes and serve.

Add 1 pound cooked, drained and crumbled Italian sausage. Experiment with the flavor by replacing rosemary or mixing rosemary with Greek oregano, garlic salt or seasoned salt for a Mediterranean twist. Create your own combination of herbs!

jelly-roll pan

Markham Reilly: Dallas, Texas

I met Markham in the Oklahoma airport en route to Kansas City during Christmas in 1998. She has been very instrumental in guiding me toward my passion and natural calling, which is the love of food, people and travel. Markham suggests playing Italian opera music when you make her father's recipe. He made this for all of his nine children when mom needed a break and he did the cooking.

Grandma's Potato Dressing

Serves: 8

6	slices bacon
1	yellow onion
5	pounds potatoes
3	stalks celery
1	package seasoned croutons
½	teaspoon sage
¼	teaspoon thyme
½	teaspoon salt (add to water used to cook potatoes)
2	eggs
1	cup reserved potato water
	Salt and freshly ground pepper, to taste

Fry 6 slices bacon until crisp. Remove from grease and drain on paper towels. Fry one chopped onion in the bacon grease until translucent. Peel and quarter 5 pounds of potatoes. Cut celery and celery leaves in 1 inch pieces. Boil potatoes and celery together in water with ½ teaspoon salt added, until tender. Do not boil until mushy because they are not to be mashed. Drain water leaving 1 cup water in pan. Mash the potatoes and celery by hand with the remaining one cup water. They should remain chunky. Add the seasoned croutons. Stir in the crumbled bacon, onion and grease. Add spices and salt and pepper to taste. Mix and refrigerate overnight to let flavors blend. Before either baking or using to stuff a turkey, add two raw eggs and mix well. Bake 30 to 45 minutes at 350 degrees. Serve with roasted turkey and turkey gravy.

vegetable peeler

Louie Scherer: Kansas City, Kansas

This is my paternal grandmother's family recipe. My Dad, Louie grew up in Atchison, Kansas and this is the only dressing we have ever served during the holidays. Don't be afraid to pepper heavily. The bacon, onion and pepper combination is quite good.

Asparagus and Mushroom Sauté

Serves: 4

1 **bunch asparagus (½ pound after ends snapped)**
¼ **cup chopped green onions**
2 **tablespoons olive oil**
½ **pound fresh mushrooms, cut in half lengthwise**
1 **tablespoon fresh thyme or 1 teaspoon dried thyme**
½ **teaspoon salt**
¼ **teaspoon freshly ground pepper**
3 **tablespoons dry white wine**
3 **ounces freshly grated Parmesan cheese**
1 **teaspoon grated lemon rind**

Snap off tough ends of asparagus. Cut asparagus (approximately 40 thin spears) into 1 inch pieces. Set aside. Cook green onions in olive oil in a large skillet over high heat, stirring constantly, one minute. Reduce heat to medium and add asparagus, mushrooms and next 3 ingredients. Cook, stirring constantly for 3 minutes. Add wine and cover. Cook 2 minutes and drain. Sprinkle with Parmesan and lemon rind. Serve warm.

cheese grater

Jane Langlais: Southlake, Texas

Jane from Dinner Club helped me proofread the cookbook and gave me this because it is such a great side vegetable as well as light dinner. The combination of lemon and thyme is wonderful.

A tip from Linda Gore, Colleyville, Texas. It is sometimes hard to know how much of the asparagus you should trim off. If you take the asparagus and bend it, it will break where the tender stalk meets the tough stalk.

Stuffed Portobello Mushrooms

Serves: 8

1 **pound zucchini, cut in
   ½ inch cubes**
2 **teaspoons thyme**
5 **cloves garlic, chopped**
2 **leeks, chopped (white and
   light green leeks only)**
¼ **cup freshly grated
   Parmesan cheese**
½ **cup Gruyère cheese**
2 **tablespoons fresh chopped
   parsley**
8 **portobello mushrooms**
3 **tablespoons butter (divided)**
½ **cup bread crumbs**
3 **tablespoons olive oil,
   divided**
   Salt and pepper

Cook zucchini in 2 tablespoons oil, about 5 minutes. Salt and pepper. Mix in 1 teaspoon thyme and turn onto cookie sheet to cool. Add one tablespoon butter to pan and cook garlic and leeks. Add another teaspoon thyme and sprinkle lightly with salt and pepper. Mix with zucchini, set aside. Add cheese and parsley to this mixture. Cut off and discard stems of the portobello mushrooms. Wash mushrooms. Put mushroom gill sides down on baking sheet and brush with 1 tablespoon olive oil. Broil mushrooms 2 to 3 inches from heat for 3 minutes. Turn mushrooms over and broil an additional 3 minutes. Mound the zucchini, leek, cheese mixture on the mushroom. Mix together the 2 tablespoons melted butter with the bread crumbs and sprinkle on top of the vegetable mixture. Broil 1 to 2 minutes. This is also good as a side vegetable without using it as a filling for portobello mushrooms. If you prefer, bake the filling in an ovenproof dish and cut into squares or wedges.

pastry brush
cheese grater

Vegetables in Puffed Pastry

Serves: 8

⅔ cup chopped onion
2 unpeeled zucchini, diced
4 peeled carrots, sliced thin
2 unpeeled yellow squash,
    diced
1 tablespoon butter
1 tablespoon olive oil
1 large garlic clove
2 teaspoons fresh thyme
¼ teaspoon *Tony Chachere's®*
    Creole Seasoning
2 (17.3 ounce) boxes frozen
    puffed pastry sheets
1 egg, beaten

Defrost puffed pastry sheets for 20 minutes and heat oven to 400 degrees. Line bottom of a jelly-roll pan and a 9 inch round cake pan with parchment. Butter parchment paper. Chop vegetables and measure. Vegetable mixture should equal approximately 7 cups before it is cooked. Heat oil and butter and sauté all vegetables with garlic, thyme and *Tony Chachere's®* for 15 minutes or until carrots are tender but not mushy. Let mixture cool. On a floured surface cut out 16 circles, 4 inches in diameter. Use scraps for the decorative leaves. Spoon the mixture of vegetables onto all circles. Gather the pastry up to form a half moon, pinching to seal edges and then pull widest part together again to form a small round purse. Brush with egg and put a decorative dough leaf on top and coat it with egg. Place on the baking dish 2 inches apart and bake 20 to 25 minutes.

You may add crumbled goat cheese to the vegetable mixture for a variation.

---

1 (4 inch) round cookie cutter
1 ½ inch leaf cookie cutter
1 piece parchment paper
pastry brush

Tomato Pie

Serves: 8

3　ripe tomatoes, sliced
1　**(9 inch) unbaked refrigerated pie crust**
　Salt and pepper
　Dried oregano
　Dried or fresh basil
　Italian seasoning
1　**bunch chopped, green onions**
1　**cup HELLMANN'S® Real Mayonnaise**
1　**cup grated sharp cheddar cheese**
3　**Roma tomatoes for garnish**

Pre-bake the pie shell according to package directions for an unbaked shell at 450 for approximately 10 minutes. Remove from oven and turn the oven down to 325 for baking filled shell. To protect the edges of the shell from getting too brown during second baking, cover with foil. Drain sliced tomatoes on paper towels for 15 minutes. Cover bottom of pie shell with the tomato slices. Cover tomatoes with chopped green onions. Sprinkle liberally with spices, salt and pepper. In a small bowl, combine mayonnaise and cheddar and spread over tomato layers. Thinly slice the Roma tomatoes and slightly overlap on the outside of the pie forming a decorative circle. Bake filled shell approximately 30 minutes or until top is golden and bubbly. Let cool 10 minutes before slicing. Garnish with a fresh basil sprig. In the summer this can suffice as a light dinner with salad and bread. This is also a delicious vegetable accompaniment to beef, fish or poultry.

Add 6 slices cooked, drained crumbled bacon for variety. Experiment with different cheeses such as Gruyère. Sauté red onion in place of green and add sautéed red or green pepper. Add sliced zucchini, squash and garlic or any other vegetables to make your own combination vegetable pie.

Mary Hutchinson: Topeka, Kansas

Mary and I met through work at my first job out of college in 1984. She was in the original Girl's Dinner Club and is a polished entertainer. Mary has traveled all over the world and has sampled a variety of cuisines, but claims nothing compares to sitting down in her home with good friends, food, wine and stimulating conversation. This is one of Mary's favorite dishes to make in the summertime with homegrown tomatoes.

Green Bean Bundles

Serves: 6

2 **pounds fresh green beans, washed and ends snapped off**
6 **strips bacon, cut in half, partially cooked**
½ **teaspoon *Tony Chachere's*® *Creole Seasoning*, divided use**
  Garlic salt
4 **tablespoons butter, melted**
3 **tablespoons packed brown sugar**

Steam beans until crisp-tender in water seasoned with ¼ teaspoon *Tony Chachere's*® seasoning. When cool, wrap approximately 6 to 10 beans with bacon. Place bundles in a 9 x 13 inch baking dish. Sprinkle bundles with garlic salt and ¼ teaspoon *Tony Chachere's*® *Creole Seasoning*. Pour melted butter over bundles and sprinkle with brown sugar. Bake at 350 degrees 15 to 20 minutes or until bacon is done. To make ahead, complete all steps except the last (pouring the butter and brown sugar over beans). Put in a glass baking dish and refrigerate overnight until ready to bake. Before putting in oven, pour melted butter over bundles and sprinkle with brown sugar.

Green Beans with Balsamic Brown Butter

Serves: 8

2 **pounds fresh green beans**
1 **slice bacon**
1 **tablespoon balsamic vinegar**
½ **cup butter**
¼ **teaspoon salt**
¼ **teaspoon pepper**

Dice uncooked bacon and add to green beans. Cook green beans in boiling water for 5 to 7 minutes or until crisp-tender, drain. Melt butter in a small saucepan over medium high heat, stirring often until deep golden brown. Remove from heat; stir in vinegar, salt and pepper. Pour over beans and serve. This is a nice alternative to steamed green beans.

Marinated Green Bean Bundles *Serves: 12*

2 cans whole green beans, drained
16 slices bacon, cut in half
1 (8 ounce) bottle French dressing
5 pimentos, cut in strips

Arrange beans in bundles of 8 to 10, wrap with a half slice of bacon. Place in 9 x 13 inch glass pan. Pour dressing over beans. Cover and chill at least 3 hours. Bake uncovered at 350 degrees for 40 minutes, turning once after 20 minutes. Remove with slotted spoon. Garnish with pimento. You can make these beans the night before since they must marinate at least 3 hours.

slotted spoon

Marla Payne: Coppell, Texas

Marla enjoys cooking and passed on the idea of keeping a separate folder of recipes "to try." It is helpful when you are not feeling imaginative to comb through the items you've cut out from various publications. If you don't want to cut up your magazines, catalogue the issue, page number, add the title of the recipe and add it to your folder. This recipe that Marla makes for our Dinner Club is one of her most requested and you should add it to your list of recipes "to try."

Curried Cauliflower *Serves: 8*

1 large head cauliflower
½ teaspoon salt
1 (10¾ ounce) can cream of chicken soup
4 ounces cheddar cheese
⅓ cup HELLMANN'S® Real Mayonnaise
½ teaspoon curry powder
3 tablespoons melted butter
½ cup dried bread crumbs

Break cauliflower into flowerets. Cook in water with salt over medium, 10 minutes. Drain. In a 2 quart casserole dish, stir in soup, cheese, mayonnaise and curry powder. Add cauliflower. Melt butter in saucepan. Stir in bread crumbs. Sprinkle on top of casserole. Bake 30 minutes or refrigerate until ready to bake. Let warm to room temperature before baking. Great with turkey or ham.

Jalapeño Broccoli

Serves: 6

4   **tablespoons butter**
2   **tablespoons flour**
3   **(10 ounce) packages frozen broccoli, cooked, drained, reserve liquid**
2   **tablespoons chopped onion**
½   **cup evaporated milk**
¾   **teaspoon celery salt**
1   **teaspoon Worcestershire sauce**
1   **(6 ounce) package jalapeño pepper Kraft® Cheez-Link**

Make a paste of 4 tablespoons butter and 2 tablespoons flour. Add all other ingredients excluding broccoli and blend in small saucepan, over low heat to make a cheese sauce. (This includes the reserved liquid.) Mix cheese sauce with broccoli and put in buttered 9 x 13 inch glass baking dish. Bake at 350 degrees, 20 minutes. This may be made 1 to 2 days ahead.

The jalapeño cheese in a tube is a processed cheese sold in the cheese section with other common packaged cheeses. The garlic Kraft® Cheez–Link may also be used. A processed American cheese or cheddar cheese and fresh or pickled jalapeños can be substituted. Add the chopped jalapeños to your taste.

Brigitte Scherer:
Kansas City, Kansas

My mother has made this for years during the holidays to serve with turkey. It is wonderful! There are never any leftovers. If you want it spicier, add an additional minced, seeded jalapeño.

Steakhouse Creamed Spinach

Serves: 4

2	**(10 ounce) boxes frozen spinach**
4	**strips bacon**
2	**tablespoons butter**
1	**bunch green onions**
4	**large garlic cloves, minced**
1	**tablespoon flour**
½	**cup chicken broth**
⅓	**cup heavy cream**
	Pinch nutmeg
1	**(3 ounce) package cream cheese**
1	**cup freshly grated Parmesan cheese**
	Salt and pepper, to taste

Thaw spinach and drain excess water. Fry bacon, drain and crumble. Set bacon aside. Melt the butter. Chop the white and pale green part of the green onion and add to butter. Sauté 8 minutes. Add garlic and sauté 1 to 2 minutes longer or until fragrant. Add spinach and sauté until the remaining liquid is gone. Add flour a little at a time. Raise the heat to medium and add broth. When this simmers, add the cream. Stir in a pinch of nutmeg and add cream cheese that has been cut in cubes. Stir until melted. Gradually add the Parmesan cheese. Stir until creamy. Add bacon and stir. Reduce heat to low and simmer 5 to 10 minutes. Salt and pepper to taste.

Goat cheese (½ cup) may be substituted for Parmesan. It is also delicious!

 cheese grater

Joe Graber: Arlington, Texas

Joe and I met years ago on a double date. He married his date, my dear friend Jeanne, and they live a short distance from me. The three of us spent quite a bit of time together while working on the photography for Good Friends Great Tastes. *Joe and I love to exchange recipes and Joe often treats Jeanne and me to gourmet meals that he prepares while Jeanne and I drink wine and visit.*

Bacon-Brown Sugar Carrots

Serves: 6

¼ **cup crumbled bacon**
3 **cups sliced carrots**
3 **tablespoons butter**
2 **tablespoons sliced green onions**
1 **tablespoon firmly packed brown sugar**
¼ **teaspoon salt**
⅛ **teaspoon pepper**

Fry bacon, drain and crumble. Slice carrots ¼ inch thick. In a saucepan bring ¾ cup water to boil. Add carrots; cover and cook over medium heat 10 to 12 minutes until crisp-tender. Drain. In saucepan, melt butter. Add green onions, brown sugar, bacon and carrots. Cover and cook over medium heat until heated through. Add salt and pepper.

Brown sugar sometimes gets hard when in the box. It is best to store it in an airtight container. If it does become hard, peel half an apple and put it in the box for several hours or overnight; or if needed immediately, microwave brown sugar (without apple) for 15 to 30 seconds to soften. It can then be transferred to an airtight container.

Corn Maque Choux

Serves: 6

3	**cups fresh kernel corn**
½	**cup oil**
1	**cup chopped yellow onion**
½	**cup chopped green pepper**
1	**cup chopped fresh parsley**
1	**tablespoon garlic, chopped**
1	**cup dry white wine**
	***Tony Chachere's® Creole Seasoning*, to taste**
	Tabasco pepper sauce, to taste
1	**chopped tomato**

Remove corn from cob, scraping close to cob to get juices. Heat the oil in a skillet and sauté the onions, pepper and parsley until the onion is translucent. Add the corn, garlic, wine and seasonings, stir again. Reduce heat and simmer for 30 minutes. Add the chopped tomato. Taste and adjust seasonings before serving. The Choux is pronounced "Shoe" and is a fancy name for smothered corn.

David Gore: Grapevine, Texas

Dave, Ryan and I enjoy spending Sunday afternoon barbecuing and inviting the neighborhood children to swim, or have our friends stop by for a casual dinner. Dave made this to accompany brisket and it is super!

To easily remove corn from the cob, set it in the center tube of a tube pan. With a knife, cut straight down and kernels will fall into pan. Scrape cob to remove extra juices.

"Jiffy's®" Cornbread Casserole

Serves: 8

- 1 **(15.25 ounce) can whole kernel corn, undrained**
- 1 **(14¾ ounce) can cream style corn**
- 1 **(8½ ounce) box "Jiffy®" Corn Muffin Mix**
- 1 **stick melted butter**
- 1 **(8 ounce) carton sour cream**
- 1½ **cups grated cheddar cheese**

Mix together all ingredients except cheese. Put in a 9 x 13 inch pan and bake uncovered, approximately 45 minutes at 350 degrees or until top is golden. Sprinkle cheese on top and return to oven. Bake until the cheese melts.

*The "Jiffy®" mix gives this casserole a slightly sweet flavor. If the meat being served is grilled and does not have a sauce, the sweetness complements the grilled meat. One cup of yellow cornmeal can be substituted for the "Jiffy®" mix, if preferred. One (10 ounce) can of drained Ro*Tel® Diced Tomatoes and Green Chiles adds extra spice to either variation.*

cheese grater

Marla Payne, Coppell, Texas

Marla and her husband Steve are part of the original "Dinner Club." We alternate homes and the hostess picks a theme and the menu. She has her choice of assigning a dish and sending the recipe to you or assigning you the course (i.e. salad, vegetable or dessert.) On the evening we had this corn, marinated pork tenderloin was served. Everyone requested the recipe.

Spicy Black Beans

Serves: 8

¼   **pound bacon, chopped**
1   **large onion, chopped**
2   **large garlic cloves, chopped**
2   **(15.5 ounce) cans black beans, drained and rinsed**
1   **(14.5 ounce) can diced, peeled tomatoes**
1   **(4.5 ounce) can diced green chiles**
2½   **tablespoons chili powder**
2   **teaspoons dried oregano**
¼   **teaspoon cayenne pepper**

Cook bacon in large saucepan over medium heat until light brown, about 10 minutes. Add onion and garlic and sauté until onion is translucent, about 5 minutes. Add all remaining ingredients. Simmer until mixture is thick, stirring frequently, about 12 minutes. Season to taste with salt and pepper. Make ahead and reheat so flavors blend.

Zucchini Pepper Squash Casserole

Serves: 4

Pepper Squash
4   **slices bacon cooked, crumbled**
2   **tablespoons butter**
¾   **cup chopped yellow onion**
½   **cup red pepper, diced**
2   **zucchini, unpeeled**
2   **yellow squash, unpeeled**
1   **teaspoon brown sugar**
½   **teaspoon nutmeg**
½   **cup grated cheddar cheese**
½   **cup grated Monterey Jack cheese**

Seasoning
1   **teaspoon sea salt**
½   **teaspoon white pepper**
½   **teaspoon onion powder**
½   **teaspoon garlic powder**
½   **teaspoon dried basil leaves**
½   **teaspoon black pepper**

Cook bacon, drain and crumble. Reserve one tablespoon of drippings and add butter. Add onion and pepper and sauté until tender. Add zucchini, squash, brown sugar and nutmeg. Toss with seasoning. Cook until slightly tender. Toss with crumbled bacon. Put in ovenproof baking dish and top with cheeses. Bake at 350 degrees for 30 minutes. You may make ahead and refrigerate. Let mixture come to room temperature before baking.

 cheese grater

Gruyère Butternut Squash Gratin

Serves: 4

2   medium butternut squash
¾   teaspoon salt
¾   teaspoon freshly ground
       pepper
1   medium leek, white part
       only
1   teaspoon olive oil
2   tablespoons water
½   cup dry white wine
½   cup low salt chicken stock
2   small cans evaporated milk
       (10 ounces total)
8   fresh basil leaves, shredded
½   teaspoon sugar
¼   cup bread crumbs
1   cup grated Gruyère cheese
1   tablespoon freshly grated
       Parmesan cheese

Preheat oven to 400 degrees. Halve the butternut squash lengthwise and remove seeds. Season each of the halves with salt and pepper. Wrap each half in foil and put on baking sheet. Bake one hour until the squash are tender, not mushy. Let cool slightly. Meanwhile, in a saucepan, combine leek, oil and 2 tablespoons water. Cover and cook over moderately low heat until the leek is soft and translucent, about 5 minutes. Uncover and stir in wine. Increase the heat to high and boil until liquid is reduced to approximately 3 tablespoons, 3 minutes. Stir in the stock, milk, sugar and remaining salt and pepper. Remove from heat. Scoop the flesh from the squash in large pieces. You can make up to this point, 3 hours ahead. Leave at room temperature. Preheat oven to 400 degrees. Spoon the squash into casserole dish. Bring the leek mixture to boil. Mix ½ of the chopped basil into squash. Spoon ½ of the leek mixture over the squash mixture. Sprinkle with ½ of the bread crumbs, and ½ the Gruyère. Repeat. Sprinkle Parmesan on top. Garnish with remaining basil. Bake 30 minutes at 350 degrees.

cheese grater

Red Cabbage

Serves: 8

1	head red cabbage
1	cup Burgundy wine
⅓	cup brown sugar
1	tablespoon salt
½	teaspoon cayenne
4	medium apples, peeled, cored and quartered
¼	cup butter
¼	cup cider vinegar
3	tablespoons cornstarch mixed with 3 tablespoons cold water

Core cabbage and cut into 4 quarters, then into strips. Add wine, brown sugar, salt, sprinkle of cayenne and apples. Cook on low for 20 to 30 minutes. Apples will get so soft, they will dissolve. While this is hot, add butter, cider vinegar and cornstarch mixture. Stir until thickened. This freezes nicely if you want to make for a later date. This is another specialty from my mother.

 vegetable peeler

"You can eat well or you can eat a lot."

Another lesson from mom on the benefits of fine dining and quality versus quantity.

Desserts

Desserts

Kitchen tools needed

May be prepared ahead

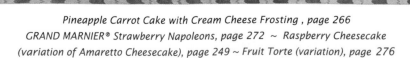

Pineapple Carrot Cake with Cream Cheese Frosting , page 266
GRAND MARNIER® Strawberry Napoleons, page 272 ~ Raspberry Cheesecake
(variation of Amaretto Cheesecake), page 249 ~ Fruit Torte (variation), page 276

Amaretto Cheesecake

Serves: 12

Crumb Crust
1½ cups graham cracker crumbs (1 inner pack of a 16 ounce box)
2 tablespoons sugar
1 teaspoon ground cinnamon
6 tablespoons butter, melted

Cheesecake
3 (8 ounce) packages cream cheese, softened
1 cup sugar
4 eggs
⅓ cup amaretto

Topping
1 (8 ounce) carton sour cream
1 tablespoon plus 1 teaspoon sugar
1 tablespoon amaretto
¼ cup toasted almonds
1 (12 ounce) chocolate candy bar, grated

Crush graham crackers in blender or food processor. Combine the graham cracker crumbs with 2 tablespoons sugar, cinnamon and butter, mix well. Press in bottom and up sides of 9 inch springform pan. Preheat oven to 375 degrees. Toast almonds until lightly golden, about 3 minutes. Beat cream cheese with electric mixer until light and fluffy. Gradually add 1 cup sugar, mixing well. Add eggs one at a time, beating well after each addition. Stir in ⅓ cup amaretto. Pour into prepared pan. Bake cheesecake for 45 to 60 minutes until set. Combine sour cream, 1 tablespoon plus one teaspoon sugar and 1 tablespoon amaretto. Stir well and spoon over cheesecake. Bake at 500 degrees, 5 minutes. Let cool to room temperature, refrigerate 24 to 48 hours. Garnish with toasted almonds and the grated chocolate. Cheesecake is best when thoroughly chilled for at least 24 hours.

This is a cheesecake recipe that can be a basic for many variations. Replace amaretto with a raspberry flavored liqueur, omit almonds and garnish the top with 2 pints fresh whole raspberries arranged neatly with pointed end up, covering top. Use ⅓ cup grated white chocolate in the crust and reduce sugar in crust to 1 tablespoon. Frangelico will work nicely as a substitute for amaretto, using chopped hazelnuts instead of almonds and white or dark chocolate can be used as a garnish.

springform pan
blender or food processor
hand mixer

Cheesecake can be cut easily with a piece of dental floss held very taut.

Chokahlúa Cheesecake

Serves: 12

Chocolate Crumb Crust
- 1⅓ **cups chocolate wafer crumbs or chocolate graham cracker crumbs**
- 1 **tablespoon sugar**
- 4 **tablespoons butter at room temperature**

Cheesecake
- 2 **tablespoons butter**
- 1½ **cups semisweet chocolate pieces**
- ¼ **cup KAHLÚA®**
- 2 **(8 ounce) packages cream cheese, softened and cut into small pieces**
- 2 **large eggs**
- ⅓ **cup sugar**
- ¼ **teaspoon salt**
- 1 **cup sour cream**

Topping
- ½ **cup sour cream**

Mocha Sauce
- 1 **cup semisweet chocolate pieces**
- ⅓ **cup KAHLÚA®**
- ⅓ **cup light corn syrup**

Combine wafer crumbs, sugar and butter. Mix well. Put mixture in a layer over the bottom of a 9 inch springform pan. Preheat oven to 325 degrees. Slowly heat butter, chocolate and KAHLÚA® in a small saucepan, stirring until chocolate melts and mixture is smooth. Cool and set aside. Beat softened cream cheese until smooth. Beat in eggs one at a time and beat in sugar, salt and sour cream. Gradually beat in the cooled chocolate mixture. Pour into chocolate crumb crust. Bake for 40 minutes or until filling is barely set in center. Remove from oven and let stand at room temperature at least one hour. Make Mocha Sauce. Combine ingredients over low heat and stir until chocolate melts. Spread with a thin layer of sour cream and drizzle with warm Mocha Sauce. If not serving until later, refrigerate cheesecake and sauce until ready to serve. Reheat sauce gently. Before serving, bring slices being served to room temperature. Serve sauce warm. Cheesecake may be made 1 to 2 days ahead and sauce one week ahead.

 hand mixer
springform pan

Betty Krenger: Abilene, Kansas

Betty is the mother of a college boyfriend. We got along well back then and loved to discuss food and recipes. We've stayed in touch and still exchange recipes today. This is a recipe she gave me back in 1982. It is a chocolate lover's dream.

Pecan Pie

Serves: 8

3 eggs, beaten
½ cup sugar
½ cup dark corn syrup
½ cup light corn syrup
½ teaspoon vanilla
⅓ cup butter, melted
½ cup pecans, halved
½ cup pecans, broken
I (10 inch) refrigerated pie crust
2 cups heavy cream, whipped

Preheat oven to 350 degrees. Press unbaked crust into glass pie plate according to package directions. Combine first 6 ingredients together. Mix in the pecans and pour into unbaked shell. Bake 45 to 50 minutes until the pie is set. Let cool and serve with whipped cream.

Add powdered sugar (I tablespoon or to taste) and vanilla (I teaspoon) to your heavy cream as you whip for flavor and sweetness.

 hand mixer

Pumpkin Pie

Serves: 8

½ cup sugar
½ cup brown sugar
¼ cup flour
½ teaspoon ginger
I teaspoon cinnamon
½ teaspoon allspice
¼ teaspoon salt
I (I pound) can solid packed pumpkin
¼ cup corn syrup
I cup heavy cream plus, extra to whip for garnish
2 eggs
I (9 inch) refrigerated pie crust

Preheat oven to 375 degrees. Combine all dry ingredients in a bowl. In another bowl, combine pumpkin and corn syrup. Mix into dry ingredients. Add I cup heavy cream and eggs; mix until well combined. Pour the mixture in an unbaked, 10 inch pie shell. Bake 45 minutes. Cool and serve with whipped cream. Can be made a day ahead, once pie is served, refrigerate any leftovers.

 hand mixer

White Chocolate, Vodka and Cranberry Cheesecake

Serves: 12

Crumb Crust

8½ **ounces butter biscuit cookies**
½ **cup hazelnuts, toasted and husked**
2 **tablespoons sugar**
½ **teaspoon ground nutmeg**
5 **tablespoons unsalted butter, melted**

Cheesecake

8 **ounces imported white chocolate, finely grated**
1 **teaspoon butter, melted**
¾ **cup dried cranberries**
¼ **cup Russian vodka**
4 **(8 ounce) packages cream cheese, softened**
1¼ **cups sugar**
4 **large eggs**
1 **cup sour cream**
2 **teaspoons vanilla extract**

For the crust, generously butter the bottom and sides of a 9 inch springform pan. Wrap the outside of the pan with a double layer of foil. Finely grind cookies, hazelnuts, sugar and nutmeg in the food processor or blender. The blender may be better for blending cookies and nuts separately and then mixing with the sugar and nutmeg in a bowl. Add butter and process until moist clumps form or melt and mix in. Press the crumb mixture in the bottom and up the sides of the springform pan. Chill while preparing filling. For the filling, grate the white chocolate and set aside. Melt 1 teaspoon of the butter in the saucepan. Sauté the cranberries one minute and add vodka. Flambé the vodka mixture until alcohol evaporates, approximately 2 to 3 minutes. There should be a liquid glaze in the bottom of the pan. Pour ¼ cup sugar into the cranberry vodka mixture. Over low heat, whisk into a glaze and set aside to cool. For filling, beat the cream cheese in a large bowl until smooth. Add 1 cup sugar and beat until well blended. Add eggs one at a time, beating just until blended and scraping the sides of the bowl as you are mixing. Beat in sour cream. Add to filling and beat until blended. Beat in vanilla. Stir in white chocolate. Pour filling into prepared crust. Add the cranberry vodka mixture in a circular motion. You want to see the swirl of the cranberry mixture, do not over mix. Place the springform pan in a large baking pan. Pour enough water to come half way up the sides. Bake at 350 degrees until center is set, 1¼ hours. Turn off oven; let cake stand in oven with door ajar, 1 hour. Remove pan from water and transfer to wire rack. Cool and serve. If serving later, refrigerate and bring slices to room temperature before serving.

To remove the brown skins on the hazelnuts heat them in a 350 degree oven for 10 to 15 minutes until

White Chocolate, Vodka and Cranberry Cheesecake continued

skins begin to flake. Place the warm nuts in a dishtowel and rub vigorously, most of the skin will be removed. Be sure nuts are fresh. To flambé is to ignite. When lighting the pan with the vodka, you barely have to get the flame near the liquid. Be sure to stand far enough back and don't have fans running. To extinguish the flame after you flambé, keep the saucepan lid in close proximity to the stove. To extinguish the flame, immediately place lid over the saucepan. Without oxygen, the flame cannot burn.

Other nuts may be used such as almonds, and they will not have to have skins removed. Dried cherries, apricots or blueberries are alternatives for cranberries. The crust can be made from gingersnaps or other cookies of your choice and cinnamon may be substituted for nutmeg. The process of wrapping the cheesecake in foil and immersing in water is a restaurant technique. You can use this procedure on other cheesecakes.

cheese grater
springform pan
blender or food processor
hand mixer
whisk

Brian Miske: Irving, Texas

Brian and I worked together and he has a reputation for awe-inspiring cheesecakes. Olga Miske, his Russian grandmother, was the inspiration for this cheesecake. Brian is a risk taker in business, so it is not surprising his recipe requires flambéing.

Pumpkin Rum Cheesecake with Praline Sauce

Serves: 10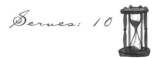

Crust
1¼	**cups honey graham cracker crumbs (1 inner pack)**
½	**cup finely chopped pecans**
⅓	**cup butter, melted**
¼	**cup brown sugar**
¼	**cup sugar**

Filling
¾	**cup plus 6 tablespoons sugar, divided use**
1	**cup canned pumpkin**
3	**eggs**
1½	**teaspoons cinnamon**
½	**teaspoon nutmeg**
½	**teaspoon ground ginger**
½	**teaspoon salt**
3	**(8 ounce) packages cream cheese, softened**
1	**tablespoon cornstarch**
2	**tablespoons heavy cream**
½	**teaspoon vanilla**
1	**tablespoon rum**

Praline Sauce
1	**cup light brown sugar**
1	**tablespoon cornstarch**
1½	**cups water**
2	**tablespoons butter**
½	**cup coarsely chopped pecans**

Crush graham crackers and chop nuts separately in processor or blender. Combine crust ingredients and mix well. Pat into bottom of 9 inch buttered springform pan. Bake 15 minutes in preheated 325 degree oven. Set aside until filling is prepared. Lower the oven temperature to 300 degrees. For filling, mix the ¾ cup sugar, pumpkin, rum, eggs, cinnamon, nutmeg, ginger and salt in a bowl. Set aside. Using an electric mixer, beat the cream cheese and 6 tablespoons sugar until smooth. Add cornstarch, heavy cream, vanilla and rum, beating well after each addition. Add pumpkin mixture to cream cheese mixture. Mix thoroughly so color is consistent. Pour filling into crust and bake one hour at 300 degrees. The center will be soft. Turn off oven and let cheesecake cool in oven with the door closed for several hours or overnight. Refrigerate until ready to serve. Serve with the praline sauce drizzled over cheesecake. Prepare sauce in saucepan by combining sugar and cornstarch. Add water. Cook over medium heat stirring constantly, until thick and bubbly, about 5 minutes. If you prefer thicker sauce, add additional cornstarch mixed with an equal amount cold water and cornstarch. Add butter and pecans. Cool slightly before serving.

Liqueurs like Frangelico or amaretto may be used in place of the rum.

blender or food processor
springform pan
hand mixer

Susan Bee: Rockwall, Texas

I reported to Susan in two different jobs, and as a result our friendship has blossomed. Dave and I enjoy restaurant outings with Susan and her husband, Russ. She and her friend Kathleen Wincorn created this tantalizing combination of pumpkin and praline. It is a unique alternative to traditional pumpkin pie.

Caramel Fudge Nut Pie

Serves: 10

Crust
1 inner package of a (16 ounce) box chocolate graham crackers
5 tablespoons butter, melted
1 teaspoon vanilla extract

Filling
1½ sticks butter
¾ cup brown sugar
¼ cup light corn syrup
3 cups pecan halves (12 ounces)
3 tablespoons heavy cream
2 ounces unsweetened chocolate

Crush graham crackers in blender or food processor. Add butter and vanilla. Press into 9 inch pie plate. Cover and freeze crust until ready to use. You may make a day ahead. Preheat oven to 350 degrees. Let pie crust return to room temperature while mixing filling ingredients. Combine butter, brown sugar and corn syrup in heavy saucepan. Bring to boil, stirring often. Boil 1 minute and stir in the nuts and cream. Boil until thickened about 3 minutes. Remove from heat and add chocolate. Stir until chocolate melts and mixture is well blended. Pour hot filling into crust. Using a spoon, spread mixture to even out. Bake until filling bubbles, about 10 minutes. Let cool slightly and serve warm with Homemade Vanilla Ice Cream.

blender or food processor

Chocolate Sacks Filled with White Chocolate Mousse on Raspberry Sauce

Serves: 2

Chocolate Sack
1   (14 ounce) bag chocolate
    candy coating
2   small gift bags (approximately
    7¾ x 4 x 2½ inches)

White Chocolate Mousse
1   cup white chocolate
    morsels
¼   cup heavy cream
1   tablespoon raspberry sauce
1   drop red liquid food
    coloring
1½ cups heavy cream, whipped

Raspberry Sauce
1   (10 ounce) bag frozen
    raspberries
2   tablespoons sugar
2   tablespoons raspberry
    flavored liqueur
    Fresh raspberries for
    garnish
    Fresh mint for garnish

Make Raspberry Sauce by putting frozen raspberries in electric blender. Pour through mesh strainer and discard seeds. Add liqueur and sugar and stir until sugar dissolves. For Chocolate Sack cut 3 inches from top of sack so sack is small enough to fit on dinner plate. Insert wooden toothpicks on outside base of bag, parallel to the short edges of the bag, tucking ends of picks under the diagonal folds. Insert long wooden skewer through center base fold of bag under the wooden toothpicks. You will suspend it between cans to dry, so try not to have wooden skewer become part of the base of the bag that will be coated with chocolate. Melt bag of chocolate candy coating in double boiler and cool with candy thermometer to 100 degrees. Pour candy coating into bag and tilt to coat interior. You may need a pastry brush or a spoon to coat inside. Shake bag over double boiler to remove excess chocolate. Heat candy coating again and cool to 100 degrees. Hold bag to light and reinforce weak areas using pastry brush. Heat chocolate and coat inside again, each time shaking off excess and suspending upside down between cans to dry. Repeat for second bag. Once the Chocolate Sack has dried, gently peel bag off. It comes off easily and any slight flaws can be disguised with the bow, mousse and garnishes. Do not refrigerate, moisture will soften coating. Handle as little as possible to avoid melting. The mousse can be made ahead and refrigerated. Combine the white chocolate morsels and ¼ cup whipping cream in saucepan. Melt over low heat, stirring constantly until chocolate melts. Cool. Stir Raspberry Sauce into

Chocolate Sacks *continued*

mousse and fold in whipped cream. Add food coloring. Spoon 2 to 3 tablespoons Raspberry Sauce onto center of 10 to 12 inch dinner plate. Position small chocolate sack diagonally across pool of sauce. Pipe about ¾ cup of mousse into open end of sack; allow White Chocolate Mousse to spill out onto sauce. Scatter fresh raspberries over mousse and sauce. Garnish with mint leaves. Make a bow of gold ribbon, leaving tails long. Place bow on top of Chocolate Sack.

Shannon Curry-Rackers from Flower Mound, Texas gave me this time saving tip. Melt the (14 ounce) bag of chocolate candy coating using microwave directions and paint the inside of paper cupcake wrappers. Place in metal cupcake holders and refrigerate. When firm, peel off the paper and use as you would the chocolate paper bag. It is quick and makes 6. The filling and raspberry sauce can be used to fill cups and garnish. The mini cupcake holders and muffin pans will also work as well and could be used for mousse or filled with liqueur to serve with coffee.

pastry tube
candy thermometer
blender
pastry brush
2 (12 inch) long wooden skewers
    and 4 toothpicks
hand mixer
double boiler
mesh strainer
4 tall cans or glasses to balance the
    drying chocolate sacks
1 inch wide ribbon for decorative bows

Chocolate Flowerpot Dessert

Serves: 8

1 **(16 ounce) package chocolate sandwich cookies, crushed**
11 **ounces cream cheese, softened**
½ **cup butter, melted**
1 **cup powdered sugar**
2 **(3½ ounce) packages instant chocolate fudge pudding mix**
3 **cups cold milk**
1 **teaspoon vanilla**
1 **(8 ounce) container Cool Whip® whipped topping, thawed**

Crush cookies in a blender a few at a time, leaving cream filling in them. They should resemble potting soil. Cover the hole in the flowerpot with foil or wax paper. Put ½ of the crumbs in the bottom of a 9 x 13 inch pan or in individual flowerpots (8 x 8 inch round or slightly smaller). With a hand mixer, beat together cream cheese, butter and powdered sugar. Add the powdered sugar. In a separate bowl, whisk together the pudding, cold milk, vanilla and whipped topping. Mix the pudding mixture with the cream cheese mixture and pour over crumbs. Top with the remaining chocolate cookie crumbs. Let chill 10 hours. This may be served chilled or frozen.

Top the chocolate crumbs in the flowerpot with gummy worms for a boy's birthday party. For a more feminine touch, use small individual flowerpots and insert a flower into the center. For a more sophisticated look, layer in brioche dishes. This dessert is very versatile. Graham cracker crumbs can be substituted for chocolate cookies, use vanilla pudding and layer with strawberries. It is delicious and can also be layered in a 9 x 13 inch pan.

flowerpot, whisk
blender
hand mixer

Barb Homer: Houston, Texas

Barb is a teacher in Houston and has been a friend of mine since junior high school. I love her contribution because the ingredients are simple but make a creative dessert. The tips for serving may lead you to your own discovery...adding nuts, fruit or cookie variations.

Rum Bundt Cake

Serves: 10

Cake

1	**cup chopped pecans**
1	**package yellow cake mix (without pudding added)**
1	**package vanilla instant pudding and pie filling**
4	**eggs**
½	**cup cold water**
½	**cup vegetable oil**
½	**cup 80 proof rum (can be white or amber)**

Glaze

½	**cup butter (1 stick)**
¼	**cup water**
1	**cup sugar**
½	**cup rum (white or amber)**
	Whipped cream (optional)

Preheat oven to 325 degrees. Grease and flour a Bundt cake pan. Sprinkle nuts over bottom of pan. Combine all cake ingredients. Blend well. With a hand mixer at medium speed, beat 2 minutes. Pour batter over nuts. Bake one hour. Cool. Invert onto serving plate. Prepare glaze by melting butter over medium heat, stir in water and sugar and boil 5 minutes. Remove from heat and stir in rum. Prick top of cake with fork. Pour glaze evenly over cake, allowing cake to absorb glaze. Repeat until all glaze is used. Serve with a side of whipped cream.

hand mixer
nut chopper
Bundt cake pan

Lonie Scherer, Kansas City, Kansas

Dad and I have some fun memories of eating popcorn with a side of tart apples and his special pancakes with peach filling! He likes food with nice presentation. When I was a child he would make eating an orange fun by inserting toothpicks into each segment. This recipe is one of my dad's favorites. We have had this recipe in the family since I was ten years old. It is a very moist and flavorful cake.

Add a festive touch to this Bundt cake by filling the center with fresh flowers. Crumble foil and place it in the center of the cake so you have a base for the stems and fewer flowers will be needed.

White Chocolate Bread Pudding *Serves: 12*

Pudding

6 **cups heavy cream**
1 **cup milk**
1 **cup sugar**
20 **ounces white chocolate, broken into pieces**
4 **whole eggs**
15 **egg yolks**
1 **(24 inch) loaf stale, French bread, sliced (1 inch slices)**

Sauce

8 **ounces white chocolate broken into pieces**
½ **cup heavy cream for whipping**
1 **ounce dark chocolate for garnish**

If you are not able to use stale bread, then dry bread out in oven at 275 degrees. Preheat oven to 350 degrees. In a large pan heat the heavy cream, milk and sugar over medium heat. When hot, remove from heat and stir in the 20 ounces white chocolate. Stir until melted. Whisk together the whole eggs with the yolks in a large bowl. Slowly pour the hot cream mixture into the eggs in a steady stream, whipping the eggs as you combine. In a 9 x 13 inch pan sprayed with cooking spray, place half of the bread in a single layer. Pour one half of the egg mixture over the bread. Be sure all parts of the bread are saturated. Layer other half of bread on top of other layer. Pour the remaining egg mixture on top to saturate bread. Cover with foil and bake at 350 degrees for one hour. Take the foil off and bake an additional 30 minutes, until pudding is set and golden brown. To make the sauce, bring the heavy cream to a boil in a small saucepan. Remove from heat and add the 8 ounces white chocolate, stir until smooth and completely melted. Using a cheese grater, make chocolate shavings. This can be served immediately from pan topped with the sauce and chocolate sprinkles. To make ahead, the bread pudding can be baked, then refrigerated for 6 to 8 hours. Loosen bread pudding from sides with a knife and invert the pudding on to a clean surface. Cut the pudding into 4½ x 4 inch squares and then cut again diagonally into triangles. Heat the triangles on a cookie sheet at 275 degrees for 15 minutes and serve with warm sauce and sprinkle with grated dark chocolate. Recipe may be cut in half.

whisk
cheese grater

Jamie Seelye: Dallas, Texas

Jamie and I met at work and we get together to "catch up" over dinner and cocktails. Jamie has supported me in my networking dinners. The purpose of these dinners is to bring people together whose paths may never cross to discuss fresh topics. Jamie's bread pudding contribution is easy to make and quite decadent!

Flourless Chocolate Almond Torte with Vanilla Cream and Fresh Berries

Serves: 12

Torte

I	**cup whole almonds, toasted, cooled**
4	**tablespoons plus ⅓ cup sugar**
2	**tablespoons oil**
I½	**sticks unsalted butter**
½	**cup heavy cream**
8	**ounces bittersweet chocolate (broken into pieces)**
8	**ounces semisweet chocolate (broken into pieces)**
6	**large eggs, separated and at room temperature**
I	**cup whipped cream for garnish**
2	**tablespoons amaretto Powdered sugar**
½	**cup almond slices, toasted**
I	**pint raspberries, for garnish**

Vanilla Cream

2	**cups milk**
6	**egg yolks**
I	**cup sugar**
2	**tablespoons vanilla**

Preheat oven to 350 degrees. Butter and flour a 9 inch springform pan. Shake out excess flour. Line the bottom of the pan with parchment paper and butter the paper. Toast all almonds on a cookie sheet 3 to 4 minutes at 350 degrees. Separate the whole almonds from the sliced almonds since they are for two separate purposes. Combine ½ cup of the toasted whole almonds with 2 tablespoons sugar in processor or blender. Transfer to a large bowl. Combine remaining ½ cup almonds and vegetable oil in processor or blender. Process until mixture is pasty, about 3 minutes. Put butter and ½ cup heavy cream in saucepan and heat until mixture simmers and butter is melted. Remove from heat and add the chocolate bars. Whisk until smooth. Stir in both almond mixtures and cool slightly. Using a hand mixer beat egg whites in large bowl until soft peaks form. Gradually add ⅓ cup sugar and beat until stiff peaks form. Beat the egg yolks in another bowl until very pale yellow and thick, about 5 minutes. Gradually beat chocolate mixture into egg yolks. Fold the egg whites into this mixture in three additions. Pour batter into the prepared pan. Bake until the top side of the cake cracks and tester inserted in center comes out with batter attached, about 35 minutes. (The lack of flour causes the batter to attach to the tester.) Let cake cool a minimum of 2 hours at room temperature before serving. For the whipped cream, whip the chilled heavy cream and add 2 tablespoons amaretto and remaining 2 tablespoons sugar until soft peaks form. Keep chilled until ready to serve. To make the Vanilla Cream, simmer the milk in a medium saucepan.

Flourless Chocolate Almond Torte continued

In a separate bowl, whisk the egg yolks and sugar together until a ribbon forms when lifted from the bowl. Whisk constantly while slowly pouring hot milk into the mixture. Return the mixture to the saucepan. Over low heat, continue to stir with a wooden spoon. The sauce is finished when you can dip a spoon into the sauce then draw your finger over the back of the spoon and there is no sauce where you drew your finger across spoon. Sauce is slightly thick but will thicken a little more once refrigerated. Be careful not to overcook or particles of cooked egg will appear. If this happens, strain to remove egg. Remove from heat and stir in vanilla. Chill until ready to use. The Torte, whipped cream and Vanilla Cream can be made earlier in the day. Loosen cake from sides of pan with a knife and release pan sides. Sprinkle lightly with powdered sugar and sprinkle almonds across the top of cake. Serve at room temperature on a bed of the Vanilla Cream with a dollop of whipped cream on the side and a few raspberries over the top of the whipped cream.

---

hand mixer
blender or food processor
whisk
wooden spoon
fine mesh strainer
springform pan
parchment paper for baking (grocery
bakery may give you a sheet, if
unable to find within store)

Gingerbread with Brandy Pear Sauce

Serves: 12

Gingerbread

1	**teaspoon baking soda**
1	**cup buttermilk**
2	**eggs**
1	**cup sugar**
1	**cup vegetable oil**
1	**teaspoon vanilla**
2	**cups flour**
3	**teaspoons ginger**
1½	**teaspoons nutmeg**
2	**teaspoons cinnamon**
1	**teaspoon salt**
1	**cup molasses**
	Powdered sugar for garnish

Brandy Pear Sauce

1	**lemon**
2	**cups water**
½	**cup sugar**
¼	**cup lemon juice**
4	**ripe Bartlett pears, peeled**
⅛	**cup brandy**

Put the soda in the buttermilk to dissolve. Mix eggs, sugar, oil and vanilla. Sift all dry ingredients and then measure them. Add the measured sifted ingredients to the sugar, oil, egg mixture and add buttermilk mixture and molasses. Pour into a greased and floured Bundt cake pan and bake at 350 degrees, 30 to 35 minutes. Let cool slightly and turn onto cake plate. To make Brandy Pear Sauce, peel the lemon and cut peel into strips. Put the lemon strips, sugar, water and lemon juice in a pan. Cook over medium heat until the sugar dissolves. Add the peeled pears cut into quarters. Cook for 20 minutes until pears are tender. Remove pears with a slotted spoon and reserve the liquid. Simmer the reserved liquid until reduced to ¾ cup. Remove the lemon strips. Reserve half of the lemon strips and put in a blender. Add the pears and the reserved liquid. Process until smooth. Strain this liquid and squeeze as much liquid out as possible by pressing the solids with the back of the spoon. Stir in the brandy. Serve the pear sauce over warm Gingerbread. You may prepare the sauce ahead of time and bring to room temperature before serving. Sprinkle cake with sifted powdered sugar just before serving.

A warm caramel sauce (such as the one that is on the Pecan Crusted Ice Cream Pie) is very good served with the Gingerbread if you are unable to serve the Gingerbread warm.

slotted spoon
blender
fine mesh strainer
vegetable peeler
sifter

Chocolate Cake with Whipped Cream Filling

Serves: 8

Chocolate Cake
1   cup cocoa
2   cups boiling water
1   cup butter, softened
2½ cups sugar
4   eggs
2¾ cups flour
2   teaspoons baking soda
½   teaspoon baking powder
½   teaspoon salt
1½ teaspoons vanilla extract

Whipped Cream Filling
1   cup heavy cream
1   teaspoon vanilla extract
¼   cup powdered sugar, sifted

Chocolate Frosting
1   (6 ounce) package
      semisweet chocolate
      chips
½   cup half-and-half
¾   cup butter
2½ cups powdered sugar, sifted

Combine cocoa and boiling water, stirring until smooth; set aside. Cream butter and gradually add sugar, beating well at medium speed with electric mixer. Add eggs one at a time, beating well after each addition. Combine flour, soda, baking powder and salt in medium bowl. Add to the creamed mixture, alternately with the cocoa mixture, beating at low speed, beginning and ending with the flour mixture. Stir in vanilla. Do not overbeat. Pour batter into greased and floured cake pans. Bake at 350 degrees for 20 to 25 minutes or until toothpick inserted in center comes our clean. Cool in pans 10 minutes; remove from pans and cool completely. For Whipped Cream Filling, beat heavy cream and vanilla until foamy. Gradually add powdered sugar while beating. Beat until soft peaks form. For Chocolate Frosting, combine first 3 ingredients in saucepan; cook over medium heat, stirring until chocolate melts. Remove from heat and add powdered sugar. Set saucepan on ice and beat at low speed until the frosting holds its shape and is no longer glossy. Add a few more drops of half-and-half to make spreading consistency. Spread Whipped Cream Filling between layers and Chocolate Frosting on top and sides of cake. Refrigerate until ready to serve.

Lisa Taylor, a friend in Dallas gave me this recipe. She decorates this cake with fresh Gerber daisies for a colorful presentation.

3 (9 inch) round cake pans
hand mixer
sifter

Pineapple Carrot Cake with Cream Cheese Frosting

Serves: 8

Cake
- 1½ cups corn oil
- 2 cups sugar
- 5 eggs
- 2½ cups flour
- 2 teaspoons baking powder
- 1 teaspoon baking soda
- 2 teaspoons cinnamon
- 1 teaspoon salt
- 2 cups grated carrots
- 1 cup crushed pineapple (drained)
- 1 cup chopped pecans
- 2 teaspoons vanilla

Frosting
- 1 (8 ounce) package cream cheese
- ½ stick butter
- 1 (16 ounce) box powdered sugar
- 2 teaspoons vanilla

Mix together oil and sugar. Add eggs one at a time, beating after each addition. Sift the dry ingredients, then measure. Mix the dry ingredients together with the oil, sugar and egg mixture. Blend in the carrots, drained pineapple, nuts and vanilla. Grease and lightly flour a 9 x 13 inch pan or 3 round cake pans. Pour batter evenly into pans. Bake at 350 degrees one hour or until toothpick comes out clean. Cake is moist but should start to pull away from sides of pan. Let cool, about 10 minutes, before inverting onto wax paper, if making a layer cake. Loosen edge of pans with knife. Let cakes cool completely. For Frosting, mix together the cream cheese and butter with the mixer. Add the powdered sugar and vanilla. Frost cake.

If making in 3 layers it may take less time to bake because it is not as dense. Check cake after 25 minutes with a tester. I used 1½ times the frosting when making it a 3 layer cake. For extra spice add 1 teaspoon nutmeg and 1 teaspoon ground cloves along with the cinnamon. One cup dark raisins may be added and walnuts substituted for pecans.

sifter
cheese grater
hand mixer
3 (9 inch) cake pans (optional)

Lenette Swain: Arlington, Texas

Lenette is one of the original Knots Landing Girl's Night members. Lenette is now involved in her children's lives, plays tennis and sails with her husband, David. With her busy schedule, she still has time to make extravagant desserts for her friends at work

Amaretto Cake

Serves: 10

Cake
1   package yellow cake mix
    (without pudding added)
1   (3.4 ounce) package vanilla
    instant pudding and pie
    filling
4   eggs
1   cup cold water
1   cup vegetable oil
1   cup coconut
1   cup chopped almonds

Glaze
½   cup butter
½   cup amaretto
½   cup sugar

Preheat oven to 350 degrees. Grease and flour a Bundt cake pan. Mix first 5 ingredients together. Fold in nuts and coconut. Pour batter into Bundt pan. Bake 50 to 60 minutes or until tester comes out clean. Cool. Invert onto serving plate. Prepare Glaze by melting butter over medium heat; stir in amaretto and sugar and boil 5 minutes or until sugar dissolves. Prick top of cake with fork. Pour Glaze evenly over cake, allowing cake to absorb Glaze. Repeat until all Glaze is used.

This is an easy recipe to prepare and can be made with other liqueurs and nut combinations such as Frangelico and hazelnuts or KAHLÚA® and pecans.

hand mixer
Bundt cake pan

Sharon Cordes: Sugarland, Texas

Sharon and I lived together in college and she had many wonderful recipes, especially in her dessert collection. The basic cake can be changed up to suit your own tastes.

Strawberry Lemon Poppy Seed Cake with White Chocolate Frosting

Serves: 10

Cake

3   cups cake flour
2   teaspoons baking powder
½   teaspoon baking soda
½   teaspoon salt
2   cups sugar
1   cup butter, at room
      temperature
1   tablespoon plus 1 teaspoon
      grated lemon peel
4   eggs, at room temperature
2   tablespoons fresh lemon
      juice
1½ teaspoons vanilla extract
1   cup buttermilk
2   tablespoons poppy seeds
2   cups sliced strawberries
3   whole strawberries

Frosting

¾   cup sugar
2   eggs
6   tablespoons fresh lemon
      juice
8   ounces Swiss white
      chocolate, chopped
3   cups heavy cream
1   teaspoon vanilla

Preheat oven to 350 degrees. Combine the first 4 ingredients in a medium bowl. In a mixer bowl beat sugar, butter and lemon peel until smooth. Add eggs one at a time, beating well after each addition. Beat in the lemon juice and the vanilla. Add the dry ingredients and buttermilk, alternating in three additions. Do not over beat. Stir in the poppy seeds. Pour into 3 greased 9 inch cake pans. Bake 20 to 25 minutes and cool 10 minutes. Remove from pans. For the frosting, combine ½ cup sugar, eggs and lemon juice in a double boiler over simmering water. Whisk until very thick and foamy, about 3 to 5 minutes. Remove from heat, add chocolate and stir until smooth. Let cool to room temperature. Beat heavy cream with remaining ¼ cup sugar until peaks form. Add vanilla. Fold into lemon and chocolate mixture. To assemble, put bottom layer on cake plate and spread with 1 cup frosting. Top with 1 cup sliced berries and ½ cup frosting. Repeat with the second layer. Add top layer. Entire cake should be frosted. Place the three unhulled whole strawberries in the middle of the top of the cake, points out.

---

3 (9 inch) cake pans
whisk
hand mixer
double boiler
reamer (juicer) for lemons
cheese grater or zester

Strawberry Lemon Poppy Seed Cake *continued*

This cake does not transport well in the summer months because heat affects the frosting. This should be refrigerated until ready to serve. Insert a toothpick at one quarter intervals all the way around the cake, piercing all three layers to hold in place. If this is necessary, be sure guests are aware of toothpicks. Two large lemons should yield enough juice for the cake and the frosting.

Susan Bee: Rockwall, Texas

Susan and I traveled together for business in our last two jobs. We would share the most decadent desserts on the menu, thinking we were saving calories by sharing. She gave me this recipe after her friends raved about it! I love the way the lemon and white chocolate complement each other.

To get the most juice out of fresh lemons, bring them to room temperature and roll them under your palm against the kitchen counter before squeezing.

Strawberry White Chocolate Mousse Cake

Serves: 12

Cake

11	eggs (5 eggs plus 6 yolks)
1	cup sugar
	Pinch salt
1½	cups cake flour
3	tablespoons unsalted butter, melted and cooled

GRAND MARNIER® Syrup

⅓	cup sugar
½	cup water
⅓	cup **GRAND MARNIER®**

White Chocolate Mousse

3	cups heavy whipping cream
1	pound white chocolate, coarsely chopped

Garnishes

1	cup sliced strawberries
24	unfilled soft ladyfingers
8	medium sized strawberries, unhulled
8	ounces white chocolate, coarsely chopped

Move the rack in your oven to the middle position. Preheat to 350 degrees. Lightly butter and flour two 9 inch round cake pans. Whisk the 5 eggs and the 6 egg yolks, sugar and salt together in the top pan of a double boiler. Heat water in a double boiler to simmer but do not let water touch the bottom of the pan with the eggs, sugar and salt. Continue whisking over the simmering water until frothy and temperature reaches 130 degrees. Check with candy thermometer. Pour into bowl and use a hand mixer and beat at medium speed for 5 minutes or until this mixture has tripled in volume and batter forms a thick pale yellow ribbon when beaters are lifted. Sift one third of the flour over the batter. With a spatula, briskly but gently fold the flour into the batter. In two additions, sift then fold in the remaining two thirds of the flour. Fold in the cooled butter. Divide the batter between the two pans evenly. Bake about 30 minutes until cakes spring back when touched and edges have pulled slightly away from the pan. Invert the cakes and cool. In a small saucepan, combine the sugar and water. Stir over medium heat until the sugar dissolves. Bring the syrup to a boil and pour into another pan. Let cool. Stir in GRAND MARNIER®. For the mousse, bring one cup heavy cream to boil. Remove from heat. In a food processor or blender, finely chop the white chocolate. Pour the hot cream through the feed tube or into the blender and process 20 seconds, until smooth. Pour the mixture into a large metal mixing bowl. Cover and refrigerate for 45 minutes, stirring occasionally, until mixture starts to thicken. In a chilled mixing bowl, whip the remaining 2 cups of heavy cream until it

Strawberry White Chocolate Mousse Cake *continued*

begins to thicken. Stir ⅓ of the whipped cream into the white chocolate mixture. Fold in the remaining cream until blended. To assemble, trim off the rounded tops of the cakes with a serrated knife to make each layer flat. Place one layer on top of a cake plate and use a pastry brush to brush half of the GRAND MARNIER® Syrup over cake layer. Spread ¼ of the white chocolate mousse over this layer. Arrange a layer of the sliced strawberries over this, then add another layer of mousse. Add the next layer over this and repeat, reserving 1 cup of the mousse. Use a spatula to smooth out top and sides. Press the ladyfingers upright onto the sides of the cake all the way around. Tie the ribbon around the ladyfingers making a bow in the front. Fit a pastry bag with a star tip and fill with reserved mousse. Pipe 8 rosettes around the top of cake. Place an unhulled berry between each rosette. Refrigerate until serving time. This may be made a day ahead.

2 (9 inch) cake pans
double boiler
whisk
hand mixer
sifter
blender or food processor
candy thermometer
serrated knife
spatula
pastry bag
3½ feet ribbon, 1 inch wide
pastry brush

GRAND MARNIER®
Strawberry Napoleons

Serves: 6

1	**(17.3 ounce) package frozen puff pastry sheets, thawed**
1	**quart fresh strawberries, sliced**
1	**cup sugar, divided use**
1	**tablespoon slivered almonds**
6	**egg yolks**
	Pinch salt
4	**tablespoons cornstarch**
2	**teaspoons grated orange rind**
1½	**cups milk**
½	**cup GRAND MARNIER®**
2	**cups heavy cream**
1	**orange for garnish**
	Powdered sugar
	Mint leaves for garnish

Preheat oven to 400 degrees. Unfold the pastry on a lightly floured surface and cut the pastry into 3 strips along the fold marks. Cut each strip into 4 rectangles. Keep the shapes uniform because you will be stacking them. Place 2 inches apart on a baking sheet and bake 15 minutes, until golden. Let cool. When cool, split these pastries into 2 layers. Reserve the best halves of the baked puffed pastry for the top, since they will be most visible. All steps of recipe may be made ahead and assembled before serving. In a nonstick pan, heat ⅓ cup sugar, swirling the pan over moderate heat until sugar is a caramel color. Remove from heat and stir in almonds and pour into a lightly greased saucepan. This will be like a hard candy after it cools. When cool, chop in blender to make a powdery mixture. In medium bowl, whisk together the yolks with the pinch of salt, cornstarch and the rind. Set aside. In another saucepan, scald the milk with ⅔ cup sugar. Add scalded milk and sugar mixture to yolks and cornstarch mixture, whisking continually. Return mixture back to saucepan and heat to boil, whisking constantly 2 minutes. Mixture will become consistency of pudding. Pour into bowl and stir in GRAND MARNIER®. Refrigerate until ready to use. Whip 2 cups heavy cream to form soft peaks and fold ½ of whipped cream into the GRAND MARNIER® pastry cream. The additional whipped cream will be used for garnish. Keep refrigerated. To assemble, just before serving spread pastry with pastry cream, sliced strawberries, and sprinkle with caramelized sugar. Top with another pastry and repeat. Take reserved piece of puff pastry and spread pastry cream underneath, so that it will adhere to the

GRAND MARNIER® *Strawberry Napoleons continued*

last layer. Sprinkle with sifted powdered sugar and decorate the top of the Napoleon with piped whipped cream, mint leaves and a thin orange slice. Serve immediately.

To make this a child friendly dessert, use a 3½ ounce package of instant vanilla pudding mix but mix it with only 1 cup milk. Fold in 1½ cups of whipped cream and layer in the same way as recipe indicates. You may use any 3 inch diameter pastry cutter if you would like a specific puffed pastry shape for a special occasion, such as a star for Fourth of July or flower for a spring luncheon. For a Fourth of July celebration add blueberries for a red, white and blue presentation.

cheese grater or zester
blender
whisk
sifter for powdered sugar
pastry bag

"The discovery of a new dish does more for the happiness of mankind than a discovery of a new star."

Brillat-Savarin

Fresh Fruit Tarts with
GRAND MARNIER® Cream

Serves: 6

Fruit Tarts
1 **(15 ounce) package refrigerated pie crusts**
1 **cup fresh raspberries**
1 **cup fresh blackberries**
1 **cup fresh strawberries**
2 **kiwis, peeled and sliced**
1 **tablespoon sugar**

GRAND MARNIER® Cream
5 **egg yolks at room temperature**
¾ **cup sugar**
¼ **cup GRAND MARNIER®**
1 **cup heavy cream**
1 **tablespoon sugar**

Unfold each pie crust and roll out on a lightly floured surface into a 9 x 13 inch circle. Place 6 custard cups upside down on a cookie sheet and lightly grease bottoms and sides of cups. Cut out and drape a pastry circle over each cup, pinch dough to make pleats. Form pastry around each cup. Prick the bottom and sides with a fork. Bake at 425 degrees for 10 minutes until lightly brown. Carefully remove pastry cups, and turn right side up to cool. Two hours before serving, combine fruit and sugar. GRAND MARNIER® Cream can be made a day or two ahead and refrigerated. Beat egg yolks with a hand mixer in the top of a double boiler. Beat in ¾ cup sugar and place over simmering water, stirring until thickened, 20 minutes. Remove from heat and beat until smooth. Add GRAND MARNIER® and refrigerate until chilled. In a separate bowl, whip cream until it starts to thicken and add one tablespoon sugar. Continue to beat until cream is medium thick but will still pour. Fold into egg sauce and pour into serving dish. Chill until serving time. Spoon berries into tartlets and put a dollop of sauce on top. Serve immediately.

6 glass custard cups
hand mixer
double boiler

Chocolate Mango Parfaits

Serves: 8

2 **ripe mangoes**
2 **limes**
1 **pint heavy cream**
1 **dark Swiss chocolate candy
   bar**
1 **(2½ ounce) package
   pirouline cookies**
   Fresh mint
   **Granulated or powdered
   sugar, to taste**
1 **teaspoon vanilla**

Chill serving glasses (i.e., martini glasses or other stemmed glasses or dishes) in freezer for one hour before assembling. Whip the cream and add 1 to 2 teaspoons sugar or sweeten to taste. Add the vanilla. Zest the limes, green part only. Grate or shave the chocolate. Peel the mangoes and remove pit. Cut into chunks and puree in blender. Refrigerate to keep cold. In chilled dish, layer crumbled cookies, a 2 inch layer of pureed mangoes, whipped cream, another layer of mangoes and whipped cream. Cover top with chocolate shavings. Sprinkle top with lime zest.

Pirouline cookies are chocolate flavor lined wafer rolls that are sold at grocery stores with the specialty crackers and cookies and some office supply stores. Other cookies can be substituted.

hand mixer
blender or food processor
cheese grater or zester

Susan Bee: Rockwall, Texas

Kathleen Wincorn's daughter, Stacy, discovered this dessert while studying abroad. Stacy served it when the Bees and the Wincorns visited the host family. Susan brought the recipe back from Switzerland and shared it with me. It is easy and festive!

Fruit Torte

Serves: 8

Fruit Torte
1   (18 ounce) package
     refrigerated sugar cookie
     dough
1   (8 ounce) package cream
     cheese, softened
4½ ounces Cool Whip®
     whipped topping, thawed
1   pint strawberries, cut in half
     (save a few whole with
     leaves for garnish)
2   large bananas, sliced and
     dipped in lemon juice
8   ounces sliced peaches or
     small can mandarin
     oranges
4   ounces pineapple chunks
2   kiwis, sliced

Fruit Glaze
½   cup sugar
2   tablespoons cornstarch
     Dash salt
2   teaspoons lemon juice
½   cup fresh orange juice
½   teaspoon grated orange
     peel

Thaw cookie dough. Roll out into round pizza pan ¼ inch from the edges. Bake 10 to 15 minutes at 350 degrees until edges are slightly brown. Cool dough. Mix cream cheese and Cool Whip® with a mixer. Spread this over cookie dough. Arrange fruit symmetrically starting at the center with 2 to 3 whole strawberries, pineapple chunks, peaches, orange segments, bananas, kiwi and strawberries cut in ½. Use fruit of your choice. Vary the colors that sit next to each other. Blackberries and raspberries combined with kiwi slices and strawberries make an elegant tart. Line outside of pastry with sliced strawberries, then kiwi (3 kiwi instead of 2) and gently mix the blackberries and raspberries together for the center portion (1 cup of each). Make Fruit Glaze. Combine sugar, cornstarch and salt. Gradually add orange juice and lemon juice. Cook over medium heat. Boil one minute. Remove from heat and stir in orange peel. Cool and spoon sauce over pizza. Refrigerate until ready to serve.

zester or cheese grater
hand mixer
vegetable peeler for kiwi
pizza pan or other tart pan or
springform

Fruit Torte *continued*

This fruit tart can be as sophisticated as you like. If all of your desserts are round make this one in another shape. I used a 14 x 4 inch fluted tart pan with a removable bottom and also substituted 8 ounces mascarpone cheese mixed with ⅓ cup well chilled heavy cream and ¼ cup sugar in place of the Cool Whip® and cream cheese mixture. Do not beat mascarpone too long or it will turn to butter. Only ½ of the cookie dough is needed. I used strawberries, peaches and blueberries and glazed with the orange glaze, substituting ½ of the orange juice with cranberry juice. It had a slightly pink hue and was also very good. Puffed pastry sheets can also be used instead of cookie dough for a base that is not as sweet.

Mary Pat Johnston,
Overland Park, Kansas

Mary Pat has a busy schedule, but still manages to entertain family and friends. She is known for her creative and special table settings and makes it fun and entertaining for the children. Mary Pat likes this dessert because it has a colorful presentation and is easy.

Apple Cranberry Crumb Tart

Serves: 8

Dough

1	**stick unsalted butter**
¼	**cup plus 1 tablespoon sugar**
1	**egg yolk**
1⅔	**cups cake flour, sifted**

Filling

1½	**cups Granny Smith apples**
1	**cup fresh cranberries, rinsed and picked over**
2	**tablespoons plus 2 teaspoons all-purpose flour**
⅔	**cup granulated sugar**
½	**teaspoon cinnamon**

Topping

1	**cup rolled oats**
¾	**cup all-purpose flour**
⅔	**cup light brown sugar**
6	**tablespoons unsalted butter, melted**

Cream the stick of butter and sugar together on medium speed until light and fluffy. Beat in the egg yolk. On low speed, mix in the flour until dough just comes together. Turn out on lightly floured surface and knead 3 to 4 times to form a smooth ball. Pat the dough into a 6 inch disk. Press the dough evenly into the bottom and up the sides of a 9 to 10 inch springform pan or 11 x 1 inch fluted tart pan with a removable bottom. Prick dough with a fork and refrigerate one hour. Preheat oven to 375 degrees. Place the shell on a baking sheet and bake 10 to 15 minutes until it just starts to color. Remove from oven. Peel, quarter and core the apples. Slice apples ¼ inch thick and toss with remaining filling ingredients. Mound the filling in the crust. Combine the oats, brown sugar and flour. Pour the melted butter over these ingredients and crumble the mixture with your fingers. Bake the tart about 40 minutes until topping is golden, filling is bubbly and apples are tender when pierced. If apples are not tender and topping is browning, cover with foil and cook a few minutes longer. Let cool slightly before serving.

hand mixer
vegetable peeler
springform pan or fluted tart pan with removable bottom

Twila Baker: Dallas, Texas

Twila and I met the first week of college and now both live the in Dallas area. She is a member of the "Original Dinner Club" and the "Girl's Dinner Club." She gave me this recipe to make when she had a theme dinner at her house. It was a ski party and we dressed in ski clothes. The sweet tangy combination of cranberries and apples with the crumbly topping is perfect for a cozy winter gathering.

Cake flour is 27 times finer than all-purpose flour.

Butterscotch Apple Crisp

Serves: 12

Filling
8 cups peeled tart apples
1 tablespoon lemon juice
1 cup sugar
½ cup flour
2 teaspoons cinnamon
⅛ teaspoon salt

Topping
**1 (11 ounce) package
   butterscotch chips**
½ cup butter
1½ cups flour
¼ teaspoon salt
¼ teaspoon mace

Preheat oven to 375 degrees. Measure out dry ingredients for topping and filling before peeling and slicing the apples. Peel and slice apples and toss with the lemon juice. Add dry filling ingredients and toss. Grease a 9 x 13 inch pan with butter and spread apples over the bottom and bake for 20 minutes. While apple filling is baking, melt the butterscotch chips and butter in a double boiler over hot water until smooth. Add the dry topping ingredients with a fork so mixture becomes crumbly. Crumble topping over the hot apple mixture and bake an additional 25 minutes. Serve with vanilla ice cream.

vegetable peeler
double boiler

For cooking and baking, it is best to use apples that remain flavorful and firm, such as Baldwin, Cortland, Northern Spy, Rome Beauty, Winesap or York Imperial. The Granny Smith apple has a green skin that covers a sweetly tart flesh that's excellent for both eating and cooking. Mace is a spice that is a pungent version of nutmeg.

"Friends. . .they cherish each other's hopes
They are kind to each other's dreams."

Thoreau

Sour Cream Apple Pie

Serves: 8

1   egg, beaten
1½ cups sugar
1   cup sour cream
½   teaspoon cinnamon
4   tablespoons flour
      (divided use)
4   cups peeled tart apples
      (Granny Smith and
      McIntosh combination)
½   cup brown sugar
1   tablespoon butter
1   refrigerated pie crust

Combine the egg, sugar, sour cream, cinnamon, 3 tablespoons flour and the apples. Press pie crust into pan according to package directions. Pour mixture into the unbaked shell. Mix the remaining tablespoon flour, brown sugar and butter. Sprinkle over apple mixture and bake at 350 degrees for one hour.

You may also make this as a pie with a top and a bottom crust.

 vegetable peeler

Easy Cherry Pecan Crisp

Serves: 8

2   (20 ounce) cans cherry pie
      filling
½   teaspoon almond extract
¼   cup warm water
1   (1 pound 2.25 ounce) box
      white cake mix
½   cup melted butter
1   (8 ounce) package pecan
      pieces
⅛   cup warm water

Mix pie filling, almond extract and ¼ cup water. Spread in 9 x 13 inch pan. In a separate bowl mix cake mix, butter and pecan pieces and ⅛ cup water. Drop this mixture by teaspoonfuls or with fingers on top of fruit mixture until it is completely covered. Bake 40 minutes in a 350 degree oven.

Any flavor canned pie filling can be used. This is a wonderful quick dessert. Serve with vanilla ice cream.

Easy Peach Cobbler

Serves: 8

1 **(15 ounce) package refrigerated pie crusts**
1 **(29 ounce) can peaches with juice**
1 **(21 ounce) can peach pie filling**
1 **cup sugar**
1 **tablespoon ground cinnamon**
¼ **cup butter, softened**

Place one crust on the bottom of 8 or 9 inch square pan, following package directions. Press dough around edges. Combine the peaches, sugar, cinnamon and butter. Pour over crust. Top mixture with the other crust and seal the two crust edges together. Bake at 350 degrees for 25 to 35 minutes or until top of cobbler is golden. Put foil around the edges to protect them from getting too brown. Place a jelly-roll pan on the lower shelf to catch any drippings. Serve with vanilla ice cream.

 8 or 9 inch square pan
jelly-roll pan

Melissa Brown: DeSoto, Texas

Melissa and I worked together and she gave me this tasty recipe. It is as easy as 1,2,3!

Bananas Foster

Serves: 8

12 **tablespoons unsalted butter**
1½ **cups dark brown sugar**
1½ **teaspoons cinnamon**
6 **very ripe bananas, halved lengthwise, then quartered**
2 **ounces banana liqueur**
1 **cup dark rum, warmed**
1 **gallon vanilla ice cream**

In a skillet melt butter, sugar and cinnamon together until sugar dissolves. Add bananas and liqueur. Cook to coat, stirring gently. Add rum. Spoon over vanilla ice cream. Ice cream melts quickly due to warm topping, so work quickly. It is best to give guests spoons to eat this dessert.

Homemade Vanilla Ice Cream

Makes: 1 gallon

4   **eggs**
2   **cups sugar**
1½ **cups heavy cream**
4   **tablespoons vanilla**
¼   **teaspoon salt**
     Whole milk to fill line
     Ice and salt according to your ice cream freezer's directions

Beat eggs until light with hand mixer. Add sugar, cream, vanilla and salt. Stir to dissolve sugar. Pour in freezer. Whole milk is then used to fill to the ice cream freezer's fill line. Freeze according to directions. If your freezer is ½ gallon, cut this recipe in half.

hand mixer
ice cream freezer

Esther Rowley:
Overland Park, Kansas

Esther is my friend Kathryn's mother and she made this rich ice cream in the summertime, so it brings back many memories. Kathryn and I roomed together at Kansas State and to relieve our stress, we would walk to the Dairy Science building to get scoops of homemade ice cream.

Pecan Crusted Ice Cream Pie with Caramel Sauce

Serves: 8

Crust
I	**egg white, whipped**
¼	**cup sugar**
1½	**cups finely chopped pecans**

Filling
I	**pint coffee ice cream**
I	**pint French vanilla ice cream**

Caramel Sauce
⅔	**cup dark brown sugar**
¼	**cup evaporated milk**
I	**egg yolk, beaten**
⅓	**cup corn syrup**
¼	**cup butter**
½	**teaspoon vanilla extract**

Fold together the crust ingredients and press into greased 9 inch pie plate. Bake 12 minutes at 400 degrees. Chill. Spread one pint of coffee ice cream on the bottom and one pint of vanilla ice cream on top. Freeze. Make caramel sauce. In a small saucepan, mix together and heat the sauce ingredients, stirring until smooth. This sauce can be refrigerated and reheated when you are ready to serve pie. Both the pie and the sauce can be made several days ahead.

The crust is a great basic recipe so use your imagination for other combinations of ice cream and sauce. The pairing of coffee, vanilla and caramel is still my favorite. You may add ½ cup coarsely chopped pecans to the sauce. The sauce makes a great gift as an ice cream topping.

nut chopper or blender to chop nuts

Coleen Rossi: Scottsdale, Arizona

Coleen and I have known each other since the days of our parent's elaborate dinner parties. This wonderful recipe came from her mother. This is the dessert I remember sampling before the adults even sat down to eat. It is still my favorite.

Tumbleweed Ice Cream Pie

Serves: 8

Crust
**32 chocolate sandwich cookies
    with filling**
⅓ cup melted butter

Filling
**1 gallon good quality vanilla
    ice cream**
2 ounces Frangelico
2 ounces KAHLÚA®

Caramel Sauce
⅔ cup dark brown sugar
¼ cup evaporated milk
1 egg yolk, beaten
⅓ cup corn syrup
¼ cup butter
½ teaspoon vanilla extract

Crush cookies a few at a time in a blender or food processor and pour in bowl. Mix the butter in with the crushed cookies. Press into pie plate. Mix together ice cream and liqueurs. Pour into crust. Freeze. This must be made at least 24 hours ahead in order to harden. It is not necessary to thaw before serving. Make Caramel Sauce in a small saucepan. Mix together the sauce ingredients over low heat and stir until smooth.

Chocolate Sauce, (p. 285), may be substituted for the Caramel Sauce. The pecan crust from the Pecan Crusted Ice Cream Pie is good with this filling too. Liqueurs can be substituted to suit your taste.

blender or food processor

> "Yesterday is history,
> tomorrow is a mystery
> and today is a gift, that is
> why we call it the present."
>
> Brian Dyson

Almond Lace Cookie Ice Cream Torte with Chocolate Sauce

Serves: 12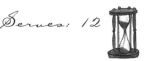

Almond Lace Cookies

⅔ **cup finely chopped blanched almonds**
½ **cup sugar**
1 **tablespoon flour**
½ **cup butter**
2 **tablespoons half-and-half**
¾ **gallon vanilla ice cream**

Chocolate Sauce

½ **cup butter**
4 **squares unsweetened chocolate**
1½ **cups sugar**
½ **cup cocoa**
1 **cup half-and-half**
   Pinch salt
1 **teaspoon vanilla**

Place chopped almonds, sugar, flour, butter, and half-and-half in a saucepan and bring slowly to a boil, stirring constantly. Drop by teaspoonfuls on a foil covered cookie sheet. (They spread and will run together.) Bake 6 to 8 minutes at 375 degrees. They should be golden, so watch carefully. When they are cool they will be easy to remove from the foil. In a 9 x 13 inch pan place a layer of cookies, layer of ice cream and repeat ending with cookies. Cover and place in freezer. For Chocolate Sauce, melt butter and chocolate. Mix together the sugar and cocoa. Add sugar mixture, half-and-half and salt. Bring to boiling, stirring constantly. Add vanilla. Cut ice cream torte into squares and top with Chocolate Sauce. Entire dessert can be made several days ahead. Keep sauce refrigerated until ready to use.

Baklava

Baklava

3	**sticks butter (1½ cups)**
½	**cup vegetable oil**
1	**pound phyllo pastry**
4	**cups shelled pistachio nuts, chopped in blender**

Syrup

1½	**cups sugar**
¾	**cup water**
1	**tablespoon lemon**
1	**tablespoon honey**
1	**tablespoon rose water**

Cut the butter into small pieces. Clarify butter. (Melt butter at a low heat, skimming foam off the top as it melts.) Let rest 2 minutes. Pour butter into another pan leaving solids behind. This will be your clarified butter that you will work with for making Baklava. Add oil to this. Using a pastry brush, grease the bottom of a 9 x 13 inch pan. When working with phyllo (filo) you need to keep it moist. Take a clean dishtowel and wet it and ring it out so it is just damp and cover the dough while working with it, otherwise it will crumble. Fold a sheet of dough in half crosswise, lift it gently and put into prepared pan and unfold. Press the pastry flat, press down the excess around the sides and flatten it against the bottom. Brush entire surface with the butter and oil mixture and repeat. Sprinkle with 3 to 4 tablespoons of the chopped pistachios. Repeat with another sheet in the same fashion. Sprinkle with 3 to 4 tablespoons of the pistachios. Repeat with 2 sheets buttered phyllo and 3 to 4 tablespoons pistachios. Repeat until you have only 2 sheets of phyllo left. Put the last two sheets on top and brush with the remaining butter and oil mixture. With a sharp knife score the top of the pastry with diagonal lines ½ inch deep and 2 inches apart both lengthwise and widthwise then cross them diagonally to make diamond shapes. Bake in the middle of a 350 degree oven for 30 minutes. Reduce oven to 300 degrees and bake 45 minutes longer until top is crisp and golden. Make the syrup while this is baking. Combine the sugar, water and lemon juice in a small saucepan, stirring constantly. Cook over moderate heat until the sugar dissolves. Increase the heat to high and cook 5 minutes, uncovered. Mixture should be thick enough to coat the back of a spoon.

Baklava *continued*

Remove from heat and stir in honey and rose water. Let cool. Pour over Baklava as it is removed from the oven. Cool and cut into diamond shaped pieces with a sharp knife.

Rosewater has been a popular seasoning for centuries in the cuisines of the Middle East. You can find it in gourmet stores.

You may substitute walnuts or pecans for pistachios. Orange blossom water may be substituted for rose water in this recipe. For a party you may serve the triangle of Baklava with a small scoop of vanilla ice cream and fresh berries. You may also top the entire surface with a layer of vanilla ice cream and freeze. To serve, cut it into squares or other desired shape.

pastry brush
blender or nut chopper

Sami El-Beheri:
Colorado Springs, Colorado

This was a big hit at a Greek dinner club we had. I also won a bake-off at work with this recipe. It looks more difficult than it is so don't be intimidated. Twila's father, Sami, gave me this recipe.

Pecan Lace Tacos with Margarita Mousse Filling

Serves: 4

Mousse

1	teaspoon unflavored gelatin
2	tablespoons tequila
2	tablespoons **GRAND MARNIER®**
2	teaspoons grated lime rind
¼	cup fresh lime juice
1	drop green food coloring (to make mousse pale green)
1½	cups whipping cream
¾	cup sugar
	Grated lime rind (do not grate until ready to use or it will dry up and turn brown)

Pecan Lace Shells

2	tablespoons firmly packed brown sugar
2	tablespoons butter, melted
2	tablespoons light corn syrup
¼	cup flour
¼	cup finely chopped pecans
¾	teaspoon vanilla extract

Make the pecan shells first. To make pecan lace shells, cook first 3 ingredients in a saucepan over high heat, stirring constantly until mixture boils. Remove from heat. Add flour, chopped pecans and vanilla, stirring until well blended. Drop batter by level teaspoons on well-greased cookie sheet, spacing 3 inches apart. Do not bake more than 3 at one time. Bake at 350 degrees for 8 minutes or until golden brown. Cool one minute. When you remove the shell from cookie sheet after one minute, drape over greased handle of a wooden spoon so it takes the shape of a taco shell. Two should fit on the end of the wooden spoon handle. Repeat with remaining batter. The shells can be made one week ahead and stored in an airtight container. The mousse can be prepared 24 hours before serving. To make mousse, sprinkle gelatin over tequila and GRAND MARNIER® in small saucepan and let stand one minute. Cook over low heat, stirring until gelatin dissolves. Stir in lime rind, lime juice and food coloring, if desired. Cool. Beat whipping cream until foamy, gradually add sugar and gelatin mixture, beating until soft peaks form. Cover and chill. Pipe into Pecan Lace Shells. Sprinkle with grated lime peel for additional color. I kept this recipe in my file for years before trying. This is a fun dessert especially if the meal is not overly complicated.

Approximately 2 shells will fit on one wooden spoon. You will need to make 2 shells for each guest. Grease the handles of the wooden spoons so shells are easily removed once hard and cool. You may need 4 cans of same height for cooling the hardening

Pecan Lace Tacos continued

shells. Suspend the wooden spoon between the two cans while they are hardening. Garnish dessert plates with mango and kiwi slices.

2 wooden spoons
pastry tube
cheese grater or zester
hand mixer

KAHLÚA® Bars

Serves: 16

8 **tablespoons butter, softened**
1 **(16 ounce) box dark brown sugar**
2 **eggs**
1¼ **cups flour**
2 **teaspoons baking powder**
1 **teaspoon salt**
3 **tablespoons KAHLÚA®**
1 **teaspoon vanilla**
1 **cup chopped pecans or walnuts**

Preheat oven to 350 degrees. Butter an 11¼ x 7½ x 1½ inch pan. Cream butter and sugar until fluffy and add remainder of ingredients. Stir together. Batter will be stiff. Pour into prepared pan and bake 30 minutes or until tester comes out clean. Cool before slicing. This is an elegant dessert when topped with vanilla ice cream, drizzled with KAHLÚA® or chocolate sauce and garnished with chocolate leaves.

Dress up simple desserts with Chocolate Leaves. Mix 8 ounces bittersweet chocolate with 1½ teaspoons shortening. Melt in double broiler. Paint the underside of a camellia, ivy or gardenia leaf. Lay natural leaf side down on pan and put in refrigerator or freezer to harden. Peel leaf away and use as garnish.

hand mixer
11¼ x 7½ x 1½ inch pan

Tiramisu

Serves: 6

1   cup brewed expresso, cooled
2   tablespoons brandy
18 hard Italian ladyfingers
3   eggs, separated
3   tablespoons fine sugar
½   pound mascarpone cheese
½   cup good quality bittersweet chocolate, finely grated
    Fresh raspberries
6   mint leaves

Combine expresso and the brandy. Lay ½ of the ladyfingers in the bottom of a 3 quart serving dish. Using a pastry brush, brush expresso mixture over each ladyfinger. In a mixing bowl, beat the egg yolks with the sugar until fluffy. In another bowl, beat egg whites until they are stiff, fold in the mascarpone cheese. Gently combine the two egg mixtures. Cover the ladyfingers with half the egg mixture and sprinkle them with half the chocolate. Top with the remaining ladyfingers that have been soaked with expresso mixture. Add another layer of egg mixture. Sprinkle with the remaining chocolate. Cover and refrigerate one hour before serving.

To serve, spoon Tiramisu into footed goblets or put 2 scoops onto a plate and garnish with 3 raspberries in the middle and a sprig of mint.

pastry brush
hand mixer
cheese grater

Mascarpone is a buttery-rich double to triple cream cheese made from cow's milk. Mascarpone can be found in the specialty cheese section of the grocery store and is sometimes packaged in an 8 ounce plastic container.

Coconut Cherry Bars

Makes: 48 bars

Crust
2 cups flour
1 cup softened butter
**6 tablespoons powdered
   sugar**

Filling
4 eggs
2 cups sugar
½ cup flour
2 teaspoons vanilla
1 teaspoon baking powder
½ teaspoon salt
1½ cups chopped pecans
1 cup flaked coconut
**1 cup chopped maraschino
   cherries, drained**

Mix crust ingredients together. Press into greased 9 x 13 inch pan. Bake 10 minutes in preheated 350 degree oven. Beat eggs and stir in next seven ingredients. Spread over baked layer. Sprinkle cherries on top. Bake an additional 30 to 40 minutes or until the center is set. Cool. Cut into 2 x 1 inch bars.

If you cut in half, you may use 8 x 8 x 2 inch pan.

Lynn Holcomb,
Huntersville, North Carolina

Lynn and I worked together years ago and she brought this decadent dessert to work. They taste like a pecan pie cookie with chewy coconut and cherries. Superb!

Buttermilk Brownies with Buttermilk Icing

Serves: 12

Brownies
I	**stick butter**
I	**cup water**
¼	**cup cocoa**
½	**cup oil**
2	**cups flour**
2	**cups sugar**
½	**teaspoon salt**
½	**cup buttermilk**
2	**eggs, beaten**
I	**teaspoon baking soda**
I	**teaspoon vanilla**

Frosting
I	**stick butter**
¼	**cup cocoa**
⅓	**cup buttermilk**
I	**(16 ounce) box powdered sugar**
I	**cup chopped pecans**
I	**teaspoon vanilla**
	Dash salt

Combine butter, water, cocoa and vegetable oil in a medium saucepan. Bring to boil and pour over mixture of flour, sugar and salt. Add buttermilk, beaten eggs, soda and vanilla. Bake at 400 degrees for 20 minutes in a greased and floured jelly-roll pan. For Frosting, combine butter, cocoa and buttermilk in pan. Bring to boil and add powdered sugar, nuts, vanilla and salt. Spread over brownies while warm.

jelly-roll pan

"I've taken my fun where I've found it."

Rudyard Kipling

Peanut Butter Crispy Rice Cookies

Makes: 12

1   **cup sugar**
1   **cup corn syrup**
1   **cup peanut butter**
6   **cups crispy rice cereal**
1   **(6 ounce) package semisweet chocolate chips**
6   **ounces butterscotch chips**

In a saucepan heat the sugar, corn syrup and peanut butter until melted together. Bring to boil but only for a short time so the peanut butter mixes with the corn syrup. If you cook too long it will reach a candy state and cookies will be difficult to bite into. Remove from heat and pour over 6 cups crispy rice cereal. Press into lightly buttered 9 x 13 inch glass pan. Melt chocolate chips and butterscotch chips together in double boiler. Spread the chocolate and butterscotch mixture over cereal and refrigerate until top hardens. Remove from refrigerator 10 minutes before cutting. Cut into squares when ready to serve. I prefer to serve these at room temperature once top is hardened.

double boiler

Marla Payne, Coppell, Texas

I have collected quite a few recipes from Marla over the years. This recipe is from one of the first invitations to her house. She made these and I ate more than a first time guest should! They can be addicting to those of us with a sweet tooth!

If you spray your measuring cup with nonstick cooking spray, sticky ingredients like corn syrup will slide right out.

Chewy Chocolate Bars

Serves: 16

1   (14 ounce) bag of caramels
    or 60 unwrapped light
    caramels
½   cup evaporated milk
1   German chocolate cake mix
¾   cup butter, melted
⅓   cup evaporated milk
1   cup chopped pecans
1   cup semisweet chocolate
    chips

Preheat oven to 350 degrees. Grease and flour 9 x 13 inch pan. In a double boiler melt the unwrapped caramels and the evaporated milk over low heat, stirring constantly. In a large bowl mix together cake mix with the melted butter, ⅓ cup evaporated milk and nuts, mix by hand. Press half the dough in pan. Bake for 8 minutes. Sprinkle chocolate chips over baked dough. Spread caramel over chips. Crumble remaining dough over caramels and return to oven for 18 to 20 minutes. Cool before cutting.

There are easy to unwrap caramels called classic caramels and also classic caramels with chocolate filling that work nicely for this recipe.

Kids love these if you leave out the nuts.

 double boiler

Jody Amerter
Kansas City, Kansas

In 1978 Jody gave me my first recipe holder. It seemed so difficult to fill up at the time. Her oldest daughter Susie and I wrote out some of Susie's favorite recipes from Jody's collection. This recipe is still on the original card that matches the book and continues to be a favorite.

When a recipe using a cake mix requires you to flour the pan, use a bit of the cake mix instead.

Mini Pecan Pie Cookies

Makes: 24

4½ ounces cream cheese
¾ cup butter, melted
2¼ cups flour
2 eggs
1½ cups brown sugar
Pinch salt
2 tablespoons melted butter
¼ teaspoon vanilla
1 cup chopped pecans
Cooking spray

Make a dough of the cream cheese, butter and flour. Roll into balls. Spray mini muffin tins with oil and press a dough ball into each individual muffin tin, forming mini pie crusts. In a separate bowl, stir eggs with a fork but do not beat. Add sugar, salt, butter, vanilla and pecans. Fill shells ¾ full. Bake at 350 degrees for 25 to 30 minutes.

mini muffin tins

Sift powdered sugar lightly over the cooled Mini Pecan Pie Cookies for a special touch. A few semi-sweet chocolate chips in the bottom of each shell before pouring batter into shell makes this a cookie for chocolate lovers. This dough can be the base for other fillings as well.

Chewy Oatmeal Cookies

Makes: 2 dozen

1 cup brown sugar
1 cup white sugar
1 cup vegetable oil
2 eggs
2 teaspoons vanilla
3½ cups oatmeal
1 cup coconut
½ teaspoon salt
1 teaspoon baking soda
1 cup flour

Mix the first 3 ingredients together. Add eggs and vanilla. Mix in the oatmeal and coconut. Add salt, soda and flour to batter. Drop by teaspoonfuls onto ungreased baking sheet. Bake approximately 10 minutes at 350 degrees.

Amy Carro: Wichita, Kansas

I met Amy at Kansas State through her sorority sister Mary Pat Sasenick (now Johnston). We ran into one another at an alumni function in Dallas and decided to live together. Amy made these cookies regularly and I would eat the batter by the spoonful, therefore the yield is approximate. This is one of my favorite cookie recipes because of the chewy texture and rich flavor.

Mexican Wedding Cookies

Makes: 3 dozen

3 cups sifted flour
1½ teaspoons baking powder
½ teaspoon salt
½ pound lard (do not substitute)
1 cup sugar, divided use
½ teaspoon chopped anise seeds (chop in blender or chopper)
1 egg
2 tablespoons Frangelico, amaretto or brandy (may not need entire amount)
2 teaspoons cinnamon (to mix with the ¼ cup sugar for topping)
1 tablespoon water (if needed)

Preheat oven to 350 degrees. Sift flour, baking soda and salt. Cream lard with ¾ cup sugar. Add anise seed and beat at medium speed with mixer. Beat egg separately with blender and add to mixture. Add dry ingredients and just enough liqueur that batter is stiff. Water may or may not be needed. If batter does not stick together, add 1 tablespoon water. Knead slightly and pat into ¼ to ½ thickness. Cut into small shapes. I use a 1½ inch heart. Mix ¼ cup sugar with the 2 teaspoons cinnamon. Generously sprinkle cookies with cinnamon and sugar mixture. Bake approximately 9 minutes on ungreased cookie sheet.

blender
flour sifter
1½ inch cookie cutter
hand mixer

Baking powder goes flat fairly fast, so buy it in small tins.

Sylvia Muñoz: Garland, Texas

I used to buy 5 dozen for 5 dollars from my friend Sylvia when she brought these cookies back from her hometown of Edinburg, Texas. I had difficulty sharing these because I loved them so much and only got them a couple times a year. They are traditionally served at Hispanic weddings and are called by many different names, all meaning small pastry.

Mimi's Congo Cookies

Makes: 5 dozen

2 eggs
⅔ cup shortening
1 (16 ounce) box brown sugar
2¾ cups sifted flour
2½ teaspoons baking powder
½ teaspoon salt
1 cup chopped pecans
1 (12 ounce) package semisweet chocolate chips
¼ cup water

Mix together eggs, shortening and sugar with hand mixer. Add other ingredients and drop by teaspoonful on greased cookie sheet. Bake at 350 degrees until light brown, 10 to 12 minutes.

Spread into a greased jelly-roll pan or 9 inch square pan for bar cookies to save baking time. Bake 30 to 35 minutes until golden brown.

 hand mixer

Melissa Weikel, Topeka, Kansas

Melissa lived across from me in the dorm at Kansas State. She got this recipe from her grandmother, Mimi. She had never made these cookies because she thought they had a silly name. Now that Mimi has passed away, she makes them in her memory.

Chocolate chip cookies taste better when they are made with shortening rather than butter. A few drops of butter flavoring can be added or butter flavored shortening can be used. Cookies hold up better over several days and stay moist without tasting stale.

Crunchy Chocolate Peanut Cookies

Serves: 8

1 (12 ounce) package
  semisweet chocolate
  chips
1 (11 ounce) package
  butterscotch chips
1 (12 ounce) can shelled
  salted peanuts
2 (3 ounce) cans or
  1 (5 ounce) can chow
  mein noodles

Melt chocolate chips and butterscotch chips together over simmering water in a double boiler. Pour over nuts and noodles. Stir to coat. Drop by tablespoons on wax paper to harden.

 double boiler

Heather Gray:
Kansas City, Missouri

Heather and I have been friends since junior high and have always loved chocolate. We would buy candy by the piece from a specialty chocolate store when we went shopping together. She gave me this recipe years ago when I was making holiday cookies. These are easier than baking cookies when you want to take a treat to a friend.

Praline Grahams

Makes: 24

1   **inner package of a (16 ounce) box honey graham crackers**
3   **sticks butter**
2   **cups brown sugar**
¼   **teaspoon cream of tartar**
2   **cups coarsely chopped pecans**
¼   **teaspoon cinnamon (optional)**

Break the graham crackers into their natural rectangles and lay them out on a jelly-roll pan. Melt butter in medium size pan and add brown sugar and cream of tartar. Stir until mixture comes to boil. Add 2 cups coarsely chopped pecans and boil 3 minutes stirring frequently. Pour this mixture over the graham crackers and bake at 350 degrees for 10 to 12 minutes. Let cool and cut into bars following the outline of the graham crackers, keeping bars somewhat uniform in size. These are decadent! Serve with Homemade Vanilla Ice Cream for an extra special treat.

jelly-roll pan

Beth Martell
New York, New York

Beth and I have been friends since college and have been able to stay in touch since my career often took me to New York. Beth is a residential and commercial decorator and we have spent numerous hours over dinner discussing design details for the two homes she has helped me decorate. When I fly into the Big Apple, it is off to SoHo for shopping, but we always make plenty of stops for good food along the way!

Elizabeth's English Toffee

 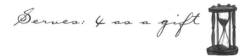

3½ sticks butter
2 cups sugar
1 teaspoon lecithin
1 tablespoon light corn syrup
¼ teaspoon salt
1 cup chopped pecans
1 pound chocolate summer
  coating

Melt butter over low heat in a 3 quart pan. Add the sugar and lecithin. Stir constantly with a wooden spoon over medium high heat until the mixture comes to boil. Add the corn syrup and continue to cook over medium heat, stirring constantly to prevent burning until temperature reaches 295 degrees. Remove from heat and add salt and nuts. Pour into a well buttered shallow pan or jelly-roll pan. Smooth out with a spatula. Let cool. Melt the chocolate and spread on cooled toffee. Additional ground nuts may be sprinkled on top. Break into irregular pieces.

Lecithin can be purchased at health food stores. Summer coating is not almond bark but comes in round disks. Stores that sell candy making supplies or hobby shops carry summer coating. Candy thermometers are sensitive. If you haven't used yours in a while, invest in a new one so the recipe turns out with the best results.

candy thermometer
wooden spoon
jelly-roll pan
spatula

Elizabeth Fast,
Kansas City, Missouri

Elizabeth, a family friend gave me this buttery, crunchy candy store toffee recipe. She suggests making it for an open house or to give the toffee as a holiday gift in a decorative tin. Elizabeth and her father, Albert, took a candy making class together over 20 years ago and have spent years perfecting this toffee. Elizabeth's mother, Janice, helps with clean up. The three of them have many fond memories of making toffee together over the last 20 years.

Wine Basics

One of the highlights of my career was working as a buyer in a gourmet food store, Caviar to Cabernet. The customers were friendly and interested in food and wine. My day consisted of helping with menu selections, wine pairings and offering entertaining ideas. Wine sales represented a large portion of the business, so it was necessary to taste many of the wines to recommend to the customers. This section covers wine basics and some reasonably priced wine recommendations.

Cooking with Wine

I recommend cooking with wines you enjoy that are moderately priced. An inexpensive Merlot can be used for red wine sauces unless a certain grape variety or region (i.e. Burgundy) is specified. A Sauvignon Blanc is a nice dry white wine for cooking; Sauternes is a nice sweet white wine that can be used in recipes. It is best to cook with a wine that you would drink with dinner and that complements the food with which it's paired. I do not recommend using cooking wines sold in grocery stores, because they contain salt and affect the recipe's flavor.

When dining out in a restaurant, you can expect to spend anywhere from 1½ to 3 times what you would pay at a wine merchant for a bottle of wine. Be sure the wine is the same year as the wine you ordered on the menu, otherwise you may find a difference in price when the bill arrives. Inhale the bouquet of the wine once poured in the glass. Swirl and taste the wine. Allow yourself two tastes before judging a wine. The cork is given to you not to smell, but so you may check it for moistness. The cork will tell you if the wine has been stored properly. If the cork is dried out, the wine may have been improperly stored. Air may have entered the wine bottle, causing oxidation, which may cause the wine to have an unpleasant flavor. This often happens when wines are served (by the glass) in a restaurant and they have been open several days. A "corked" wine smells strongly of mold, this is due to a bad cork, not poor winemaking. A wine that tastes more like a sherry or Madeira, may have been exposed to heat or poorly stored. In any of these cases, if the wine is unpleasant you should send it back.

White Wines

American Sauvignon Blanc

The Sauvignon Blanc grape produces crisp wines with fresh flavors. Certain styles taste slightly of herbs. Those aged in oak barrels resemble a Chardonnay. Robert Mondavi introduced Fumé Blanc, an oak-aged wine made with Sauvignon Blanc which has increased in domestic popularity. The Fumé Blanc is no different than a Sauvignon Blanc. Sauvignon Blanc is the second bestselling white wine, just behind Chardonnay. Sauvignon Blanc goes

well with appetizers, poultry, sautéed or grilled fish, oysters, veal, pasta and light cream or tomato based sauces. Acidic wines such as these are also recommended with salads that have vinegar or lemon in the dressing.

Recommendations:

Benziger	Markham	St. Supéry
Hogue	Murphy-Goode	Voss

American Chardonnay

The Chardonnay grape was for centuries the only grape used to make all French White Burgundy wines and is a primary source for champagne. Chardonnay was transplanted to American climates with great success. American Chardonnay ranges from light-bodied, delicate and crisp to full-bodied, rich and oakey. The light-bodied varieties are fruitier, sometimes tasting of melon or apple. Identify which type you prefer, and your wine merchant can then accommodate your taste. Chardonnay goes well with appetizers, spicy foods, salmon and shellfish when not served with a cream sauce. Smoked fish is excellent with an oak-aged Chardonnay. Buttery Chardonnay complements sauces made with butter.

Recommendations:

Ferrari-Carano	Clos Du Bois	Morgan
Flora Springs	Benziger	Markham
Joseph Phelps	Morro Bay	Château Ste. Michelle
		Geyser Peak

American Viognier

Viognier is a rare varietal that was brought to the Rhône Valley of France over 2000 years ago by either the Greeks or Romans. It was only planted in California in the late 1970's. In the 1990's plantings in California increased from 10 acres to 1,000 acres with 90% planted in the late 1990's. It is medium-bodied and known for its spice, floral, citrus, apple and peach flavors. Typically the younger the wine the better. This wine is great before dinner or with fish or chicken.

Recommendations:

Cline Cellars

Arrowwood

American Gewürztraminer

Gewürztraminer wines are golden in color with distinctly floral scents that vary from dry to very sweet. The grape is slightly pink and is similar to that of the Alsace region. When it is allowed to ripen late, it can take on a slight clove flavor and is often described as spicy. Gewürztraminer complements appetizers, turkey, salmon, slightly spicy foods and Asian food.

Recommendations:

Alderbrook	Fetzer
De Loach	Geyser Peak

American Pinot Blanc

This wine is often made with tart orchard fruit and can vary from a crisp acidic taste to an oak-aged flavor, and is similar to a Chardonnay. Grown most often in California, its roots lie in Burgundy where this variety was used as a less expensive alternative to Chardonnay. Most consider Pinot Blanc an all-purpose wine that can be served with appetizers, brunch or fish in a white sauce.

Recommendations:

Mirassou

Murphy Goode

Lockwood

Australian Chardonnay

Australia produces a huge volume of competitively priced, high quality Chardonnay. Many of their wines have more vibrant citrus flavors and less oak flavors. These wines proudly state "unwooded" on the label. Australian Chardonnay can easily be paired with poultry, ham, salmon and buttery pasta sauces.

Recommendations:

Penfolds

Yalumba

Seppelt

New Zealand: Sauvignon Blanc

Marlborough on the South Island of New Zealand has a region that lies southeast of the north coast on a wide flat area called the Wairau Plains. It is now the largest grape growing region in New Zealand and consists of 5,110 acres. This has only been achieved since 1973 when Montana, the largest wine group in the country, planted the vines. This area is the sunniest and driest part of the whole country and the conditions are suitable for white varieties including Müller-Thurgau, Sauvignon Blanc, Chardonnay and Riesling. Watch for these wines to become more popular. Appetizers, sautéed or grilled fish, veal, pasta and light cream or tomato sauces go well with these wines.

Recommendations:

Cloudy Bay

Allan Scott

Grove Mill

Bordeaux, France: White Bordeaux

These wines are a blend of Sauvignon Blanc and Sémillon in varying proportions. The wines are typically oak-aged and have a distinct toasted vanilla flavor. Serve with seafood and poultry dishes or enjoy them without a meal.

Recommendations:

Maitre d' Estournel	Verdillac
Marquis de Chasse	Château Bonnet
Mission St. Vincent	(entre deux mers)

Burgundy, France: Pouilly-Fuissé

Pouilly-Fuissé is a region located in southern Burgundy where they grow Chardonnay grapes exclusively. The soil is a key element to the creation of these wines that are rich, ripe and tinged with oak. These wines are moderately expensive, but those made by top wine producers are well worth the price. This wine goes well with scallops, whitefish (mild-flavored white fish, a member of the salmon family) and veal with a light cream sauce.

Recommendations:

Louis Latour

Antonin Rodet

St. Veran

Northern Italy: Pinot Grigio

Pinot Grigio is Italy's favorite white wine. It is crisp, refreshing and acidic. In America we have a similar wine called Pinot Gris which is grown in Oregon. These wines complement smoked salmon, spicy food and pasta with seafood.

Recommendations:

Alois Lageder

Zenato

Ecco Domani

Tuscany Italy: Vernaccia Di San Gimagnano

This white wine comes from vines surrounding the medieval city of San Gimagnano. It is a soft white wine with a crisp acidity. This is an affordable everyday table wine that can be purchased for less than $20. Most Italian whites are easy to drink and a good value. This wine is enjoyed with poultry, fish and pastas in a light cream or tomato sauce.

Recommendations:

Teruzzi & Puthod

Mormoraia

Red Wines

American Pinot Noir

Pinot Noir is grown in cooler climates. Oregon and cooler parts of California are known for this variety. There is a delicate balance between fruit and acidity and these wines are very food friendly. In a Pinot Noir that has not been aged long, there is often a plum or cherry flavor, but as they age the flavor leans toward spices, fig or chocolate. This wine is a nice complement to pork loin, salmon and veal.

Recommendations:

Carneros Creek	Sokol Blossor	Saintsburg
David Bruce	Bethel Heights	Testarossa

American Rhône Style Reds

American winemakers introduced the less popular Syrah and Mourvèdre grape varieties to the United States. These grapes make a full-bodied and flavorful wine while the Grenache is a lighter wine. California also has a Petite Syrah that continues to remain a good value with its rich and tannic characteristics. All of these varieties fall within the Rhône style red wines. They are good with poultry in a light sauce or with cheese.

Recommendations:

Bonny Doon Blends	David Bruce: Petite Sirah	Guenoc: Petite Sirah
Joseph Phelps: Blend; Syrah	Carignane; Syrah	Zaca Mesa: Cuvée Z, Syrah
Swanson: Syrah	Fess Parker: Syrah	

American Merlot

Merlot and Cabernet Sauvignon are the two most popular grapes planted in Bordeaux. Merlot was often blended with Cabernet to add fruit and softness to the Cabernet. California wine makers began experimenting with the Merlot on its own and it quickly became America's red wine of choice. These are usually medium to dark red and have predominant flavors of currants and cherries. They are not as tannic as Cabernets and do not have the long range aging potential of Cabernets. Merlot is paired well with lamb and grilled duck.

Recommendations:

Kunde	Ferrari-Carano	Merryvale
Rombauer	Columbia Crest	Shafer
Newton	Markham	Shafer
		Swanson

American Cabernet Sauvignon

The Cabernet Sauvignon grape is originally from Bordeaux and is a chief ingredient in California and Washington red wines. It is full-bodied, deeply colored and aged in oak. The Cabernet Sauvignon improves with age because of the heavy tannins that give the wine its longevity and dryness. This flavor comes from the skin, pit, and stems of the grapes as well as the French oak barrels. For this reason, Cabernet Sauvignon complements lamb, duck, beef and game.

Recommendations:

Arrowood	Joseph Phelps: Bachus	Shafer
Flora Springs	Ridge	Markham

American Red Zinfandel

This red grape was brought to the United States from Italy. This grape produces a wine with a spicy, yet fruity flavor that can rival a Cabernet Sauvignon. A great wine for steaks and kabobs.

Recommendations:

Storybook	Ravenswood	Ridge
Kenwood	Rabbit Ridge	

Australian Shiraz

Shiraz has been a widely planted red grape since cuttings were brought from France's Rhône Valley Syrah vines. The vines date back to the nineteenth century and produce a slightly spicy wine similar to those France produces in Rhône. Americans have since discovered the quality of Australian reds, which has driven the price up. Larger producers will have more reasonable prices on Shiraz. The Shiraz grape is wonderful with barbecue and spiced chicken.

Recommendations:

Penfolds: Grange	Penfolds	McGuigan Bros.
Rosemount: Balmoral	Lindemans	Tyrell's
St. Hallet	Kingston	Peter Lehmann

Australian Cabernet Sauvignon and Merlot

Cabernets in Australia gained popularity by blending with Shiraz, known as the Syrah grape in France. In more recent years it has gone back to the traditional pairing with Merlot. The finer quality Bordeaux styled wines come from a cooler climate and are rich and fruity in character. These wines have a higher alcohol content than their American counterparts. Serve with duck, lamb or beef.

Recommendations:

Henschke	Rosemount
Penfolds: All Bin Numbers	Yalumba

Spain: Rioja

Forty percent of all exported wine coming from Spain to the United States is from Rioja. Winemaking in this region dates back to the Romans. Tempranillo is Rioja's primary grape followed by Grenache (Garnacha Tinta,) Garignan (Mazuelo) and Graciano. Because they are oak-aged they have a vanilla aroma. There are regulations as to the aging specifications; Crianza and Reserva must spend one year in the cask and Gran Reserva requires a minimum of two years. They can be consumed upon release or can be cellared for years. Rioja can be paired with paella, pizza and tapas.

Recommendations:

Conde de Valdemar	Sierra Cantabria
Faustino	Bodegas Montecillo

Spain: Ribera del Duero

The local grapes of this area (Tinto Fino, or Tinto del Pais [Tempranillo]) are grown following the course of the Duero River from Soria to Valladolid. Although wines have been made in this region since 1846, it was not until 1982 that this region was recognized for having world class wines. Now wines from this area are becoming more popular. The high altitude and climate allows Ribera del Duero to produce a wine of balanced acidity and complexity without the addition of other grapes. Only red wines and rosé wines are produced in this region. Wines from this region are good with paella, pizza and manchego cheese.

Recommendations:

Pesquera

Arzvaga

Vega Sicilia

Italy: Chianti

A Tuscan wine made in the area between Florence and Sienna. This region extends to six outlying regions that also produce wines identified as Chianti. These wines vary from light hues to dark and age worthy. This is due to the variety of grapes used including Sangiovese, Canaiolo Nero, Trebbiano, Malvasia, and Cabernet Sauvignon. If it states reserve on the label it has been aged in oak at least three years. Chianti pairs well with grilled foods, pasta with a red sauce, some rich cream sauces (such as Carbonara) and pizza.

Recommendations:

Badia a Colitbuono	Querceto	Fontodi
Monsanto: Il Poggio	Terrabianca	

France: Côtes du Rhône

Most of the vineyards in the Rhône valley comprise the Côtes du Rhône region that is responsible for 80% of wines produced. This region makes some white and rosé wines but red wines made with the Grenache grape are most prevalent. Syrah, Carignan and Mourvèdre are sometimes used for blending. These wines vary from light and fruity to full and dark. They do not require aging. Cheese, mild meats and chicken in a light sauce go well with this wine.

Recommendations:

Coudelet de Beaucastel	Domaine de Mont Redon
Guigal	Perrin Reserve
La Vielle Ferme	

France: Pomerol and Saint-Emilion

Between the city of Bordeaux and the Medoc lie two of the finest wine producing areas in France. These regions are Pomerol and Saint-Emilion and they produce softer, less tannic wines than Cabernet Sauvignon. The grapes used are predominantly Merlot and Cabernet Franc. Pomerol uses Merlot that has a great concentration of fruit. Cabernet Franc is grown more often in Saint-Emilion and the characteristic of the wine from this region is the herbal and mineral flavors. Saint-Emilion is a larger region than Pomeral, so Saint-Emilion wines tend to be less expensive than wines from Pomerol. Try roast or grilled beef with wines from these regions.

Recommendations:

Château Gazin

Château La Fleur Petrus

Rhône, France: Châteauneuf-du-Pape

Châteauneuf-du-Pape means "new castle of the Pope." This region lies in the region near Avignon, France. Avignon was a summer residence used by the Avignon popes. This wine can be a blend of 13 varieties of red or white grapes, but some of the finest contain high percentages of Syrah, Grenache and Mourvèdre. These wines are rich, ripe and heady and can be enjoyed with steak, venison and ripe cheeses.

Recommendations:

Château Beaucastel	Guigal
Domaine du Vieux Telegraphe	Perrin

South America: Chile and Argentina

The wines of Argentina and Chile definitely deserve mentioning. The climate found in the southern belt that encompasses Chile and Argentina is the same climate by latitude that allows southern Australia, South Africa and South America to produce wines at low or moderate prices. The Argentinean varietal, Malbec, is usually used in a blend and introduces interesting and spicy flavors to the wine. It has become quite popular. Grilled meats, spicy sauces and paprika are notable in South American cuisine and pair nicely with these wines.

Recommendations:

Argentinean/Catena

Chilean/Casa Lapostolle/Los Vascos

South Africa: The Cape Area

Jan Van Riebeeck, a former ship's surgeon, sent for vines from Europe believing they prevented scurvy. He was able to plant these vines in 1655 in an area called the Cape. During the 18th century the wine industry flourished and today this area of South Africa produces most of the country's wines. The wines produced today span the spectrum from good dry whites to tannic reds and sparkling wines. Port and sherry is also produced. The vintner's recent focus has been on reassessing wine styles and making the reds softer and richer and some of their harsh whites fruitier. The white grape varieties include Chenin Blanc, Colombard, Chardonnay and Sauvignon Blanc. The red grape varieties include Pinotage, Merlot, Shiraz and Cabernet Sauvignon. Pinotage is unique to South Africa and produces some of the most exciting wines. The Pinotage grape only accounts for 5% of their production. A cross between Pinot Noir and Cinsaut, these 2 grapes combined produce complex fruity wines with age, but can also be enjoyed when young. Cinsaut is South Africa's most widely planted grape. The Steen also known as Chenin Blanc is the most widely planted grape for white wines.

Germany: The Rhine and Mosel

The Riesling grape produces the best German wines of the Rhine (Rhein) and Mosel as well as the Alsace wines of France. This grape yields very dry wines to very sweet dessert wines. The finest have a fragrant nose that is fruity and flowery. The level of sweetness is determined by the length of time the grapes are left on the vine. The label will indicate degree of sweetness.

Champagne

True champagne comes only from the Champagne region in northeast France. Sparkling wines may be labeled as "Spumante" in Italy and "Sekt" in Germany. French champagne is made from a blend of Chardonnay, Pinot Noir or Pinot Blanc grapes. Good champagnes are not expensive because of the grapes used, but because a second fermentation process in the bottle is required, which requires up to 100 manual operations, some of which are mechanized today. Thus the high price.

Champagnes vary from dry to sweet. A sugar and wine mixture called a dosage is added just before corking and determines how sweet a champagne will be. The label indicates the level of sweetness. Brut is dry, extra sec or extra dry (slightly sweeter), sec (medium sweet), demi sec (sweet) or doux (very sweet). It is recommended to use champagne glasses because the shape of the glass allows the champagne to hold bubbles longer. If you open a bottle of champagne and don't drink it all, stick a metal handle in the bottle, letting the bowl of the spoon rest on top. It will remain drinkable stored in the refrigerator for 1 to 2 days this way. Pair champagne with brunch entrées, fruit desserts or with caviar.

Recommendations:

Roederer	Carousel
Taittinger	Marwood Brut
Rotari Brut	

Port; Porto

Port is a sweet fortified wine often served after a meal. Grape alcohol is added to the wine part way through fermentation, stopping the process at a point where the wine has plenty of sweetness and alcohol. Vintage Ports are the most expensive, and are made from a single vintage bottled within 2 years. The best age 50 years or more. Late-Bottled Vintage Ports and Single Vintage Ports are not made from as high of quality of grapes as the Vintage Ports.

Tawny Ports are a blend of grapes from several different years that can be aged in wood as long as 40 years. They are ready to drink when bottled. Ruby Ports are considered the lowest quality of port. They are blended from several vintages and wood-aged. Port is traditionally served after dinner with walnuts and Stilton or enjoyed with cigars. It is also good with chocolate, a dessert or alone.

Recommendations:

Dows	Fonseca
Taylor	Grahams

Madeira, Marsala and sherry wines have a higher alcohol content and therefore cannot be sold where only beer and wine is sold. Marsala is from the western tip of Sicily and can range from sweet to dry. Madeira can be used for both sweet and savory recipes. Sherry is made in the Andalusia region of southern Spain. They range from dry to sweet. Sherry is often served with traditional Spanish appetizers (tapas), as an apéritif, after dinner drink, or used in recipes.

Vermouth is a white wine that originated in Italy that has been flavored with herbs and spices. It is used as an apéritif, in cocktails, and for cooking. Fortified wines such as vermouth, Madiera, Marsala and sherry have had brandy or another spirit added to them, increasing the alcohol content.

Common Wine Terms

Corked-wine tastes of a bad cork. Slightly musty taste and unpalatable with an unpleasant smell.

Oxidized-exposed to air, flavor has changed. Open too long.

Tannin-identifies a dry sensation with flavors of leather and tea. Excess tannins can cause wine to be bitter.

Balance, Acid-alcohol, fruit and tannins should be balanced. The right amount of acidity and tannins means the fruit is refreshing and flavor lingers. Time will alter this balance.

Tasting Terms

Color-is largely due to grape variety but age and region of origin also play a part. The color of wine comes from the skin of the grapes. White wines can be made from red grapes when the skins are removed immediately after picking.

Smell-or nose of the wine will reveal the condition and character. Swirl it around in the glass and inhale deeply. What flavors do you smell? Swirling the wine aerates the wine and allows oxygen to mix with it, creating the bouquet. The "nose" is the term tasters use to describe the bouquet and aroma of the wine.

Length-the way in which flavor lingers in the mouth and is considered a positive description. The quality and sensation of the wine's aftertaste, combined with how it lingers, is described as finish.

Artichokes and asparagus are difficult to pair with wine because the acid called cynarin in artichokes makes wines taste sweet, and phosphorus and mercaptan in asparagus makes the wines taste bad. Avoid these foods if guests are wine connoisseurs.

Flavors-have a lot to do with the scientific basis of the wine. You may not recognize the characteristics but these flavors may make the identification easier.

Banana or pear-will indicate wine was fermented at a low temperature which is common for inexpensive whites and Beaujolais.

Black pepper-often a flavor from a Syrah grape.

Toast-can be a sign of new oak barrels or bottle aged Chardonnay or Sémillon.

Peach or apricot-suggests a Chardonnay, ripe Riesling or Muscat.

Honey-found in dessert wines or wines that were subject to noble rot. Noble rot is a mold that grows on the grapes and is necessary to make Sauternes and sweeter German dessert wines such as Beerenauslese and Trockenbeerenauslese.

Nutty overtones-hazelnut or walnut is present in a mature white burgundy.

Green pepper-designates an inexpensive young red from Cabernet Sauvignon or Cabernet Franc.

Lemon or lime-is found in wines made from Sémillon and American Riesling.

Cherries, strawberries and red currants-are often associated with Pinot noir grapes.

Chocolate-may be sensed in a fine full-bodied red wine. These wines are ripe, mature and low in acidity.

Vanilla-is often associated with wine being aged in new oak barrels.

Raspberry flavors-are apparent in expensive red Rhône wines, often those from Syrah grapes.

Litchis-are found in wines made from Gewürztraminer grapes. This small fruit from China is deliciously sweet.

Rose petal-will be noticed in a Gewürztraminer.

Butter-is a distinct flavor of all styles of Chardonnay.

Gooseberries-are distinctive of Sauvignon Blanc.

Mint and eucalyptus-are indicative of Cabernet Sauvignon from Australia, South Africa and California.

Tasting Basics

Swirl wine and take a generous amount in your mouth, but do not swallow. Roll it around in your mouth and breathe over it to further release the flavors. Assess acidity, sweetness and alcohol content. There are 4 flavors you will taste on the different parts of the tongue. The back and top of the tongue recognize bitterness, possibly from the tannins. The sides of the tongue detect sharpness and acidity and the tip registers sweetness.

The oak from wood barrels imparts tannins to the wine and gives the wine a vanilla characteristic. The limited exposure to oxygen coming from the pores in the wood helps to mature the wine. You may hear the term oak-aged frequently. Corks are used to stop

air from entering the bottle. and have no affect on the wine. An older wine may have some air trapped between the wine and the cork. Mature wines are best if opened a half hour before serving, young wines will not benefit from opening early.

Wineglasses

Glasses should not obscure the color of the wine. A clear glass bowl is most appropriate for tasting wines, and a large enough glass is important for swirling. Ideally, a 10 ounce glass is the appropriate size. Large balloon-shaped glasses are more appropriate for red wines. A smaller glass, closed slightly at the top, is used for white wines and helps to concentrate on the bouquet and to keep the wine chilled.

Malolactic Fermentation

Malolactic fermentation is the fermentation of wine in a cask or tank that occurs naturally or is induced artificially by the vintner. This process will impart an oak flavor to the wine. Determine whether this process has caused too much oak flavor for your liking and ask you wine merchant to help you determine which wines would better serve your taste.

Storing Wine

Fluctuations in temperature can be harmful to wine. Store bottles horizontally, away from sunlight to ensure corks remain moist. The optimum temperature to store wine is 52 degrees, but wine is safe anywhere from 40 to 65 degrees. Expensive wines age well. Cabernet Sauvignon, Zinfandel, Merlot and Syrah benefit from the aging process. Modestly priced reds should be enjoyed within two years and modestly priced whites within six months.

Chilling Wine

Immersing a bottle of wine in a bucket of ice and water for 30 minutes is the best way to chill a white wine or champagne and keep it cool while drinking. White wines and champagne should not be left in the refrigerator more than a few hours or they may oxidize.

Below are some guidelines for the correct temperature to serve wines:

Sparkling: 40 to 45 degrees

White wine: 45 to 50 degrees

Reds, rosé and light reds: 50 to 55 degrees

Medium-bodied: 55 to 60 degrees

Full-bodied: 60 to 65 degrees

Light Reds-Rioja, Beaujolais, Chianti

Medium bodied reds-Beaujolais-Villages, wines from Burgundy, Pinot Noir, Merlot, Red Zinfandel, Cabernet Sauvignon, Chianti Classico, Rioja-Riserva.

Full bodied-Barbaresco, Barolo, Bordeaux wines, Rioja Gran Riserva, and some Cabernet Sauvignon, Merlot and Red Zinfandel from California.

In the summer it may be necessary to slightly chill a warm red wine. Chill in the refrigerator for 30 minutes. It is a recognized practice since temperatures for wine storage are based on properly cooled cellars, not our homes today.

Reading Labels

Wines from United States winemakers are required by law to state on the label the brand name and the year the wine was bottled. It is required that 100% of the grapes must come from the area stated on the bottle. The label may also indicate a broad growing area such as the northern coast in California. The county such as Napa or Sonoma may be stated and even a township such as Carneros. After branding and location are stated, the grape variety is named and by law the wine must contain 75 percent of that variety. If the grape of origin is identified, the wine may also reflect a higher cost. The vintage year is listed which determines the year the grapes were harvested although the wine may have been stored several years. This Is Important because the conditions of a particular year determine the quality and readiness of the wine for drinking.

The same information appears on the French labels, but order of emphasis varies. In France, the place the grapes were grown takes precedence over the vintner or grape variety since each region has ratings according to the excellence of the wines. The name of the proprietor is next followed by the location. Having the proprietor's name on the bottle places his or her reputation on the contents. Estate bottled means the proprietor has watched over the entire production.

Italian wine labels fall somewhere between the French and the California labels with the emphasis placed on the vintner and the region the grapes were grown. Italian wine has a government designation on the label that is either DOC or DOCG. The DOC is the name of the agency that controls the wine production in Italy. The DOCG on the label denotes that it is the finest of red wines. The G at the end is a guarantee that it is a premium wine and only 5 qualify for this label (Barbaresco from Piedmont, Barolo from Piedmont, Brunello di Montalcino-Tuscany, Chianti-Tuscany and Vino Nobile di Montepulcino from Tuscany.) Following the DOCG, the label will identify a prestigious site within a particular growing zone from which this wine originated. A regional DOC and the grape's variety will be listed on the label. When you find an Italian wine you like, try other wine varieties from that maker and use it to measure other wines.

The producer's name is most important aspect on Australian labels. If the variety of grape is stated on the label, then the contents must contain 80% of that kind of grape. When the

origin is listed, 80% of the grapes must come from that region. Australian wines are a very good value. If it was a good vintage year in California, it will also hold true for that year in Australia since they have similar climates.

On Spanish labels, the reputation of the Rioja wine producer and shipper is most important. After the shipper buys the grapes, they blend wines from several vintages to keep the style consistent. The label may give you the style of wine, but grape varieties are not found on the label. The label identifies appellation or region, (i.e. Rioja or Penedes.) DOCA is the top quality and then DO. VdM is considered table wine. Reserva on a Spanish label indicates that the shipper specially selected this wine and gave it further aging in cask or bottle.

The fancy artwork and crests on German wine labels are somewhat misleading. The important information is alongside or beneath the art. The greater degree of particularity the greater the quality of wine. The label may state all of the specifics (producer, vintage, township and the vineyard from which it comes, and the grape variety) and have a high price tag. The less detailed the information, the less expensive the wine. The sweetness of a German wine will depend on how long the grapes are left on the vine and will be denoted on the label. The driest German wine is a Kabinett followed by Spätlese, "spät" meaning late (as in late pick.) The next level is even sweeter, which is Auslese, Beerenauslese and Trockenbeerenauslese or the picking of trocken (dry almost raisin-like grapes.) Eiswein is the sweetest because the grapes are harvested after the first freeze. Qualitätswein or Qualitätswein mit Prädikat with the addition of Prädikat is a climb up the ladder of sweetness. The wine grade will be listed at the bottom of the label.

The History of Wine

Winemaking encompasses a period of over 7000 years. Tom Haas, one of my previous employers informed me that turning water into wine in Cana is the first recorded miracle in the Bible. There is little recorded about the early years, but it is generally accepted that wine was made for the first time in Asia Minor in the Caucasus and Mesopotamia, around 6000 to 4000 B.C.. From there, winemaking spread to Egypt where there are written references dating back to 5000 B.C. At about the same time, they began making wine in Phoenicia. By 2000 B.C. the Greeks and Cretans began experimenting with winemaking. By 1000 B.C. the inhabitants of Sicily, Italy and most countries in North Africa had begun planting vineyards, and 500 years later wine production began in Spain, the south of France and Arabia. By about 100 B.C., wine was made in northern India and China. Shortly after the birth of Christ the practice spread to the Balkan States and Northern Europe. The history of wine halted during the next 1000 years due to the decline of the Roman Empire and Europe's Dark Ages. Explorers in the 16th century accelerated the pace and by 1530 vine plantings had spread to Mexico and Japan. In 1560, Argentina imported plantings, and later Peru. South Africa planted vines in 1655 followed by Australia in 1697 and New Zealand in 1813. The birth of wine in America began in California when vines

were planted in 1849 during the Gold Rush. Those that had no luck panning for gold turned to farming and the most popular crop was grapes. Many Europeans that settled in California planted grapes and brought their winemaking tradition with them. In the 1970's California wines evolved into national and international prominence. Oregon, Washington, New York State and Texas are a few other states that produce wines in the United States.

Just some wine funnies from the Internet...

Women say:
"Men are like fine wine. They all start out like grapes,
and it's our job to stomp on them and keep them in the dark until they mature
into something you'd like to have dinner with."

Men say:
"Women are like fine wine. They all start out fresh and fruity
and intoxicating to the mind and then turn full-bodied with age until they
go sour and vinegary and give you a headache."

Cheese Basics

Cheese is always appropriate as an appetizer. It is great for quick and elegant gatherings even when dinner does not follow. Choosing cheese can be confusing if you don't purchase them for appetizers on a regular basis. In this section I explain flavors of the different varieties I purchase most often.

When arranging your cheese tray include red and green grapes cut in small bunches and piled on top of one another so the tray looks full in the empty spots. If fruit and cheese is your preference, sliced apples, pears and melon are a nice accompaniment. Sprinkle apples and pear slices with lemon juice so they don't turn brown. Grapes are also appropriate when you include olives and cornichons as garnish. Wine and cheese are a wonderful choice for an appetizer before a meal.

Premium olives cured in oil with herbs or brine (from a specialty grocer) complement cheese and cleanse the palate. The common black olive is called a Mission olive. This olive is a ripe green olive that obtains its color from lye curing and oxygenation. Olives that are tree ripened turn dark brown or black naturally. Two of the most popular imported olives are the niçoise and the kalamata. Spanish olives are picked young and are therefore green. They are lye fermented and are usually aged about 6 to 12 months. Dry-cured olives have been packed in salt, which removes moisture and they become wrinkly in texture. Some of my favorite olives include amfissa, lucques, nyon, niçoise, kalamata and gaeta. Gourmet food stores usually have many choices. For the best flavor, it is recommended to buy olives with the pit.

Once you unwrap cheese, it spoils quickly. When arranging a cheese platter, cheese should be removed from refrigeration 1 to 2 hours before consuming to experience the true flavor. In the summer, you may want to remove only one hour ahead since the soft cheeses may change in consistency. Serve with water crackers or a thinly sliced baguette to allow the palette to experience the flavor. Allow approximately 4 ounces of cheese per person for a cheese tray. Cut cheeses for your serving platter while they are cold. Do not cut cheese in cubes or slices, serve with the appropriate utensil. (Use a spreader for soft cheeses and a knife or cheese cutter for harder cheeses.) If the group is large, some cheeses (such as manchego) can be sliced to make the buffet line move more quickly. When wrapping leftover cheese, wrap each individual piece of cheese with a new piece of plastic wrap or place in a self-sealing plastic bag.

Popular Cheese Varieties

Feta Cheese from Greece is made from sheep's milk and has a distinct strong, slightly acidic flavor. Feta is crumbly in texture and white in color. True feta should be stored in brine in the refrigerator and is usually found only in cheese stores and some supermarkets. This is wonderful with crackers. Today, feta cheese is also found packed without brine, and makes a great salad topping or can be used for making spreads.

Goat Cheese is made from goat's milk and comes in a variety of shapes (cones, cylinders, and pyramids). A mild or more profound flavor depends on the aging process. Today many are made from a mixture of goat, cow and sheep's milk.

Stilton is a blue veined cheese with a rich and mellow flavor and a pungent taste similar to blue cheese. The wrinkled rind is not edible. Stilton is milder than Gorgonzola or Roquefort and is excellent on salads. It can also be served with port after dinner.

Roquefort is made from sheep's milk that has been aged 3 months or more in a limestone cavern near the village of Roquefort in southwest France, near the Spanish border. It is creamy in texture and has a pungent somewhat salty flavor. Blue veins throughout a creamy white interior characterize Roquefort. The name Roquefort is protected from imitators by law. True Roquefort has a red sheep emblem on the wrapper, but many retailers will repackage the original wheel so you may not see this label of authenticity.

Cambozola is a German cheese, creamy in texture with an edible, white, velvety rind. The flavor is a cross between a blue cheese and Brie.

Brie is compact, even textured, pale yellow in color, with an edible white rind. As it ages it takes on a nutty flavor. This creamy cheese is made from cow's milk and is noted as the French cheese "king of kings." The French exported Brie is stabilized and the maturing process stopped so it has a longer shelf life. Brie must be served at room temperature to enjoy its full flavor.

Camembert is made from raw cow's milk. True Camembert comes from only five parts of Normandy, France. Although often copied, a good Camembert mentions "affine" which means it is matured to the heart of the cheese. It is clean yellow with a subtly salty taste and has a white edible rind like Brie.

Saint André is a triple cream soft cheese that has been heavily enriched with cream during the manufacturing process. The double and triple cream cheeses have an exceptionally rich and creamy texture and are higher in fat content. This one is outstanding!

Explorateur is rich triple cream cheese that has a delicate picquant flavor. It is a wonderful appetizer substitute for Brie.

Boursin cheese is a triple cream cheese with a buttery texture. It is usually flavored with garlic, herbs or black pepper.

Gouda has a yellow rind covered by a red or black paraffin wax. This coating allows the cheese to breathe while losing some humidity. Gouda accounts for 50% of the cheese produced in Holland. The flavor is sweet and fruity and as it ages is more pronounced. Gouda is firm and supple and essentially mild tasting. This cheese goes well with fruit.

Port-Salut is a semi-soft cheese that was originally made by the Trappist monks in France. This cheese is made from cow's milk and has a pale yellow interior. It has a savory flavor and a satiny texture. Fruit complements the flavor of Port-Salut.

Manchego is Spain's most popular cheese that comes from the milk of the Manche sheep in the La Mancha region. The Manche sheep survives on shrubs and grass and produces an aromatic milk. It is a well-ripened hard cheese with ivory color. The taste is creamy, nutty and sharp to the palate. The exterior is decorative but not edible. This cheese can be thinly sliced for a cheese tray with the exterior intact or as a wedge with the proper utensils for slicing.

Gloucester is a natural hard English cheese with a creamy yellow almost orange color. It has a rich smooth flavor. Gloucester is often layered with Stilton, which is referred to as Huntsman. Gloucester is a form of cheddar.

Gorwood Caerphilly is mild, yet tangy and is made from cow's milk. It is produced in England but gets its name from the village in Wales where it was first made. It may be one of the more difficult cheeses to find, but is truly worth the search if you can locate it at a specialty grocer or cheese shop.

Cheddar Cheese, originally made in the English village of Cheddar, is now produced all over the English speaking world. It is made from cow's milk and varies in color from white to deep yellow and has a mild to sharp taste. Colby is a mild cheddar. Other types of cheddar include Gloucester, Cheshire, Leicester, Lancashire, Derby, Wensleydale and Gorwood Caerphilly.

Cabot Cheddar Cheese is one of the best known American types of cheddar and has won every major cheese-making prize in America. The Cabot Classic Private Stock and Vintage Choice are sold in specialty food stores.

Gruyère is famous for its use in Swiss fondue. Gruyère is a hard cheese that is similar to Emmentaler with smaller holes but with the characteristic tough outer rind. The holes in these Swiss cheeses are caused by an expansion of gas within the cheese curd during the ripening process. Its texture is chewy and it melts evenly. The flavor is mild and nutty.

Parmigiano-Reggiano is the finest of Parmesan cheese and is made in Italy. It comes in a 75 pound wheel. This cheese has a pungent smell. It is primarily a grating cheese with a granular texture. It is recommended to buy this in a small wedge and grate it yourself. The outside coating states Parmigiano-Reggiano and ensures you won't get an imitation.

Sage Derby has a greenish hue due to sage being introduced to the cheese during the production. It is a mild hard cheese with a slight sage flavor.

Buffalo Mozzarella is made in the south of Italy from a mixture of water buffalo and cow's milk. It is pure white and hand formed into balls. The consistency is soft and rubbery and it is stored in whey brine. To serve, slice and alternate with fresh sliced tomatoes and fresh basil, sprinkle with salt and pepper and drizzle with extra virgin olive oil and balsamic vinegar.

Fresh Mozzarella is made today predominately from whole milk instead of from the milk of water buffaloes. It is usually packaged in whey or water and is labeled "Italian style." It can be found in Italian markets, cheese shops and some supermarkets. It differs

from the regular mozzarella, which is factory produced. It has a much softer texture and a sweet delicate flavor and can be used in the same way as the buffalo mozzarella. You may order this cheese and a variety of other wonderful cheeses from The Mozzarella Company in Dallas. Visit their web site at www.mozzco.com or contact them at 1-800-798-2954.

Havarti is a pale yellow Danish cheese that is semi-soft with irregular holes. It is considered a mild cheese, but slightly tangy. It intensifies and sharpens with age.

Mascarpone is a cheese that is usually mixed with sugar and used in desserts. It is a solidified cream that has been whipped to a velvety consistency. Mix with whipped cream to make a delicious topping for fruit. It is also used in Tiramisu.

An odd assortment of cheeses on a tray is most appropriate. If choosing 5 cheeses for a platter, select a hard, a crumbly, a blue, a semi-soft and a goat cheese. This provides a variety to the milk types used and presents an array of flavors. Duplication will occur if Cambozola is paired with Stilton or Roquefort since they are all from the blue family. It would be acceptable to have a feta or goat cheese with a Stilton or Roquefort.

Crumbly Cheese	Hard Cheese	Soft Cheese	Semi-Soft
Feta	Manchego	Cambozola	Gouda
Goat Cheese	Gloucester	Brie	Mozzarella
Stilton	Cabot Cheddar	Camembert	Havarti
Roquefort	Cheddar	Saint André	Port-Salut
	Gruyère	Explorateur	Gorwood Caerphilly
	Parmigiano-Reggiano	Boursin	
	Sage Derby	Mascarpone	

There are several cheeses, which are used more often for cooking than on a cheese platter, i.e. Gruyère, mascarpone, mozzarella and Parmigiano-Reggiano.

Processed cheeses are not appropriate for a cheese tray. These cheeses have had the ripening process stopped at some point with a heat treatment and are usually a blend of varieties. A chemical process is used to smoke cheeses. Originally smoked cheeses were hung over a fire to develop the taste. I don't recommend placing smoked cheeses on a cheese tray unless you know the traditional process was used.

Grilling

Grilling is searing the outside of the meat while keeping the juices inside. Grilling time depends on the cut of meat, grid position, temperature of coals and desired doneness. You can grill both meats and vegetables. There are some simple instructions to follow for success. Trimming excess fat from meat keeps the flame from flaring up. Foods will cook faster if you cook with the grill covered. Tongs and spatulas are better for turning meat, as forks pierce and allow juices to escape.

Cooking times are helpful but the internal temperature is more important. A meat thermometer is imperative. For successful grilling you should have a flashlight on hand for reading the thermometer when grilling in the evening. David Gore offers one of his best tips for testing doneness. Hold your hand out flat and bring your thumb to the base of your index finger. Feel the pad of your hand at the base of your thumb, with your index finger from your other hand. This is the same feeling a rare piece of meat should have when pushed with tongs. It will be soft and yielding. Then, touch the base of your middle finger with your thumb, the pad of your thumb is what medium rare feels like. Touch the ring finger to see what medium feels like and touch the pinky finger to see what well-done feels like. Each time you must use your index finger from your other hand to feel the difference. The skin tightens as you move up the scale. This trick works for all meats.

Marinades are mixtures of vinegar, oils and spices that serve a dual purpose of tenderizing and adding flavor. If your marinade does not include oil, it can be mixed and refrigerated until ready to use. If oil is one of the ingredients, then it is best to mix all ingredients except oil in a blender or processor. Once other ingredients are blended, slowly add oil while the motor is running to emulsify or thicken the mixture.

Your charcoal coals should be stacked 2 to 3 inches deep. When using lighter fluid, allow the coals to heat 30 minutes in order to let the fluid taste burn off along with any chemicals on the briquettes. After the fire has died down and coals are gray, you need to spread them evenly along the bottom of the grill. Next, place the grate over the grill and let it heat. You may use a spray oil on the grate before placing over the fire to keep food from sticking. This is especially helpful for chicken. It is also acceptable to brush meats and fish with oil before grilling to keep them from sticking. The length of time needed for grilling depends on the temperature of the coals. Allow approximately 30 minutes to prepare the fire. Many cooks prefer a wood fire that burns down to embers on the grill because they don't like the charcoal taste. There is a hardwood charcoal that is 100 percent natural that many restaurants use because it burns fast and hot. Gas grills continue to be the cheapest and easiest method for grilling because they heat up and cool down quickly.

When Using Charcoal

Low is a temperature of 250 degrees; coals are totally gray. You will be able to hold your hand over coals for 10 seconds.

Medium is a temperature of 350 degrees; coals are gray with a tinge of red. You can hold a hand over coals for 7 seconds.

High is a temperature of 450 degrees; coals are glowing red. You can only hold your hand over coals for about 3 seconds. Be careful!

Keep a mixture of baking soda and water in a spray bottle near by to handle flame flare ups.

Chicken on the Grill

Cook chicken over medium hot coals. Turn chicken with tongs every 5 minutes to ensure doneness.

Juices should run clear when pricked with a fork. Internal temperature should register 170 to 175 degrees for white meat and 180 to 185 degrees for dark meat.

Cook with skin on to leave moisture in, remove skin after cooking if desired.

Chicken doesn't need to marinate long, a half hour will boost flavor. Only one cup of marinade is needed for 6 breasts.

For a whole chicken or a duck half, the inside temperature should register 180 degrees. Cooking time will be 40 to 50 minutes.

A skinned chicken breast should reach an internal temperature of 170 degrees and should cook 12 to 15 minutes. A ground chicken patty should reach 165 degrees and takes 14 to 18 minutes.

Pork

Pork tends to be overcooked. Pork found in the store is leaner and overcooking will dry it out. When cooked perfectly, pork should be juicy with a little pink in the center, reaching an internal temperature of 160 degrees. Just as with chicken, the juices should run clear.

Basting meats while cooking will keep them from drying out. They can be basted with their own drippings, fruit juice or a sauce. When cooking ribs, do not add barbecue sauce until the last 30 minutes or sauce will burn while ribs are cooking.

Grilling Times (4 inches from heat)

Chops, bone in, ¾ inch thickness for 6 to 8 minutes, depending on grill and could take up to 11 minutes.

Chops, boneless, ¾ inch thickness for 6 to 8 minutes, depending on grill and could take up to 11 minutes.

Thicker chops take approximately 25 to 30 minutes.

Tenderloin, ½ to 1 pound for 15 to 25 minutes.

Kabobs, 1 inch cubes for 10 to 20 minutes.

Beef

Beef has a variety of fancy names but the best you can buy is USDA Prime. The standards for this beef are so high, only 1% to 2% of the beef produced each year earns this mark, so it will of course be more expensive. When this beef is inspected and passed by the department of agriculture it receives the USDA Prime stamp. If it doesn't have the stamp it can't be prime.

Look for marbling in the steak as it enhances the flavor and creates a more tender and juicy cut of meat. Appearance should be shiny and bright red, firm to the touch, with a slight aroma.

The most tender cuts of beef are as follows:

Tenderloin	T-bone/Porterhouse	Top Sirloin Steak
Chuck Top Blade Steak	Rib-Eye Steak	Round Tip Steak
Top Loin Steak	Chuck Eye Steak	Chopped Steak

A top blade steak is derived from the top blade roast. The roast is separated into two pieces by removing the heavy connective tissue. It takes approximately 14 to 16 minutes on the grill for medium rare and 18 to 20 minutes for medium doneness.

Grilling Times

Rib-eye Steak ¾ inch thickness for 8 to 11 minutes.
Rib-eye Steak 1 inch thickness for 11 to 14 minutes.

Porterhouse/T-bone ¾ inch thickness for 10 to 12 minutes.
Porterhouse/T-bone 1 inch thickness for 14 to 16 minutes.

Tenderloin 1 inch thickness for 13 to 15 minutes.
Tenderloin 1½ inch thickness 14 to 16 minutes (grill covered.)

Boneless Top Sirloin Steak ¾ inch thickness for 13 to 16 minutes.
Boneless Top Sirloin Steak 1 inch thickness for 17 to 21 minutes.
Boneless Top Sirloin Steak 1½ inch thickness for 22 to 26 minutes.

Steaks including rib-eyes, porterhouse, sirloin, T-bone, top loin or tenderloin (otherwise known as filet mignon) reach medium rare at 145 degrees and medium at 150 degrees. It takes approximately 8 to 12 minutes for medium rare and 12 to 15 minutes for medium.

Marinated Flank Steak

1½ to 2 pounds for 17 to 21 minutes, medium will be 160 degrees in the center.

Beef Patties

4 ounces @ ½ inch thickness and 4 inches in diameter for 11 to 13 minutes.

6 ounces @ ¾ inch thickness and 4 inches round in diameter for 13 to 15 minutes.

At 160 degrees no pink remains and grill time is 14 to 18 minutes.

Lamb

Lamb is best when cooked to a medium rare temperature of 150 degrees when tested with a meat thermometer. Americans have a tendency to overcook lamb. Use a meat thermometer to ensure doneness. Insert thermometer in thickest portion and do not let it rest against fat or the bone. 160 degrees is optimum for medium; 145 degrees for medium rare.

Approximate Cooking Time for Grilling (over moderate heat)

Shoulder Chops for 11 to 13 minutes.

Loin Chops for 9 to 10 minutes.

Rib Chops for 9 to 10 minutes.

Sirloin Steaks for 9 to 10 minutes.

Center Cut Leg Steaks for 9 to 10 minutes.

Cubes for kabobs (1 inch) for 7 to 8 minutes.

Lamb Patties for 5 to 7 minutes.

Butterflied Leg for 40 to 50 minutes.

Fish

Fillets ½ to 1 inch thickness for 4 to 6 minutes (per ½ inch thickness.)

Sea scallops for 5 to 8 minutes.

Shrimp (medium) for 6 to 8 minutes.

Shrimp (large) for 10 to 12 minutes.

These are based on 160 degree temperature readings.

Safety Tips

Throw away leftover marinade.

Marinate meats in the refrigerator.

Clean all cutting surfaces well.

Do not use the knife used for raw meats for other dinner items without washing first.

Do not use the same platter for raw and cooked meats.

Leave meats in the refrigerator until ready to grill.

Do not marinate in aluminum.

Lettuce and Salads

Salad adds such a wonderful balance to a meal whether served before the main course or with dinner. You can be creative with salads and develop your own combinations. Mixing lettuce helps to incorporate color and texture. Nuts take on a more interesting flavor when toasted. Here is an abbreviated list of possibilities and tips for the combinations. Allow approximately 1¼ to 1½ cups of slightly packed lettuce per person, as a side dish. When you have a fruit and lettuce combination you may want a dressing with a touch of sugar.

Lettuce	Nuts	Fruits	Vegetables	Cheese
Butterhead or Boston	Pine Nuts	Kiwis	Artichokes	Asiago
Crisphead	Pecans	Strawberries	Olives	Parmesan
Romaine	Walnuts	Apples	Hearts of Palm	Mozzarella
Red Leaf or Green Leaf	Macadamia Nuts	Grapes	Red Onions	Gorgonzola
Frisée	Cashews	Avocados	Green Onions	Stilton
Mesclun	Sunflower Seeds	Oranges	Tomatoes	Blue
Spinach	Pistachios	Pears		Monterey Jack
Arugula	Almonds	Dried Cherries		Brie
Radicchio				Goat
				Feta

Lettuce should be washed in lukewarm water and drained completely or blotted with a paper towel to remove excess moisture before refrigerating. Do not soak. I like to wash lettuce ahead of time and roll it in paper towels to remove excess water. Store this way in the refrigerator for several hours before serving. Lettuce can be stored 3 to 5 days in an airtight bag once washed and dried.

Butterhead other wise known as Bibb or Boston lettuce is a delicate lettuce. This lettuce is a small round head that is usually pale yellow green on the inside to pale green on the outside.

Crisphead Lettuce is a tightly packed head otherwise known as iceberg lettuce. It is not very flavorful but is good for Mexican dishes because it is so crisp. This lettuce is not recommended for formal gatherings.

Leaf Lettuce ranges in color from medium to dark green with some tipped in red (oakleaf or red leaf) lettuce. Look for any wilting or yellowing of leaves when selecting.

Romaine lettuce is the common choice for Caesar salad. The elongated head is crisp with green leaves that go to pale green at the center. There is little waste with romaine lettuce. Tear off any brown that may be on the edges and cut off the root end in a v shape. Wash in lukewarm water and dry off. This lettuce gets crisper if it is stored in the refrigerator ½ hour to an hour after washing, wrapped in paper towels.

Mesclun lettuce is sold in most grocery stores. It is a mixture of young small salad greens and is also referred to as gourmet salad mix. Even if the whole salad is not made from this, it is nice to mix a few handfuls with other lettuce for variety in color and texture. Baby spinach, frisée, arugula and radicchio are usually included in this mix.

Frisée is a member of the chicory family and has a slightly bitter flavor. Leaf color ranges from yellow white to yellow green and the ends are feathery. Curly endive can be used as a substitute for frisée.

Endive is closely related to, and often confused with chicory. Belgian endive, curly endive and escarole are the three main varieties. Belgium endive is a small (6 inches long,) cigar shaped head of cream colored, tightly packed, slightly bitter leaves. Curly endive, often mistakenly called chicory, grows in loose heads of lacy, green-rimmed outer leaves that curl at the tips. The off white leaves in the center form a compact heart. Escarole has broad, slightly curved, pale green leaves and has a milder flavor than either Belgian or curly endive.

Radicchio is a red-leafed Italian chicory often used for its pink to dark red color. It is slightly bitter and comes in a small loose head.

Arugula is an aromatic salad green with a bitter flavor that comes in small bunches. It must be thoroughly washed before using.

Keeping Things Interesting

It is always good to expand your social circles and mix people up to make events more entertaining and exciting. Sometimes a lull in the conversation, whether before or after dinner, requires a little encouragement from the host! Included in this section are some favorite games to help energize the party. Most games you can only use once with the same guests, but they are sure to stimulate lively conversations with each new group! One game per event is usually enough. There are also books on games that offer additional options. (I have found many of these games through the internet, the original author is unknown.)

Activity 1

The Language of Birthdays is a great book that gives the characteristics of people born on a certain day. As the host, you will know enough about the guests to look for characteristics they may recognize in themselves. Type a few sentences about each guest, then cut and paste to the inside flap of a place card. Once guests arrive and have time to drink a cocktail, randomly pass out the place cards. This alone will have people mingling and searching for the one card that bests suits them. Another option is to have one person take all of the cards and start by picking out one with characteristics they think best suits him or her. Pass the remaining cards on to the next person. When everyone has a card, let each person read it aloud. After everyone has finished you can then reveal to each person whose card they picked. Few people see themselves as they really are, so the conversation can be very engaging! Afterwards, you can write the correct name on each card and set them on the dinner table.

Activity 2

This game needs the host to organize answers for all of the players, so he or she will not participate. Have each guest start by drawing a cross on an index card to separate the four quadrants. In the upper left box ask the guests to list four descriptive words that identify their favorite color. They are to keep their answers and adjectives to themselves until they are revealed later. Next in the upper right box have guests list four adjectives to describe their favorite animal. In the left lower box have them describe their favorite body of water (which can be an ocean, pond or even the bathtub). They can be imaginative! Finally in the fourth box they should describe how they would feel in a dark room with no windows or doors.

Starting with the upper left box, have each guest reveal what their favorite color is and the four words used to describe it. Go around to each person. You then can tell them that these words describe how they see themselves. Once the first box is done repeat the process, revealing the meaning after they have revealed the animal and 4 words to

describe the animal. Their favorite animal describes how others see them. Their favorite body of water describes their intimate life, and the dark room with no windows describes their view of death. Tell them what it means after everyone has disclosed their word and 4 words to describe the word. Other than the room with no doors or windows they all have an object and adjectives. This activity works well in groups that are not too large.

Activity 3

For this game you will need paper and pen for each guest. First ask each guest to write down the following five animals, starting with their most favorite to least favorite: Cow, Sheep, Horse, Tiger, Monkey. Second, ask them to write down one word to describe each of these words: Dog, Rat, Cat, Coffee, Ocean. Third, have them write down the name of a person with whom they relate to each of the following five colors: Yellow, Orange, Red, White, Green. Finally, you can reveal the special meanings found in what they wrote.

1.) The animals from part one relate to the following and the order is how they prioritize things in their life.

Cow is career

Tiger is pride

Sheep means love

Horse means family

Monkey means money

2.) The description of each object in part two reveals how you view certain personalities:

Dog implies your personality

Rat implies your enemy's personality

Cat implies your partner's personality

Coffee implies how you interpret your intimate life

Ocean implies how you interpret your own life

3.) The colors in part three describe where people stand in your life according to which color you associated them with:

Yellow is someone who will never forget you

Orange is someone you can consider a real friend

Red is someone you really love

White is your soul mate

Green is a person whom you will remember for the rest of your life

Whether these descriptions are accurate or not, they certainly will liven up the group as each guest shares their answers!

Activity 4

You can either type out the next game, or copy and give to each person or just read it aloud to the group. If you decide to read aloud, give each guest paper and pen to write down the numbers 1 through 10. With each question they will write down their answer a, b, c, or d. Each answer corresponds to a certain amount of points, which when added up will reveal something about each guest's habits and personality.

1.) When do you feel your best?

    a.) in the morning

    b.) during the afternoon and early evening

    c.) late at night

2.) You usually walk:

    a.) fairly fast with long steps

    b.) fairly fast but, with short, quick steps

    c.) slower, head up, looking the world in the face

    d.) slower, head down

3.) When talking to people, you:

    a.) stand with arms folded

    b.) have hands clasped

    c.) have one or both hands on your hips

    d.) touch or push the person to whom you are talking

    e.) play with your ear, touch your chin or smooth your hair

4.) When relaxing, you sit with:

    a.) your knees bent and your legs neatly side by side

    b.) your legs crossed

    c.) your legs stretched out or straight

    d.) one leg curled under you

5.) When something really amuses you, you react with:

    a.) a big appreciative laugh

    b.) a laugh, but not a loud one

    c.) a quiet chuckle

    d.) a sheepish smile

6.) When you go to a social gathering, you:

    a.) make a loud entrance

    b.) make a quiet entrance, looking around for someone you know

    c.) make the quietest entrance, trying to stay unnoticed

7.) You are working hard, concentrating hard, and then you are interrupted. How do you react?

    a.) welcome the break

    b.) feel extremely irritated

    c.) vary between the two extremes

8.) Which of the following colors do you like most?

    a.) red or orange

    b.) black

    c.) yellow or light blue

    d.) green

    e.) dark blue or purple

    f.) white

    g.) brown or gray

9.) When you are in bed at night those last few moments before going to sleep, you lie:

    a.) stretched out on your back

    b.) stretched out face down on your stomach

    c.) on your side, slightly curled

    d.) with your head on one arm

    e.) with your head under the covers

10.) You often dream that:

    a.) you are falling

    b.) fighting or struggling

    c.) searching for something or somebody

    d.) flying or floating

    e.) you usually have dreamless sleep

    f.) your dreams are always pleasant

Here is the point system for what each answer means. Read aloud and have each guest keep track of their own points.

    1.) a-2,b-4,c-6

    2.) a-6,b-4,c-7,d-2,e-1

    3.) a-4,b-2,c-5,d-7,e-6

    4.) a-4,b-6,c-2,d-1

    5.) a-6,b-4,c-3,d-5,e-2

    6.) a-6,b-4,c-2

    7.) a-6,b-2,c-4

    8.) a-6,b-7,c-5,d-4,e-3,f-2,g-1

    9.) a-7,b-6,c-4,d-2,e-1

    10.) a-4,b-2,c-3,d-5,e-6,f-1

Have guests add up their score and read what the points reveal about their personality. They can choose what to share about themselves, since they do not have to read their answers out loud.

Over 60 points:
Others see you as someone that they should "handle with care." You are seen as self-centered and extremely dominant. Others may admire you and wish they could be more like you, but they do not always trust you and hesitate to become too deeply involved with you.

51 to 60 points:
Your friends see you as exciting, highly volatile, with a rather impulsive personality. You are a natural leader, quick to make decisions (although not always the right ones.) They see you as bold and venturesome, someone who will try anything once. They enjoy being in your company because of the excitement you radiate.

41 to 50 points:
Others see you as fresh, lively, charming, amusing and always interesting. You are seen as, someone who is constantly the center of attention, but sufficiently well balanced not to let it go to your head. You are seen as kind, considerate and understanding, someone who will cheer them up and help them out.

31 to 40 points:
Others see you as sensible, cautious, careful and practical. They see you as clever, gifted, and talented but modest. Not a person who makes friends too quickly or easily, but someone who is extremely loyal to the friends that they have and expects the same loyalty in return. Those who really get to know you realize it takes a lot to shake your trust in your friends, but it takes equally as long to reestablish the trust if broken.

21 to 30 points:

Your friends see you as painstaking and fussy. You are extremely cautious and careful, a slow and steady plodder. It would really surprise them if you ever did anything impulsively or on the spur of the moment. They expect you to examine everything carefully from every side and then usually decide against it. They think this reaction on your part is caused partly because of your careful nature and partly due to laziness.

Under 21 points:

People think you are shy, nervous and indecisive. You are someone who needs to be looked after, who always wants someone else to make the decisions and who does not want to become involved with anyone or anything. They see you as a worrier who sees problems that do not always exist. Only those that know you well know that you are not boring. The problem is that you let very few people get close to you.

Activity 6

(Especially recommended for couples.) For evenings with married or unmarried couples, or even wedding showers, it is fun to do a take off of the old Newlywed Game. Think of funny questions for the group before they arrive and be as imaginative as possible. Have one mate of each couple leave the room and put them somewhere where they cannot hear the host asking the questions. Have pen and paper ready for the mates remaining in the room, so they can write a single answer on a piece of paper. Ask questions such as:

> What does the other one usually order in a restaurant?
> beef, chicken, pork or fish?
>
> What is their favorite show on TV?
>
> Where did you go on your first date?
>
> What size shoe does the other one wear?
>
> What does your mate do when lost? immediately ask for directions,
> look up directions before even leaving, try to convince you that
> they know what they are doing?

The group answering the questions can write down either an abbreviated or complete version of the answer they think their mate is most likely to use. Once done, have them turn the answers upside down on their lap in the same order the questions were asked. Four questions are usually enough, but you can ask more depending on the crowd's interest. The point is to see how well the guests know their mate, so be creative!

Bring the mates back into the room and start asking questions. Points accumulate when the one who left the room answers the same as their mate. Conversations can get exciting and lively, especially when couples differ in their answers! Continue the game by having the other mate leave the room, asking the new contestants four new questions.

Activity 5

The last game is a quick one. Have the guests imagine there are five things going on at the same time that they need to take care of. They must decide what to take care of first. Once they have listed each of the 5 in the order they would prioritize them, reveal what each incident means in terms of their own priorities.

The events are:

The telephone is ringing.

The baby is crying.

Someone knocks on the front door or rings the doorbell.

There is laundry hanging outside and it begins to rain.

The water faucet in the kitchen is running.

Each answer represents a different aspect of life and your priorities:

Phone represents job or career.

Baby represents family.

Visitor represents friends.

Laundry represents your intimate life.

Running water represents money or wealth.

All of these fun, quick games inspire women and men to interact, laugh and discuss topics that we can all relate to. Sharing anecdotes with each other about children, politics, sports and other personal interests encourages guests to relax in each others' company and ultimately to enjoy the party!

Organized Shopping List

Meats/Deli/Seafood	Produce	Dairy/Specialty Cheeses

Baking/Crackers/Chips Nuts/Bakery	Frozen Foods	Jars/Cans/Bottles/Tubes

Rice/Beans/Pasta/ Spices/Tea/Coffee	What do I need to check if I already own?	Errands and Supplies

Measurements to Remember

3 teaspoons	=	1 tablespoon
4 tablespoons	=	¼ cup
8 tablespoons	=	½ cup
16 tablespoons	=	1 cup
4 ounces	=	½ cup
8 ounces	=	1 cup
16 ounces	=	1 pound
2 cups	=	1 pint
1 pound butter	=	2 cups or 4 sticks
2 pints	=	1 quart
4 cups	=	1 quart
1 quart	=	32 ounces
2 quarts	=	½ gallon
4 quarts	=	1 gallon

Sifting passes ingredients through fine mesh to remove large pieces. It incorporates air and will change measurements. When a recipe calls for sifting, measure ingredients after they are sifted.

Instead of relying on package labels, use a measuring cup instead. It is best to measure liquids in glass measuring cups and solids in metal or plastic measuring cups. Solid and dry ingredients can then be leveled off with a knife to ensure proper measurements.

Trademark Credits

The TABASCO® marks, bottle and label designs are registered trademarks and servicemarks exclusively of McIlhenny Co., Avery Island, LA 70513.

HELLMANN'S® is a registered trademark of BestFoods, Englewood Cliffs, NJ 07632.

KNORR® is a registered trademark of BestFoods, Englewood Cliffs, NJ 07632.

KITCHEN BOUQUET® BROWNING AND SEASONING SAUCE and HIDDEN VALLEY® ORIGINAL RANCH® DRESSING are both registered trademarks of Hidden Valley Products Company.

Ro*Tel® is a registered trademark of International Home Foods, Inc.

SHAKE N' BAKE® Perfect Potatoes, Cool Whip® Whipped Topping and Kraft® Cheez-Links are registered trademarks of Kraft Foods, Inc.

My Secret™, The Original Honey Sauce™ is a trademark of Orb Enterprises, Layfatette, LA 70596.

Tony Chachere's® Creole Seasoning is a registered trademark of Creole Foods of Opelouses, Inc.

Briannas® is a registered trademark of Del Sol Food Co., Inc., Brenham, TX.

"Jiffy®" Corn Muffin Mix is a registered trademark of Chelsea Milling Company, Chelsea, Michigan.

True Crystals® Cocktail Mixers is a division of Crystals International Foods, Plant City, Florida.

GRAND MARNIER® is a registered trademark of Société des Produits Marnier-Lapostolle.

MAGGI® is a registered trademark of Société des Produits Nestlé S. A.

A.1.® STEAK SAUCE is a registered trademark of Nabisco, East Hanover, N.J. 07936 ©Nabisco, Inc.

Bibliography

Anderson, Jean, *1001 Secrets of Great Cooks*. The Berkley Publishing Group, 1995.

Food Epicurious.com

Herbst, Sharon Tyler. *Food Lover's Companion*. Barron's Educational Series, 1995.

Maresca, Tom. *Mastering Wine*. Grove Press, 1992.

Stevenson, Tom. *101 Essential Wine Tips*. DK Publishing, 1997.

Zraly, Kevin. *Windows On The World Complete Wine Course*. 1994 Updated Edition. Sterling Publishing Co. Inc., 1994.

Index